Earth, Fire and Sea

God's Story in Genesis

R. Russell Bixler

Treasure House
An Imprint of
Destiny Image® Publishers, Inc.
P.O. Box 310
Shippensburg, PA 17257-0310

"For where your treasure is,
there will your heart be also." Matthew 6:21

ISBN 1-56043-342-6

(Previously published under ISBN 0-9617094-0-5)
by Baldwin Manor Press)

For Worldwide Distribution
Printed in the U.S.A.

First Printing: 1999   Second Printing: 2000

This book and all other Destiny Image, Revival Press, Mercy Place, Fresh Bread, and Treasure House books are available at Christian bookstores and distributors worldwide.

For a U.S. bookstore nearest you, call **1-800-722-6774**.
For more information on foreign distributors, call **717-532-3040**.
Or reach us on the Internet: **http://www.reapernet.com**

Acknowledgments

With their reactions ranging from enthusiastic to indignant, many scholars across the nation—even across the sea—have made countless valuable suggestions concerning this book. Some of their critiques seemed devastating at first glance; they repeatedly demanded further research and innumerable revisions. The basic premises, however, have remained unshaken through all these rigorous examinations. Without these special friends, this book would not have been possible.

I also acknowledge the two secretaries who worked so diligently for countless hours, typing and retyping: Ruth Coles and Irene Plutto.

Endorsements

"You are on to something so important I have an inner stir unlike any before. I have verified your understanding of the keys...Your understanding sparkles."

Karl D. Coke, Ph.D.
Biblical Languages and Church Administration
The Karl Coke Evangelistic Assn.

"Your book is overdue in the Chrisitian Community. I believe it could be the juncture point for a whole new series of studies on creation and for biblical studies in general...You have given much food for thought."

Charles McDowell, Ph.D.
Professor-Emeritus of History and Geography
Cuyahoga Community College

"I hope this will reach a broad readership among biblical creationists. The cause of creationism and the good of bringing people into a personal relationship with their Creator will be well served if you do."

R.H. Brown, Ph.D.
Professor-Emeritus of Physics

"I am very, very grateful for this chance to read your book. I pray that it will find its mark and make its true contibution to this very hotly debated area of inquiry."

Chalmer Faw, Ph.D.
Professor-Emeritus of Biblical Studies
Bethany Theological Seminary

"With considerable exegetical and historical support Russ Bixler relates numerous passages of scripture to contemporary mythological accounts, while maintaining a commitment to a recent six consecutive day creation. He offers an issue worh much further study by Christians interested in true science."

William E. Stillman, Ph.D.
Former Senior Engineer, Research and Development
Westinghouse Electric Corp.

"*Earth, Fire and Sea* is a fresh, provocative, scholarly and solidily biblical treatment of the riddle of the universe. Author Russ Bixler's thesis is carefully documented from scripture and natural science and is presented with clarity and compelling logic."

Joseph Hopkins, Ph.D.
Professor-Emeritus of Religion
Westminister College

Contents

Foreword by a Scientist

The doctrine of creation will be a strong stimulus to research and may become a source of revitalization in the Church of the twenty-first century. Some scholars predict that the doctrine of creation will become as pivotal for future reformation as was the doctrine of salvation by faith in the sixteenth century. Therefore this book—which is a treatise on creation—is a harbinger of good things to come in the world of Christian literature and theology.

Furthermore, this work is of outstanding intrinsic merit. It is written with directness, with enthusiasm, with competency and with in-depth quality research. The author has a wide-ranging mind, and he does not hesitate to draw from the wells of thought dug by early Church Fathers, medieval Jewish scholars and contemporary liberal theologians. Notwithstanding, his approach is essentially and clearly conservative. He proceeds from an unswerving commitment to scripture as the word of God and understands the panorama of Earth history as displaying the works of God. His book will deepen the thought and strengthen the faith of many, including those who may disagree with, or reserve judgment on, his conclusions.

Ex nihilo creation is a long-standing doctrine of the Church in the matter of origins. In their eagerness to exclude evolutionists, several vigorous creationist parachurch organizations have included in their statement of faith this doctrine as a "litmus test" of orthodoxy. Mr. Bixler subjects this doctrine, *ex nihilo* creation, to a rigorous examination and comes up with a most interesting and surprising conclusion.

His historical research is careful and thorough, and he demonstrates an evident competency in dealing with the textual materials in their original languages, Hebrew and Greek. His exegesis of the first verse of Genesis is of particular interest and of crucial importance to his main thesis.

In writing on the doctrine of creation, in depth, the author has taken into account the great texts of Genesis, plus related texts in the Psalms, the Prophets and the New Testament. However, he draws rather sparsely from the Book of Job. One would hope that perhaps a sequel volume will address more thoroughly the great texts in the Book of Job, especially God's speech, chapters 38–41, both for their textual import and for the nature of Job's response to that revelation experience. Nevertheless, the treatise as it stands is an exciting, well-conceived, remarkable work.

Donald W. Patten
Founder, Microfilm Service Company
Author, *The Biblical Flood and the Ice Epoch* (1966)
Author, *The Long Day of Joshua and Six Other Catastrophes* (1973)
with Ron Hatch and Loren Steinhauer
Author, *The Recent Organization of the Solar System*
with Samuel R. Windsor
Editor, *Symposium on Creation*, 6 vols.
Contributor, *Catastrophism & Ancient History*,
Creation Research Society Quarterly and *Kronos*

Foreword by a Biblical Scholar

In a day when the Bible-science controversy rages more hotly than ever, Russell Bixler endeavors to goad evangelical scholars to reconsider biblical creationism. He presents a strongly reasoned case to challenge the traditional exegesis of Genesis 1:1-3, which for 18 centuries has fallen in line with *creatio ex nihilo*—the doctrine that God created the Earth out of nothing. The reader finds himself asking whether the allusions to the mythological terms in Job, Psalms and Isaiah are in reference to God's struggle with the forces of chaos at Creation, to the global cleansing of evil in the Deluge, or to Yahweh's victory over the forces of Pharaoh at the Red Sea.

For one who is not a professional scientist, Mr. Bixler evidences widespread knowledge of the various pertinent disciplines. His study is especially valuable in retrieving for us the conclusions of Jewish and Christian teachers ever since the close of the biblical canon. This is no mere academic ax to grind but the formulation of devoted research in Bible and science over several decades. He is burdened for truth—God's truth as revealed primarily in scripture but also in nature. Boldly he provokes us to listen again to what the lines of ancient scripture are really proclaiming as well as to the most recent theories of geology and astronomy.

Let not the admittedly speculative interpretations of various lesser issues deter us from setting aside our preconceptions long enough to take another careful look at Creation and the age of the Earth.

John Rea, Th.D.
Emeritus Professor of Old Testament
School of Biblical Studies
Regent University

Introduction

Curiosity about our beginnings continues to haunt the human race. It will not call off the quest for its origins.[1]

The ancient Israelite (as well as all of his contemporaries) was also deeply concerned about his origins. Of course, he knew quite well the drama of his own story; it is we today who are not certain of our story. Our origins have been sorely confused by a return to paganism in the name of science. Therefore, we moderns must redefine our earliest genealogy anew.

Scientific creationism is helping us to accomplish that quest by enthusiastically restating our heritage for this generation. Tragically, a great amount of that effort must be dedicated toward exposing the massive fallacies of those twin nineteenth-century philosophies, uniformitarianism[2] and evolution.[3]

---

1. Henri Blocher, *In the Beginning*, trans. David G. Preston, Downers Grove, IL: Inter-Varsity Press, 1984, p. 15.

2. *Uniformitarianism*: The theory that all geological phenomena may be explained as resulting from a continuity of currently observable processes and rates, such as erosion or volcanism; global natural catastrophes in recent times are excluded from consideration.

3. *Evolution*: Generally, the theory that all life is explained by the initial chance appearance of simple forms of life followed by increasing organization and complexity through immense periods of time. A divine Power may or may not be involved; if so, the word *chance* might be deleted.

In opposition to these two erroneous philosophies, the Bible presents natural history as brief and catastrophic, and the supporting historical and geological evidence for such recent catastrophism is overwhelming. Scientific creationism is beginning to fulfill its promise as we look ahead to a new millennium.

Nevertheless, creation science is seriously divided within itself. The most controversial issue is the age of the universe and in particular the Earth. Some creationists, examining the scientific data indicating long ages, have attempted various means of reinterpreting Genesis 1 in order to accommodate the natural evidence for an *old* Earth. Other creationists, just as competent in their science, hold to the traditional translation—and literal interpretation—of Genesis 1, pointing to the vast array of valid indicators of a *young* Earth.[4]

As a result of this conflict, the growing creation science movement is experiencing difficulty in establishing its credibility.[5] Surprisingly, both sides may be right, and both may also be wrong. The many scattered biblical allusions to the Creation can resolve at least a significant area of disagreement when scriptures are studied in context, without prejudice.

The key is 900-year-old Jewish scholarship, which provides the primitive intent and interpretation of Genesis 1:1-3. The correct syntax of these verses, more acceptable grammatically than that to which we are accustomed, implies for creationists a distinctly different approach to the question of Earth's age. Coupled with the other catastrophic events portrayed in the Bible *passim*, the original Hebrew understanding of Creation provides a most satisfying resolution of many of the major biblical and scientific difficulties.

Many valid observations about the sense of Genesis 1 and 2 are preserved in older, prescientific viewpoints. "New" is not always "better."[6]

---

4. A "creationist" is defined as one who accepts a special, one-time divine creation based upon biblical statements while denying the theory of organic evolution of life. There is limited room for disagreement about ages within creationism.

5. See, e.g., *Christianity Today*, Vol. XXVI, No. 16, October 8, 1982, pp. 22-26.

6. John Sailhamer, *Genesis Unbound*, Sisters, OR: Multnomah Books, 1996, p. 158.

This research explains—biblically—why some scientific indicators suggest an old Earth and other data picture a young Earth. Nothing is forced; the exegesis flows smoothly when perceived in context. Theology and geology, we shall find, are more compatible than usually acknowledged. In fact, the present work moves easily throughout from theology to geology and back again.

God's word is Truth. If "the facts" disagree with the Bible, then there must be something wrong with either our perception of the facts or our perception of the Bible. "It is a frequent dictum in works on Bible and Science for the writer to affirm that the Bible never contradicts 'true' science."[7] Ramm's statement was made with a strong note of irony; nevertheless, it is true. As one reads recent creationist literature, he cannot help being impressed with the quality of some of the serious research being done. Creation scientists usually get their natural facts straight; they are keenly sensitive to erroneous interpretation of those data. Their weaknesses lie more in either improper biblical exegesis or religious traditionalism. The exegesis and the traditionalism are the primary concerns of this treatise.

The Earth is both old and young!

Consider carefully this seeming paradox as we journey through an investigation together. Scriptural exegesis is discussed only in terms that can be understood by the intelligent, non-Hebrew-reading student. References are made to the commentators for technical aspects whenever appropriate.

Questions and objections will arise in the reader's mind during this study. It is urged that final judgments not be made until after reading the chapter entitled "Questions." Presumably all reasonable objections will be answered satisfactorily there.

All biblical and apocryphal references are, unless otherwise noted, from the Revised Standard Version. The questions of authorship and dating of the composition of Genesis 1 are avoided. The emphasis is upon the age of the inorganic earth rather than life on the earth.

Many knowledgeable friends (both creationists and evolutionists) have read the manuscript and have made numerous criticisms. I have seriously considered their every comment,

---

7. Bernard Ramm, *The Christian View of Science and Scripture*, Grand Rapids: Eerdmans, 1955, p. 42.

incorporating some and rejecting others, all the while stubbornly refusing to yield ground in controversial areas where I felt that the weight of evidence upheld my positions. I invite readers to do as the writers of the Forewords, who had both critiqued this work seriously, yet also contributed much helpful information toward the project.

Following its initial publication in 1986, *Earth, Fire and Sea* was reviewed in print by four creationist writers, only one of whom wrote favorably about the book.[8] This revision takes into consideration each of their objections, plus those of many others, and I have woven every valid concern into it. The negative reviews included a "straw-man" indictment, a charge that the language was overly aggressive, an attack on the use of "liberal" sources, and numerous nitpicking comments on rather peripheral issues. After considering the reviews and correcting all the errors I could detect, the basic premise of the treatise still remains unshaken.

This basic premise is vitally important to the credibility of biblical creationism. Will the tragic silence of *Earth, Fire and Sea's* first dozen years be duplicated during the next 12?

---

8.   *Creation Research Society Quarterly*, Vol. 24, No. 4, pp. 197-200; *Bible-Science Newsletter*, Feb. 1988, p. 18. One reviewer revised his critique following the editor's reception of my response.

Preface

One of the reviewers of the first edition of *Earth, Fire and Sea* concluded with this statement:

> **I have never understood why some people write books that say the same thing as others have said before them. A book is a lot of work to achieve nothing more than redundancy. Bixler's book is novel and its message is well worth considering.**[1]

If this reviewer is correct, then I have accomplished what I always set out to do when I write. His words are an appreciated compliment.

I am a "recent" creationist. I accept a literalistic view of Genesis 1, affirming the statement that God did indeed create the heavens and the earth in six actual "earth days"—as the text quite clearly tells us.

Creation science today includes many broad disciplines, requiring its students to be polymaths, with interdisciplinary interests and skills. I have been astonished by the number of creation scientists who are studying the biblical languages and the number of clergymen who are studying creation science. I approach this challenge as a student of the Bible with an interest

---

1.   *Creation Research Society Quarterly, op. cit.*, review by Glenn Morton, p. 200.

in the philosophy of science, writing as a non-specialist, a non-scientist, for heuristic purposes, asking the specialists to pursue the pertinent subjects further. I apologize in advance for being incompetent to remove all vestiges of inconsistency.

I also write to Christians. This book is not an attempt to convince anyone of the truths of scientific creationism. Rather, it assumes that the reader is already convinced. Further, the reader will notice that I am eclectic, choosing materials here and there—always in proper context—from writers who might disagree sharply with my conclusions. Some sources are modern, some older and some ancient. Christians should not fear truth wherever it may be found.

Unfortunately, much of the good biblical scholarship of the past 100 years has been accomplished by "liberal" Bible scholars. In the midst of excellent liberal writings, however, are often found erroneous conclusions, usually indicating a post-Enlightenment, post-Darwinian worldview. The "conservatives" (with whom I tend to identify), on the other hand, seem to be limited by certain religious doctrines that may or may not be scriptural. So I have tried to remain alert constantly to intrusions of non-scriptural, pious assumptions, to modern myths and half-truths and to rationalistic worldviews, yet always sensitive to biblical truth. The best of both worlds—liberal and conservative—has provided a most delightful study.

Many liberal Bible commentators would tend to agree with the biblical exegesis contained here. Those same scholars, however, would call "myth" that which I accept as historical fact dressed in ancient cultural clothing. Liberals are uncritically committed to a uniformitarian, evolutionary worldview. When I attended seminary 40 years ago, a uniformitarian, theistic evolution was generally accepted by faculty and students alike, so much so that the subject was scarcely mentioned in any classes. In fact, liberalism in the Church is largely the result of having forced the theories of uniformitarianism and evolution upon the Bible. Thus liberal scholars normally think of these most ancient biblical narratives as mythological. Liberal commentators will not—indeed, cannot—apply the same critical tools to their uniformitarian worldview that they apply to the scriptures. Although quite appreciative of the early narratives of Genesis, they perceive these verses as ancient (read, primitive) man's less-than-adequate understanding of physical reality. These scholars are simply unable to grasp what creationists are about as they delve into the scriptures; such a work as this present one would be received with disdain. Creationism is pejoratively labelled "anti-science."

Thus liberal Bible scholarship often contributes, not purposefully, but unwittingly, to a better understanding of the Old Testament for creationists. The *caveat* is to recognize the diamonds among the cut glass. I ask the conservative reader, please do not be offended by the extensive use of liberal scholars' materials; although liberals' conclusions derived because of western perceptions of reality may sometimes be unsound, their biblical scholarship is often quite sound. Von Rad states the liberal view well:

> **Without doubt, there is to be found here [in Genesis 1] a great deal of the knowledge of the origin of the world that had been worked out and taught at the same time, and as knowledge it is largely obsolete today.**[2]

Liberal commentators, with such assumptions, are offended by our attempts to integrate Genesis and modern scientific discoveries.

> **It is a naive and futile exercise to attempt to reconcile the biblical accounts of creation with the findings of modern science. Any correspondence which can be discovered or ingeniously established between the two must surely be nothing more than mere coincidence.**[3]

The liberal attitude was the same a century ago: "To seek for even a kernel of historical fact in such cosmogonies is inconsistent with a scientific point of view."[4]

Liberal biblical scholars are usually identifiable by their negative attitudes toward the miraculous, and they tend to dispute the revelatory aspect of the scriptures.

---

2.   Gerhard von Rad, *Genesis*, Philadelphia: Westminster, 1961, p. 48.

3.   Nahum M. Sarna, *Understanding Genesis*, New York: McGraw Hill, 1966, pp. 2-3.

4.   Heinrich Zimmern and T.K. Cheyne, art. "Creation," *Encyclopedia Biblica*, Vol. I, ed. T.K. Cheyne and J. Sutherland Black, New York: Macmillan, 1899, p. 938. Cf. Conrad Hyers, *The Meaning of Creation*, Atlanta: John Knox Press, 1964, esp. Chapter 1.

How ironic that many modern scholars are so eager to demythologize Genesis, yet are quite unwilling to subject uniformitarianism and evolutionism to the same process of falsification! So great a scholar as William F. Albright would have disagreed sharply with contemporary liberal writers regarding Genesis 1: "In fact, modern scientific cosmogonies show such a disconcerting tendency to be short-lived that it may be seriously doubted whether science has yet caught up with the Biblical story."[5] We who have such great respect for truth must not allow ourselves to be intimidated by changeable human worldviews!

Tradition, on the other hand, also limits sound biblical interpretation. Wagner wonders anxiously "...if being a Christian means knowing in advance what the Bible will say...."[6] The liberal German Westermann adds, "We have some extremely deeply rooted notions regarding the creation of the world and of man which...do not come from the text of the Bible, but from the history of its interpretation."[7] It is strongly urged that the reader remember Westermann's perceptive words throughout this study. Tradition may be helpful or it may be harmful; the question always to be asked is whether the particular tradition is *biblical*.

The fideism of American fundamentalism is commendable; it is largely responsible for the exciting explosion of scientific creationism in our generation. But fideism to this author is insufficient; faith must also vindicate itself in actual experience. Remanent signs of the catastrophic events depicted in Genesis 1 through 11 should also be found in the geological record. Our faith should stand upon the Bible and doctrines properly derived from its study, and we ought also to expect God to authenticate those scriptures in his natural world. "Jesus Christ is the same yesterday and today and for ever" (Hebrews 13:8). True biblical faith is not blind faith. We should also challenge doctrines whose roots are found in improper exegesis or in the interaction of the Church and human culture. American fundamentalism needs to

---

5.　W.F. Albright, "The Old Testament and Archaeology," *Old Testament Commentary*, ed. Herbert C. Alleman and Elmer E. Flack, Philadelphia: Muhlenburg Press, 1948, p. 135.

6.　Claus Westermann, *The Genesis Accounts of Creation*, trans. Norman E. Wagner, Philadelphia: Fortress Press, 1964, p. iv.

7.　*Ibid.*, p. 1. Cf. Ramm, *op. cit.*, pp. 40-42.

reassess some of its tenets, discarding those portions that are mere products of post-Enlightenment thinking.

I make two points. First, I reject any attenuation of scripture: compromising God's word in order to accommodate man's word produces erroneous results. Second, I reject the forcing of a nineteenth-century pietism upon the Bible. The Bible should be allowed to speak for itself, on its own terms. As Eichrodt says,

> **In deciding...on our procedure for the treatment of OT thought, we must avoid all schemes which derive from Christian dogmatics....Instead, we must plot our course as best we can along the lines of the OT's own dialect.**[8]

That word of wisdom will guide us throughout this work.

---

8.   Walter Eichrodt, *Theology of the Old Testament*, Philadelphia: Westminster, 1967, p. 33.

Chapter 1

The Debate Among Creation Scientists

The King James Version of the Old Testament is based upon very late manuscripts of the Hebrew (Masoretic) text. It provides a chronology from which the seventeenth-century bishop, James Ussher, calculated a "creation" date of 4004 B.C. Other students using the Hebrew Bible have arrived at variant dates, all of which are within a few hundred years of Ussher's.[1] The Samaritan Torah, however, dating from several centuries after the final break with the Jews in the fifth century B.C., provides a somewhat longer chronology; the third-century B.C. Greek Septuagint presents a yet more extended chronology.[2] However, all three textual traditions agree on one fact: The date of the Creation described in Genesis 1 and 2 can be placed no more than a

---

1.   Ussher had many predecessors: see Andrew D. White, *A History of the Warfare of Science with Theology in Christendom*, Vol. I, New York: D. Appleton & Co., 1898, pp. 249f.

2.   Sir Walter Raleigh, in his *History of the World* (1603-16), chose the Septuagint for his chronology because it provided an older and (to him) seemingly more reasonable date for creation: ibid., p. 254. Augustine (A.D. 400) debated with himself in *The City of God* concerning the dependability of the two versions, Greek and Hebrew; he too chose the longer chronology of the Septuagint (XII, 10; 12; XV, 10-15).

few thousand years ago. Certainly proposals of millions or billions of years fly in the face of the biblical testimony.

Yet scientists who are Christians are sharply divided over this chronology solely on the basis of the available scientific data.[3] Some appear to be ignoring the natural evidence; those who disagree seem to be ignoring the biblical evidence.

The scientific data do appear to be contradictory. Published radiometric dates, for example, put the Earth's age at billions of years. Old Earth supporters often accept uncritically most of these dates as reasonably accurate. However, competent challengers have called into question some of the basic assumptions of radiometric dating: long ages are *assumed*; original conditions are *assumed*; conditions through the centuries are *assumed*. Measurements can often be challenged because of known selectivity in eliminating samples that disagree with predetermined dates.[4] Radiometric dating is clearly based uncritically upon the uniformitarian hypothesis.

---

3.   For example, a Bible conference scheduled two competent creation scientists (among other speakers), one proposing a "young" Earth and the other just as firmly contending for an "old" Earth.

4.   Physical chemist Melvin A. Cook, author of *Prehistory and Earth Models* (London: Parrish, 1966), said in a letter dated May 5, 1976: "One *must* handle K-A dating, consistent with all the facts dealing with it, by simply dismissing it as unscientific and completely unreliable, indeed absurd. They simply don't publish the sort of facts they know about that would kill K-A dating once and for all if they are [sic] known" (Alfred de Grazia, *Homo Schizo 1*, Princeton: Metron Publications, 1983, p. 50).

For a critique of *radiocarbon* dating and the methods of its enthusiasts, see Robert E. Lee (not a creationist), "Radiocarbon: Ages in Error," *Anthropological Journal of Canada*, Vol. 19, No. 3, 1981, pp. 9-29; reprinted in *Creation Research Society Quarterly*, Vol. 19, No. 2, Sept. 1982, pp. 117f. Lee says, with a touch of irony, "Radiocarbon dating has somehow avoided collapse onto its own battered foundation, and now lurches onward with feigned consistency. The implications of pervasive contamination and ancient variations in carbon-14 levels are steadfastly ignored by those who base their argument upon the dates" (CRSQ, p. 125).

An excellent presentation on this subject for laymen is found in Curtis Sewell, Jr., "The Faith of Radiometric Dating," *Bible-Science News*, Vol. 32, No. 8, pp. 1-6.

The Bible could well be addressing this matter of radiometric dating by the uranium-thorium-lead, potassium-argon and rubidium-strontium "yardsticks." Lead is rather volatile; rubidium and, especially, argon are even more volatile; in case of great amounts of heat during the "Creation catastrophe" or the Flood catastrophe, highly significant amounts of these volatile elements would have been dissipated, immediately contaminating all possible samples for later measurement. Perhaps such severe phenomena were involved in the Creation, the Flood, and/or the events surrounding the Exodus from Egypt. Later the eighth-century prophet Isaiah seems to be describing a similar contemporary or imminent catastrophic event:

> *Behold, the* LORD *will lay waste the earth and make it desolate, and he will twist its surface and scatter its inhabitants....The earth shall be utterly laid waste and utterly despoiled; for the* LORD *has spoken this word. The earth mourns and withers, the world languishes and withers; the heavens languish together with the earth....[T]herefore the inhabitants of the earth are scorched, and few men are left....The city of chaos is broken down....For the windows of heaven are opened, and the foundations of the earth tremble....The earth is utterly broken, the earth is rent asunder, the earth is violently shaken. The earth staggers like a drunken man, it sways like a hut...* (Isaiah 24:1-20).

This event may have coincided with proposed meteoritic impacts, which perhaps affected much of the Solar System.[5] Thus the Bible suggests that age estimates based upon the decay rates of the more volatile elements are untrustworthy.

A worldwide pluvial *and* igneous event—the Flood—is described in Genesis 7:11. The scripture tells vividly how "...all the fountains of the great deep burst forth." Liberal Bible scholars

---

5. See Carl R. Froede, Jr. & Don B. DeYoung, "Impact Events within the Young-Earth Flood Model," *Creation Research Society Quarterly*, Vol. 33, No. 1, June 1996, pp. 23-34. Also see Michael J. Fischer, "A Giant Meterorite Impact & Rapid Continental Drift," *Proceedings of the Third International Conference on Creationism*, ed. Robert Walsh, Pittsburgh: Creation Science Fellowship, Inc., 1994, pp. 185-197; Wayne R. Spencer, "The Origin and History of the Solar System," *ibid.*, pp. 513-523.

usually assume that this verse refers to the lowest, watery level of a "three-tiered" universe. However, such an interpretation is based upon the pagan, Aristotelian, medieval worldview—*not* that of the Old Testament! In physical terms, what else could Genesis 7:11 be portraying but sudden, universal *volcanic* eruptions on the ocean floor and massive tectonism, sending enormous tsunamis (popularly known as tidal waves), hundreds or even thousands of feet high, crashing over the land?[6] Would not volatile elements have been dissipated from the Earth's crust during this period?

Radiometric dating is generally acknowledged to be greatly affected by volcanism, sometimes multiplying true ages exponentially, so distorting the results that hundreds of years can appear to be millions.[7] Recent eruptions of Mount St. Helens are already being dated in hundreds of thousands of years.[8] The incredible scope of volcanic activity suggested by Genesis 7:11 would have rendered the totality of Earth's crust utterly contaminated for purposes of radiometric dating. In the light of this book, however, it will be seen that, right or wrong, radiometric dating is less relevant to a study of origins than previously thought.

The late rabbinic *Book of Jasher* suggests that earthquakes occurred and volcanoes erupted globally during the Deluge.[9] Ginzberg notes ancient Jewish traditions that insist "...the punishment *by fire* during the flood is connected with the conception of the world *conflagration* which then took place for the first time" (italics added).[10] The oxygen content of the pre-Flood atmosphere would have been so high as to intensify greatly the already-universal fires. Further, an enormous heat load would

---

6.   Cf. Joseph C. Dillow, *The Waters Above*, Chicago: Moody Press, 1981, pp. 267f.

7.   Lee, *op. cit.*, (CRSQ), p. 119.

8.   Steven A. Austin, "Excess Argon within mineral concentrates from the new dacite lava dome at Mount St. Helens Volcano," *Creation Ex Nihilo Technical Journal*, Vol. 10 (3), 1996, pp. 335-343.

9.   *The Book of Jasher, faithfully translated from the Original Hebrew into English*, Salt Lake City: J.H. Parry & Co., 1887, p. 12. Although written in a traditional rabbinic style, most scholars insist it is only several centuries old.

10.   Louis Ginzberg, *The Legends of the Jews*, Vol. I, Philadelphia: The Jewish Publication Society of America, 1947, p. 178.

have been generated by the latent heat of condensation (of water vapor) and by the interaction of the raindrops and the atmosphere.[11] Ginzberg accordingly, quoting additional ancient Jewish records, says that God sent scalding rain during those 40 days in order to burn the human race as it struck.[12] Recent creationist research confirms from scientific evidence that, indeed, the raindrops would have been scalding. Too great an amount of hot rainfall might have destroyed even those in the ark.[13]

Research has also revealed what is apparently a global layer of soot at the Cretaceous-Tertiary boundary. Found in samples from Denmark, Spain and New Zealand, the carbon is quantitatively equal to that of 10 percent of the Earth's present biomass, indicating the enormity of the fires. Previous hypotheses of a cometary or meteoritic encounter seem to be ruled out by these finds, in that the researchers felt that such a limited impact could hardly ignite global fires of this magnitude, although the pre-Flood atmosphere contained oxygen in excess of 30 percent, establishing the atmospheric condition needed for extensive wildfires.[14] Further, the expected meteoritic noble gases were not present in the tested samples.[15]

Tropical rain forests with a large annual rainfall are usually considered unlikely to suffer destruction by

11. Dillow, *op. cit.*, p. 271.

12. Ginzberg, *op. cit.*, Vol. V, p. 159.

13. Larry Vardiman & Karen Bousselot, "Sensitivity Studies on Vapor Canopy Temperature Profiles," *Proceedings of the Fourth International Conference on Creationism,* ed. Robert E. Walsh, Pittsburgh: Creation Science Fellowship, Inc., 1998, pp. 607-618.

14. Air bubbles trapped in Flood-era amber were found to contain more than 30 percent oxygen. Robert Berner and Gary Landis, *Science,* Nov. 13, 1987, p. 890, noted in Mace Baker, *Dinosaurs,* Redding, CA: New Century Books, 1991, pp. 6, 168-70. Cf. *Time,* Nov. 9, 1987, p. 82. Bio/tech News, Portland, OR, 1996, reported a 38 percent concentration of oxygen, which would seem to be dangerously high, possibly threatening precipitate combustion.

15. Wendy S. Wolbach, Roy S. Lewis, Edward Anders, "Cretaceous Extinctions: Evidence for Wildfires and Search for Meteoritic Material," *Science,* Vol. 230, No. 4722, Oct. 11, 1985, pp. 167-70. W.S. Wolbach, I. Gilmour, E. Anders, "Major Wildfires at the Cretaceous/Tertiary Boundary," in V.L. Sharpton & P.D. Ward (editors), *Global Catastrophes in Earth History,* Boulder, CO: Geological Society of America Special Paper 247, pp. 391-400.

forest fire. However, a large percentage of soil cores taken in the Amazon Basin in Venezuela show charcoal layers. Human occupation of the area is dated back to only 3700 years ago, whereas some of the charcoal gives radiocarbon dates up to 6300 years BP. The fires which formed the charcoal cannot therefore have been started by human slash-and-burn cultures.[16]

The so-called "iridium layer" was found by the Alvarezes (and others) at the same Cretaceous-Tertiary boundary,[17] suggesting that it may have been due to an enormous meteoritic encounter. However, this layer might also be explained (as the carbon layer) by the universal, simultaneous eruptions of numerous volcanoes. A meteorite attack alone does not explain the full evidence. Thus modern science inadvertently strengthens the case for the authenticity of the ancient Deluge records. Psalms 18:7-15 may be reminiscent of this event.

"...All the fountains of the great deep burst forth..." of Genesis 7:11 pictures the initiation of the Flood, explaining why relatively immobile marine fossils are generally found at the bottom of Earth's sedimentary strata. The rains followed as dust particles from the global eruptions provided nuclei for raindrops to form. Earthquakes, volcanic eruptions, torrential rains and tsunamis persisted, tearing loose and reshaping Earth's entire surface during seven-and-a-half catastrophic months. Then "the fountains of the deep and the windows of the heavens were closed" (Genesis 8:2a). The staggering violence of the continuing ebb and flow had torn up and redeposited sedimentary strata as deep as several miles or more. Coal was at least in part produced by trees and plants that were burning when entombed by the sediment-laden tsunamis. "The evidence strongly supports a process of carbonisation in forest fires, which were extensive, but were checked by flooding before destruction of the forests was complete."[18]

---

16.   *Workshop*, Society for Interdisciplinary Studies, Vol. 6, No. 3, February 1986, p. 26, based on an item in *New Scientist*, January 24, 1985, p. 35.

17.   Luis W. Alvarez, *et al.*, "Extraterrestrial cause for the Cretaceous-Tertiary extinction," *Science*, 208, 1980, pp. 1095-1108.

18.   Wilfrid Francis, *Coal: Its Formation and Composition*, second ed., London: Edward Arnold, 1961, p. 625. Cf. John C. Whitcomb, Jr. and Henry M. Morris, *The Genesis Flood*, Grand Rapids: Baker, reprinting 1978, p. 122.

Evolutionists claim that the main period of coal deposition ended about 280 million years ago. "Yet fossilized wood and coal from a Carboniferous deposit in Spain were subjected to radiocarbon tests and produced the seemingly incredible results of 5025, 3930 and 4250 years BP."[19] Thus may be seen some of the evidences for a young Earth and a recent Flood.

On the other hand, proponents of an old Earth, beginning with astronomer William Herschel nearly two centuries ago, have been describing the great distances of remote stars, even to some billions of light-years. Such a simple proof seems to eliminate the possibility of a youthful universe. Yet many creationists counter by insisting that God created a "mature" world.[20] Adam, for example, was an adult when created, not a helpless baby; the universe likewise, they say, was created fullblown.[21] This "apparent maturity" or "functioning completeness" theory includes the most distant star—*and* its light! Such an argument frustrates old Earth creationists, eliminating immediately another possibility; the dialogue ends right there! Occasional young Earth appeals to Riemannian curved space impress very few scholars, although Setterfield has proposed a hotly disputed case for a slowly decreasing speed of light.[22]

While young Earth advocates hurry past those troublesome stellar distances,[23] they bring up the argument based on Earth's weakening magnetic field, a fact apparently demanding a very

---

19. *Radiocarbon*, Vol. I, 1966, pp. 198-278; quoted by Peter James in *Society for Interdisciplinary Studies Review*, Vol. IV, 3,4.

20. First proposed by Chateaubriand in 1802: Francis C. Haber, *The Age of the World: Moses to Darwin*, Baltimore: The Johns Hopkins Press, 1959, p. 190. Blocher, *op. cit.*, p. 216, credits Philip H. Gosse with the origination of this idea in 1857.

21. So said René Descartes in the early seventeenth century; cf. Stanley L. Jaki, *Genesis 1 Through the Ages*, London: Thomas More Press, 1992, p. 193.

22. Barry Setterfield, "The Velocity of Light and the Age of the Universe," *Ex Nihilo*, Vol. 4, No. 1, March 1981, and Vol. 5, No. 3, Jan. 1983. Cf. Paul M. Steidl, "The Velocity of Light and the Age of the Universe," *Creation Research Society Quarterly*, Vol. 19, No. 2, Sept. 1982, pp. 128-31. The present work renders moot the question of the velocity of light.

23. Cf. David J. Krause, "Astronomical Distances, the Speed of Light, and the Age of the Universe," *Journal of the American Scientific Affiliation*, Vol. 33, No. 4, December 1981, pp. 235-39.

limited history.[24] Old Earth proponents counter that paleomagnetic data indicate a weakening magnetic field only during the past two millennia; earlier evidences, they claim, indicate a strengthening field.[25]

Those who insist upon long ages point to the tree-ring record, the deep sea cores, cores from the Nevada desert, the coral record, the varves, radiometric dating and especially the Greenland/Antartica ice cores. But all of these records disagree egregiously with one another. The various Greenland/Antartica drilling sites have occasionally produced age results that contradict each other![26]

Young Earth enthusiasts sometimes appeal to the results of Robert Gentry's pioneering research in "pleochroic halos." Studying pre-Cambrian rock, Gentry's work indicates that Earth's basement rock was probably formed instantly, rather than being cooled slowly from magma to rock, as the conventional theory has it.[27] The evidence is impressive. "The single evidence of the halos is that the basement rocks of the earth were formed suddenly and in a solid state...!"[28] The uniformitarian Establishment responded with scorn to Gentry's published results and, with typical emotional heavyhandedness, made certain that Gentry's research grant was cut off by the National Science Foundation and his "visiting" status terminated. But they couldn't refute his evidence.

Obviously, speaking to the question of the age of the Earth stirs violent responses. Both sides can muster impressive arrays of evidence. Paradoxically, some apparently "proven facts" indicate clearly an *old* Earth, and some just as urgently demand a *young* Earth.

24. D. Russell Humphreys, "The Creation of the Earth's Magnetic Field," *Creation Research Society Quarterly*, Vol. 20, No. 2, Sept. 1983, pp. 89-94.

25. Davis. A. Young, *Christianity and the Age of the Earth*, Grand Rapids: Zondervan, 1982, pp. 117-124.

26. Larry Vardiman, *Ice Cores and the Age of the Earth*, El Cajon, CA: Institute for Creation Research, 1993, *passim*.

27. Robert V. Gentry, *Creation's Tiny Mystery*, Knoxville: Earth Science Associates, 1986.

28. William Overn, "The Creator's Signature," *Bible-Science Newsletter*, Vol. 20, No. 1, Jan. 1982, pp. 1f.

We must learn to look to the Bible for answers. And, as faithful as ever, God's word cuts through this Gordian knot. Simply, this work's exegesis resolves much of the disagreement between the proponents of a young Earth versus those of an old Earth. Here is the key.

The concept that Genesis 1 describes a creation out of nothing, an idea so dear to many modern Christians, is *not* scriptural!

Based not upon the original Hebrew, but rather upon the earliest Greek translation of Genesis 1, *creatio ex nihilo* was first proposed in the second century A.D., and by a heretical—that's right, *heretical*—source at that!

Before responding emotionally to this statement, note carefully all the information presented in this book and make a decision based not upon tradition, but upon the biblical and historical evidence. This work proposes a translation of Genesis 1:1-3 somewhat as follows:

> *In the beginning of God's creating the heavens and the earth—the earth being a formless waste and darkness being upon the face of the deep and the Spirit of God moving over the face of the waters—God said, "Let there be light!" And there was light.*

Surprisingly, this translation accounts for the remarkable situation where—biblically—some natural evidence may point legitimately toward an *old* Earth and some may just as legitimately indicate a *young* Earth.

That incredible statement will be explained; but first, let's investigate the matter of our "traditional" English translation of Genesis 1:1-3 and how the non-biblical concept of *creatio ex nihilo* came to be near-orthodoxy. This thesis is not offering a new interpretation, but, rather, the ages-old Hebraic understanding so ignored by most creationists for centuries.

Chapter 2

The History of Old Testament Versions

The *Hebrew* Old Testament as we know it did not receive its final form until well into the Christian era. According to some vague traditions, rabbis meeting in about A.D. 90 at Jamnia on the Mediterranean coast of Palestine recognized the Hebrew canon as being limited to its now generally accepted 39 books. The sixteenth-century Protestant Reformers later concurred in this canon. About A.D. 500 the Jewish Masoretic scribes, in an attempt to standardize the text (and its vocalization), began to revise and add vowel pointings to the Hebrew Old Testament. The present form of the Hebrew text was completed by these Jewish scholars—but not before the ninth century A.D.! Other than the Dead Sea Scrolls, today we have few portions of the Hebrew Old Testament antedating the Masoretes, although most of the Dead Sea Scrolls confirm the Masoretic text rather spectacularly, in spite of nearly a millennium between the two.

The first *translation* of the Old Testament was begun in the third century B.C. Seventy Jewish scholars, working near Alexandria, Egypt, were said to have initiated a translation into Greek at the request and expense of King Ptolemy Philadelphus, one of the early successors of Alexander the Great. The project's fulfillment is lost in variant traditions, but the creation narratives—Genesis 1 and 2—would obviously have been completed early. The translation as a whole seems to be a hodge-podge of contributions from many scholars over two or more centuries. This Greek version developed into the Old Testament for most early Christians, as well as many Diaspora Jews. Even the converted Pharisee, Paul, used the Greek Bible, in addition to the oral Aramaic texts known as the Targums (much of which he had obviously memorized). Although Jerome (A.D. 400) consulted a Hebrew text liberally for his Latin Vulgate translation from the Greek, it was actually the Protestant Reformers of the sixteenth century who initiated the return to the Hebrew—away from the Greek/Latin—Old Testament by Christians.

The newly founded city of Alexandria was thoroughly Greek, the Hellenizing of the Middle East having proceeded rapidly after the Alexandrian conquest about 330 B.C. Jews began pouring into the new Greek metropolis and, by the time Jesus was born in Bethlehem, there were an estimated 300,000 Jews living in Alexandria.[1] Stubborn resistance to Hellenistic culture was found only among some religious Jews (see 1 and 2 Maccabees). Thus noticeable philosophical changes began to take place in the thinking of Jewish writers in spite of their Jewishness, especially those living in the Diaspora. Of importance to our study is the translation into Greek of Genesis 1:1 by "the Seventy" (giving this version the title of "Septuagint," usually symbolized by "LXX"). The initial verse of the Septuagint states simply, in Greek, "In the beginning God created the heaven and the earth."

This work contends that, as can occur in any translation, the LXX rendering of Genesis 1:1 was erroneous. Actually, the error would be easy to make. Biblical Hebrew had few vowel sounds until the Masoretes added their "vowel pointings" a thousand years later, and punctuation was almost unheard of. By the sixth century A.D. the traditional pronunciation and syntax would have become quite difficult to ascertain, especially since Hebrew as a spoken language had been diminishing ever since the Babylonian captivity of the sixth century B.C.; conversational Hebrew in Palestine was usually replaced or at least greatly affected by its cognate language, Aramaic. (The original writing

---

1.   Jaki, *op. cit.*, p. 38.

of Genesis 1 was more distant in time from the Masoretic scholars than the one surviving manuscript of *Beowulf* is from us today, and few modern Englishmen can understand *Beowulf*!) Improper vocalization of the Hebrew could change the whole sense of a passage and, in the case of Genesis 1:1, appears to have contributed toward just that. Origen's third-century transliteration of the Hebrew Old Testament into Greek letters (in his *Hexapla*) indicates that vocalization had indeed changed significantly before the Masoretes initiated their prodigious work.[2]

But it is suggested that the LXX error in Genesis 1:1 may have been more deliberate than accidental. The third-century B.C. Jewish translators were quite aware of Greek and Egyptian polytheistic mythologies. Eager to maintain the distinctiveness of their God, the Jewish scribes might well have made this subtle change in order to eliminate the possibility that other gods could have co-existed with the true God before the Creation. According to *Masseketh Sopherim*, "The Tractate of the Scribes," of the eighth or ninth century A.D., the translators of the LXX later altered a few selected passages of their work for Ptolemy Philadelphus. Genesis 1:1 was specifically noted as one of these emendations.[3] Abraham Geiger, a Jewish scholar of the mid-nineteenth century, suggested that it was for this very reason that Genesis 1:1 was emended by the LXX scribes.[4] However, the variance specifically noted by the Tractate would not significantly alter the meaning of verse 1.[5] Geiger was probably wrong.

There would be reason indeed for the Jewish translators to emend the intent of the text. At this early period, prior to the Masoretic protectors of "tradition," some copyists were not at all averse to adding to and emending scriptures as they copied. How much more so for the translators! Even today translators are

---

2.   Cf. Mitchell J. Dahood, *Psalms I*, p. xxii; *Psalms II*, p. xviii, Anchor Bible, Garden City, NY: Doubleday, 1966.

3.   Henry St. John Thackeray, *The Letter of Aristeas*, London: Society for the Promotion of Christian Knowledge, 1917, Appendix, pp. 89f.

4.   Abraham Geiger, *Urschrift und Verbersetzungen der Bibel...*, 1857, pp. 344, 439, 444, noted by John Skinner, *Genesis*, Edinburgh: T. & T. Clark, 1910, p. 14 (footnote); G.J. Spurrell, *Notes on the Hebrew Text of the Book of Genesis*, London: Methuen, 1904, p. 2; August Dillman, *Genesis Critically and Exegetically Expounded*, Edinburgh: T. & T. Clark, 1897, p. 54.

5.   Skinner, *op. cit.*, p. 14, note.

tempted to take such liberties;[6] the problems inherent in textual variants and canonicity occasionally seem impossible to resolve! Literate Alexandrian Jews—Philo, for example—were usually quite impressed by Greek culture and learning. But the pagan creation myths were repugnant to the Jewish mind; by making Genesis 1:1 an independent sentence, the translators may well have felt that they were distinguishing the *real* Creation and the *real* God from the crude and polytheistic Greek and Egyptian cosmogonies. Thus it was perhaps that they translated verse 1 as a sentence complete in itself.

Still more problematic is the fact that the Hebrew manuscript(s) from which the LXX was translated was/were at many points quite different from the text that ultimately became the Masoretic text, which is the Hebrew basis for today's accepted Old Testament. The Dead Sea Scrolls have shed some light. The great majority of the Hebrew manuscripts from Qumran are remarkably—perhaps miraculously—similar to the Masoretic text of nearly a thousand years later. Yet a significant number—almost ten percent—of the Dead Sea manuscripts of the Pentateuch resemble the text of these first five books of the Greek Septuagint. Apparently, at some point much earlier than 300 B.C., the two textual traditions became separated and then continued to vary ever increasingly. Again, the problems of canonicity and textual variants are enormous.

Unfortunately, it was this minority text that established the primary model for 1,500 years of future translation and interpretation of Genesis 1. The Aramaic Targums were copied no earlier than the first century A.D. and the Syriac Peshitta begun within another generation or two. Both imitated what was by then the developing Septuagintal "tradition" concerning Genesis 1:1.[7] Other translations followed, each of them making the first verse of the Bible an independent sentence.[8] All early English

---

6.   A prominent example is Isaiah 7:14: a "virgin" or a "young woman"?

7.   Cf. Joshua Bloch, "The Influence of the Greek Bible on the Peshitta," *American Journal of Semitic Languages and Literatures*, XXXVI, Jan. 1920, pp. 161-66.

8.   Skinner, *op. cit.*, pp. 12f. In his prodigious *Hexapla*, Origen (early third century) included three Old Testament translations into Greek (Aquila, Theodotion and Symmachus) in addition to the LXX, plus a Hebrew text and a transliteration from Hebrew characters into Greek.

translations also followed this now traditional pattern.[9] Their lineage proceeds from these variant Hebrew texts of Genesis 1:1 (constituting only about ten percent of the Qumran scriptures), to the Greek LXX, to the Latin Vulgate, and to most subsequent translations prior to the Protestant Reformation.

But God has wondrous ways of transmitting and preserving his written word. In the late eleventh century the celebrated Jewish scholar Rashi reintroduced what so obviously appears to have been the Genesis author's intent as well as the original Hebraic interpretation. Rashi was the first *extant* expositor after the Masoretes to note explicitly that proper exegesis should consider the first verse of Genesis to be a dependent clause, with the finite verb "said" in verse 3 as the main verb of the opening sentence. Acknowledging that "our rabbis have interpreted it [as the Septuagint]," Rashi continues,

> **But if you should come to interpret it in its plain sense, thus explain it: At the beginning of the creation of heaven and earth, when the earth was unformed and void, and darkness... (etc.), God said, "Let there be light."**[10]

According to Rashi the initial sentence of the Bible is two-and-a-half verses long.

A generation later the Jewish scholar Ibn Ezra suggested a *third* syntactical arrangement. Ibn Ezra agreed with the temporal quality of verse 1, but disagreed concerning the main verb, which he assumed to be in verse 2, making the first half of verse 3 a distinct sentence.

Suddenly, by the twelfth century, there were *three* possible translations of Genesis 1:1!

---

9.   Luther A. Weigle, *The Genesis Octapla*, New York: Thomas Nelson, 1952, pp. 2-3.

10.   Rashi, *The Pentateuch and Rashi's Commentary, Genesis*, ed. Abraham ben Isaiah and Benjamin Sharfman, Brooklyn, NY: S.S. & R. Publishing Co., 1949, p. 1.

Chapter 3

Exegesis of Genesis 1:1-3

Could the syntax of the Hebrew in verse 1 actually permit all three variant translations? Indeed it might, although Ibn Ezra's interpretation appears to contain some weaknesses; it seems to be a compromise, and compromises result in poor scholarship.

This work will not delve extensively into the technical details of exegesis.[1] One fascinating observation concerning the commentators is that many attempt to demonstrate how one or two of the three possible translations is/are improbable or impossible,

---

1. Serious students of Hebrew can find such discussions in Franz Delitzsch, *A New Commentary on Genesis,* Edinburgh: T. & T. Clark, 1888, pp. 71f; Skinner, *op. cit.,* pp. 12f; J.M. Powis Smith, "The Syntax and Meaning of Genesis 1:1-3," *American Journal of Semitic Languages and Literatures,* 44, 1928, pp. 108f; Harold G. Stigers, *A Commentary on Genesis,* Grand Rapids: Zondervan, 1976, pp. 47f; E.J. Young, *Studies in Genesis One,* Phillipsburg, NJ: Presbyterian and Reformed Publishing Co., 1979, pp. 1f; Brevard S. Childs, *Myth and Reality in the Old Testament,* Naperville, IL: Alec R. Allenson, 1960, pp. 30f; Gerhard von Rad, *op. cit.,* pp. 43f; Weston W. Fields, *Unformed and Unfilled,* Phillipsburg, NJ: Presbyterian and Reformed Publishing Co., 1978 pp. 149f; E.A. Speiser, *Genesis,* Anchor Bible, Vol. 1, Garden City, NY: Doubleday, 1964, pp. 3-13; Gerhard F. Hasel, "Recent Translations of Genesis 1:1: a Critical Look," *The Bible Translator,* Vol. 22, No. 4, Oct. 1971, pp. 154-67; Eichrodt, *op. cit.,* Vol. 2, pp. 100f. The most detailed defenses of the traditional (LXX) translation are Young, Fields and Hasel; cf. also Eichrodt; Smith and Speiser make cases for Rashi's translation, while Stigers chooses Ibn Ezra's.

thus revealing each one's own preference. This work does the same, but with good cause.

The Hebrew alphabet contains consonants with limited vowel sounds; the proper vocalization was often known only to those who spoke it, even as in modern Hebrew, in which the vowel pointings are removed early in an Israeli child's education. Many centuries after Genesis 1:1 was written, the Masoretes, in attempting to standardize their scriptures for the ages, added unclear vowel pointings—and only brought confusion to the syntax of verse 1.

> **...The few fragments [of Origen's third-century A.D. Greek transliteration of the Hebrew, the Hexapla] that remain...seem to prove...that the present [Masoretic] system of vocalization differs appreciably from the system in use at the time of the composition of the Hexapla... We must still conclude that the mode of reading the text which prevailed when the Hexapla was compiled was not precisely the same as that which is prescribed by the system of vowel points now in use.[2]**

Although the written *consonants* remained largely the same, the three to five centuries from Origen to the Masoretes obviously made quite a difference in the *vocalization* of biblical Hebrew. The Jewish scholars of the first millennium of the current era were faithful to the written text, but they were unable to recapture consistently the spoken language.

The Masoretes certainly did not make clear by their pointing how they understood Genesis 1:1. Perhaps they were unsure; more probable is the suggestion that they knew very well how to point verse 1 clearly, but that they compromised after a dispute among themselves, unsurprisingly, over the Septuagintal tradition. Rashi, writing only a few generations later, was the first (we know of) to restore the Hebraic reading to verse 1. During the nineteenth century—and often since—many biblical

---

2.   William Smith and Henry Wace, eds., *A Dictionary of Christian Biography, Literature, Sects and Doctrines*, Vol. III, New York: AMS Press, 1974, pp.15-16. However, cf. Peter C. Craigie, *Psalms 1–50* (Word Biblical Commentary, Waco: Word Books, 1983, p. 52), who disagrees, but not convincingly.

commentators seized upon Rashi's proposed syntax, arguing "that this represents the old Jewish tradition."[3] A number of these scholars have been European. Today's translators still seem to be divided all three ways (see Appendix). Representative English versions of Genesis 1:1-3 are given below (all finite verbs are in italics):

1. (Traditional) *RSV*: "In the beginning God *created* the heavens and the earth. The earth *was* without form and void, and darkness *was* upon the face of the deep; and the Spirit of God *was moving* over the face of the waters. And God *said*, 'Let there *be* light'; and there *was* light."

2. (Rashi) *Anchor Bible*: "When God set about to create heaven and earth—the world being then a formless waste, with darkness over the seas and only an awesome wind sweeping over the water—God said, 'Let there be light.' And there was light."

3. (Ibn Ezra) *An American Translation*: "When God began to create the heavens and the earth, the earth *was* a desolate waste, with darkness covering the abyss and a tempestuous wind raging over the surface of the waters. Then God *said*, 'Let there *be* light!' And there *was* light."

Note the great variation of the main verbs. All three translations *seem* possible in view of the unclear pointing of the Masoretic text.[4]

[I]t is important that we should not enter into the attempt to translate these verses with preconceived ideas about what it must or must not say. We must allow the writer to speak for himself.[5]

Would that we all might heed this counsel!

---

3. Skinner, *op. cit.*, p. 13, note; cf. Hasel, *op. cit.*, p. 157, for a partial listing.

4. Cf. Robert Davidson, *Genesis 1–11*, London: Cambridge University Press, 1973, pp. 12-13; Childs, *op. cit.*, p. 31; William F. Albright, "Contributions to Biblical Archaeology and Philology," *Journal of Biblical Literature*, Vol. 43, 1924, p. 364.

5. W.R. Lane, "The Initiation of Creation," *Vetus Testamentum*, Vol. XIII, 1963, p. 66.

Is Genesis 1:1 an independent sentence as in the traditional interpretation? If so, the opening Hebrew word of the Bible,
*b*e*reshith* ("In [the] beginning...") is said grammatically to be in
the "absolute" state. Or, is Genesis 1:1 a dependent clause, with
the main clause in verse 3 (or, 2)? If so, *b*e*reshith* ("In [the] beginning of...") is said to be in the "construct" state. The controversy
is centered upon the syntactical interpretation of bereshith,
which means, quite literally, with the definite article missing,
either "in beginning" or "in beginning of." Is *b*e*reshith* in the
absolute state or the construct state? **The resolution of this
question will tell us how to translate verses 1-3 properly.**

First, the missing definite article in the Masoretic text mil-
itates against the traditional translation (the absolute state),
which *usually* has the article present, while the second option
(the construct state) can *never* have the article present.[6] There
are four extant early Greek transliterations of Genesis 1:1 (from
the variant [Septuagintal] Hebrew text). Hasel says the
spellings of two of these four "support the view of Genesis 1:1 as
a main clause because apparently some read the definite article
and understood the first word to read [*bareshith*]."[7] (This spelling
in the transliteration implies the presence of the definite article.)
Jerome (A.D. 400) however transliterated the initial word as
bresith.[8] On the other hand, the Greek transliteration of the
Samaritan Torah is *bareshit*, which also implies the definite article.[9] But of course the LXX centuries before had established the
tradition for vocalizing the Hebrew of verse 1 for Greek-reading
Jews, all of which causes us to wonder about the lack of unanimity among the texts and the transliterations. The ancient
examples are quite inconclusive.

*B*e*reshith* is the combination of *b*e (the inseparable preposition "in") and *reshith* ("beginning" or "beginning of"). This

---

6.   Fields, *op. cit.*, pp. 152-53.
7.   Hasel, *op. cit.*, p. 159; Alexander Heidel, *The Babylonian Genesis*, 2nd ed.,
      Chicago: University of Chicago, p. 93, quoting Fridericus Field, *Origenis
      Hexaplorum Supersunt*, Vol. I, Oxford: 1875, p. 7; cf. Origen, *Hexapla*, in
      J.-P. Migne, *Patrologiae Graecae*, Vol. XV, pp. 143-44.
8.   Heidel, *op. cit.*, p. 93.
9.   Hasel, *op. cit.*, p. 159.

combined form as seen in the Masoretic rendering of Genesis 1:1 (b^e *reshith*) is found elsewhere in the Old Testament only in Jeremiah—26:1; 28:1; 49:34—and *only* in the construct state ("in the beginning of"). Even without the preposition b^e, *reshith* in its 50 Old Testament appearances is said by Rashi to be found *always* in the construct state. This is weighty evidence.

Several scholars express their insights, beginning with J.M.P. Smith.

> Even the student beginning his study of Hebrew is puzzled [by what he sees] here... The easy explanation of the difficulty lies in the fact that [*reshith*] here stands in the construct relation with the following clause. [Smith follows with numerous Old Testament examples, concluding with the synonymous t^e*chillah* in Hosea 1:2]: "At the beginning when Yahweh spoke through Hosea then Yahweh said to Hosea, etc." This case is of especial value for our purposes since the construction...is in principle exactly the same as that of Genesis 1:1-3. [Thus the first verse] is obviously incomplete in and of itself....[10]

Smith's final sentence states the case for the primary scriptural thesis of this work. Speiser agrees:

> Grammatically, this is evidently in the construct... Thus the sense of this particular initial term is, or should be, "At the beginning of...," or "when," and not "In/At the beginning"; the absolute form with adverbial connotation would be [*bareshith*]. As the text is now vocalized, therefore, the Hebrew Bible starts out with a dependent clause.[11]

The eleventh-century Rashi long ago presented that very argument:

> For the passage does not come to teach (us) the order of the (acts of) creation, to say that these (heaven and earth) came first. For if it came to teach us that, it would have been necessary to write: "at first" He created the

---

10.   Smith, *op. cit.*, p. 108.

11.   Speiser, *op, cit.*, p. 12.

heavens, etc.; for you have no (occurrence of the word) *reshith* in Scripture, which is not in (the construct state). [Rashi follows with three biblical examples] So here also you should propound: as if (it were) in the beginning of (God's) creating. [Rashi then quotes the same example as Smith, Hosea 1:2]....[12]

Another modern commentator, Cohen, says further,

If the text is rendered literally, the translation is: "in the beginning of God's creating the heaven and the earth...." This translation is necessary because *reshith* never means "the beginning" but "the beginning of" (cf. Genesis 10:10; Jeremiah 26:1).[13]

Rashi and Cohen's assertions would be disputed by some traditionalist Hebrew scholars who insist that, out of its 50 appearances, *reshith* is found at least one time (perhaps several) in the absolute state ("the beginning"),[14] although those who insist upon the absolute state are hard pressed to justify their argument with *any* biblical examples.

Brown, Driver and Briggs in their authoritative lexicon contradicted their predecessor Gesenius by stating, "[I]n the beginning when God created [is] to be preferred over the abs[olute] in the beginning God created."[15] William F. Albright lends his considerable support to a similar proposed translation (see the Appendix).

Thus the weight of evidence indicates that the first three words of the Bible, *b^ereshith bara' Elohim*, mean (with the Masoretic pointing) literally, "In [the] beginning of God created...." The best English expression to capture the meaning is, "When God began to create...."[16] This opening clause is thus

12. Rashi, *The Pentateuch and Rashi's Commentary, Genesis, op. cit.*, p. 1.

13. A. Cohen, *The Soncino Chumash*, Hindhead, Surrey: Soncino Press, 1947, p. 1.

14. Fields, *op. cit.*, pp. 153-54; Lane *op. cit.*, pp. 66-67.

15. Francis Brown, S.R. Driver, Charles A. Briggs, *A Hebrew & English Lexicon of the Old Testament*, Oxford: The Clarendon Press, 1907 (reprinted 1959). Cf. Jaki, *op. cit.*, p. 2.

16. Cf. RSV footnote to Gen. 1:1; C.A. Simpson, "Genesis," *Interpreter's Bible*, Vol. I, Nashville: Abingdon, 1952, p. 466; Cyrus H. Gordon, *Ugaritic Textbook*, Rome: Pontifical Biblical Institute, 1965, p. 56.

almost certainly in the construct state; the evidence for the absolute state is very slight. And that information tells us how to translate verse 1.

The disagreement further concerns the understanding of the verb—that most exciting Hebrew word *bara'*, "create." Is it to be understood as participial? And, does it mean creation out of nothing? In the Old Testament *bara'* is found 48 times in its simple form, most of these occurrences appearing in Genesis and Isaiah.[17] The word in its simple *qal* stem (38 times) and its *niphal* stem (10 times) is *always* found in the Bible with God— never man—as its subject. But in the *piel* stem in Joshua 17 (twice), Ezekiel 21 (twice), and Ezekiel 23, *bara'* clearly means "to cut," with man as its subject. Could *bara'* require the quality of *ex nihilo* in the *qal* and *niphal* stems, while it clearly means "cut," "sculpt," "slash," "chop down," (by man) as in the *piel* stem? Such a major distinction is highly unlikely.

The Punic (Phoenician/Carthaginian, a Semitic tongue) "root *br'* seems to mean 'a sculptor'....The Heb. root *br'* probably has the original meaning 'to separate, divide.' "[18] Comparative linguistics makes the *ex nihilo* distinction even more unlikely.

To enhance further the unique usages of the simple forms of *bara'*, "the accusative of material used" (in creating) is never specifically noted. The object that is created is always something new.[19] *Bara'* in most Old Testament provenances is truly a majestic word. Thus, at least to the modern mind, the doctrine of *creatio ex nihilo* could possibly be inferred from Genesis 1:1.

This idea, however, can be defended only with difficulty. As long ago as 1852 the scholar William Paul noted, "The most eminent Hebrew scholars are now of opinion that the idea of creation out of nothing cannot be shewn to be inherent in the word '*bara'*.'"[20]

---

17. James G. Murphy, *A Critical and Exegetical Commentary on the Book of Genesis*, Boston: Estes & Lauriat, 1873, p. 4.

18. *Theological Dictionary of the Old Testament*, Vol. II, ed. G. Johannes Botterweck and Helmer Ringgren, trans. John T. Willis, Grand Rapids: Eerdmans, 1975, p. 245.

19. Sailhamer, *op. cit.*, p. 249.

20. William Paul, *Analysis and Critical Interpretation of the Hebrew Text of the Book of Genesis*, Edinburgh & London: William Blackwood & Sons, 1852, p. 1. Roman Catholic Carroll Stuhlmueller ("The Theology of Creation in Second Isaias," *Catholic Biblical Quarterly*, Vol. 21, 1959) names a few Catholic scholars who "teach *creatio ex nihilo*. However, most [Catholic] authors, [unlike the majority of their Medieval predecessors] deny such a teaching..." (p. 462, note).

Further, "the material used" by God is usually implied by the context, e.g., "I create Jerusalem a rejoicing..." (Isaiah 65:18b); "Create in me a clean heart..." (Psalm 51:10); "...that a people yet to be created may praise the Lord" (Psalm 102:18 NASB). In addition, *bara'* is sometimes used synonymously with other Hebrew words for create, form, make, build, produce, order, stretch, etc., including Genesis 1:7,16,21,25-27,31 (see also Isaiah 45:7-12,18). There is no Old Testament basis for assuming that *bara'* denotes a creation out of nothing, even if some commentators insist upon it. It is merely a pious tradition.

The Masoretic vowel pointing of *b^ereshith* and *bara'* in verse 1 could be emended minimally to indicate definitely a dependent clause. It makes no sense to point either word in such a compromising manner as the Masoretes did many centuries after Genesis was written, so Kittel has proposed a slightly different and quite reasonable pointing that would clearly make the first verse a dependent clause.[21] Without the confusing vocalization there would be no problem; the original Hebrew consonants remain the same. Just one small Masoretic vowel change in *b^ereshith* and another in *bara'* would give a clear vocalization, demanding the dependent clause. On the other hand, several slight alternative changes would clearly require a finite quality of *bara'*. The Masoretic scholars compromised on a volatile issue.

A pertinent sidelight involves Protestant discussions of biblical inerrancy. Beginning with Luther and Calvin and continuing to our day, conservative writers who accept biblical inerrancy tend *not* to include the Masoretic vowel pointings as being without error. The Preface to the Revised Standard Version notes the translators' usual position:

> The vowel signs...are accepted also in the main, but where a more probable and convincing reading can be obtained by assuming different vowels, this has been done... [T]he vowel points are less ancient and reliable than the consonants.[22]

---

21. Rudolph Kittel, *Biblia Hebraica*, Stuttgart, Württembergische: Bibelanstalt, 1937, p. 1, note. But see E.J. Young, *op. cit.*, p. 3; and H.C. Leupold, *Exposition of Genesis*, Grand Rapids: Baker, 1950, p. 41.

22. *The Revised Standard Version of the Bible*, 2nd ed., Nashville: Thomas Nelson, 1971, p. iv.

Thus no final, indisputable resolution of the vowel pointings of Genesis 1:1 is possible unless more information becomes available.

Three synonymous Hebrew words are found in Genesis 1 and 2: *bara'* and *'asah* in chapter 1 and *yatsar* in chapter 2. All three mean to create, to make, to form. All are used together, again synonymously, in Isaiah 45:7-12,18. *Yatsar* is the Hebrew word found in Genesis 2:7 when "...the LORD God formed man of lumps of ground."[23] Observe that man was *not* created out of nothing, but explicitly "of lumps of ground," yet in chapter 1 the author used *bara'* of the creation of man—not once but *three times* in verse 27. To suggest man's creation out of nothing in chapter 1 and out of lumps of ground in chapter 2 is absolutely contradictory: *bara'* in this usage could not possibly mean *creatio ex nihilo*.

Incidentally, the opening sentence of this *second* creation narrative possesses the same grammatical structure as the proposed initial sentence of Genesis 1: dependent clause...parenthetic clauses... main clause. The second narrative's opening sentence begins with the dependent clause at 2:4b, "In the day that the LORD God made the earth and the heavens." Then follows a series of parenthetic clauses. The subject and principal verb of that sentence are not found before verse 7: "...then the LORD God formed [*yatsar*]...." The similarity of sentence structure between the openings of the two creation narratives is impressive. If the two-and-a-half-verse introduction to Genesis 1 seems long and awkward, the opening sentence following Genesis 2:4a is even longer!

The three Hebrew synonyms are translated consistently in modern versions so the non-Hebrew-reading student can ascertain which verb is being used.[24] *Bara'* is normally rendered "create," *'asah* as "make" and *yatsar* as "form." Speaking through the Old Testament prophets, the LORD often used quite colorful language that can hardly be captured in English translation. Synonymous Hebrew words and phrases appear together in delightfully creative patterns. Isaiah 43:7 displays all three Hebrew words in rapid sequence as God describes his servants, "...whom I created [*bara'*] for my glory, whom I formed [*yatsar*]

---

23. Speiser, *op. cit.*, p. 16.
24. ASV, RSV, NASB, NEB, NIV, *et. al.*

and made [*'asah*]." God did not create a people *ex nihilo!* To insist that *bara'* demands *creatio ex nihilo* is unwarranted. The varied contexts and synonymous usages of all three Hebrew words indicate otherwise. Remember too that *bara'* in the *piel* stem cannot possibly mean a creation out of nothing: it means to "cut," as "cut a tree." Only in the *qal* and *niphal* stems is God always noted as the subject of *bara'*. To find such a massive distinction of meanings among the three stems of the same verb is quite unlikely.

Weston W. Fields, whose exegesis is almost flawless elsewhere, begins to use pejorative language when dealing with the proposed dependent clause of Genesis 1:2: "This extreme view...the pantheistic notion...such a translation is very dubious."[25] Actually, Fields never does deal fully with the basic scriptural thesis of this present work. His criticisms either are directed toward a pre-Genesis ruin-and-re-creation or impatiently dismiss out of hand any view that he judges "liberal." Fields' excellent study is weak only at this point, where the evidence weighs heavily against his case; such is what happens when a great scholar tries to retain a traditional but unproven concept.

David Kimchi, the thirteenth-century Jewish commentator, also does some delicate linguistic footwork to avoid the obvious, but he is so transparent that any student can perceive the fanciful casuistry. Commenting on Isaiah 43:7, Kimchi disagrees with earlier Jewish writers by trying to defend the concept of creation out of nothing.

> I have created him, that is, produced him out of nothing. I have formed him, that is, caused him to exist in a shape or form appointed; I have made him, that is, made the final dispositions and arrangements concerning him.[26]

Medieval and modern piety, whether Jewish or Christian, so often demands that Genesis 1:1 make God to be *Creator ex nihilo*. Regardless of good scholarship, traditionalists seem to insist on retaining the concept.

---

25. Fields, *op. cit.*, pp. 161-62.
26. David Kimchi, quoted in G.H. Pember, *Earth's Earliest Ages*, New York: Fleming H. Revell, 1876, p. 24.

Genesis 1 adds an additional, almost synonymous word, *nathan*, meaning "set": "And God *set* them in the firmament of the heavens..." (1:17). This could be translated "made" also, as it is in Genesis 17:5,20 and Exodus 18:25. A fifth synonym, *qanah*, appears in Genesis 4:1, translated literally—"I have created a man...," from which word Eve named her son Cain. Elsewhere God is *always* the subject of *qanah* (as He is of *bara'*), and the word is normally translated "create" or "Creator." We might wonder what traditional theological baggage *qanah*, like *bara'*, might have acquired through the centuries if that sole usage in Genesis 4 with Eve as its subject had not been there. Its "importance" probably would have rivalled that of *bara'*!

Still another synonym appears in Genesis 2:22 where the Lord God used the man's rib to "build up" [*banah*] the woman. All six are quite similar in meaning: *nathan*, *qanah*, *banah*, *bara'*, *'asah* and *yatsar*. Three additional, almost synonymous words are used in poetic parallelism.[27] There are yet others. Fields lists at least ten different expressions from Genesis 1 and 2 that describe God's creative work.[28]

Verse 1 includes "...the heavens and the earth...." Normally, when an ancient Hebrew spoke of the heavens (when referring to what he could see), he meant "the sky"[29] and what was visible in it;[30] when he spoke of the earth, he meant "the land" as opposed to the sea. "God called the dry land Earth..." (verse 10).[31]

"Land" is a better translation than "earth" for the Hebrew term *eretz* because the term "land" extends only to what we see of the earth around us, what is within our horizons. The land is the dry ground where the

27. *Theological Dictionary of the Old Testament*, Vol. II, op. cit., art. *"Bara'"*, p. 246.

28. *Op. cit.*, p. 73.

29. *The New Century Version of the Bible* (Dallas: Word, 1993) translates Genesis 1:1 correctly, "...the sky and the earth"; see also the New International Version.

30. F.P. Ramsay, *An Interpretation of Genesis*, New York: Neale, 1911, p. 66. And of course, the Creator is enthroned above those heavens (e.g., Deuteronomy 10:14; Psalms 8:1; 57:5; 108:4; Ephesians 4:10; Hebrews 7:26).

31. *Theological Dictionary of the Old Testament*, Vol. I, op. cit., art. *"erets,"* p. 397.

man and the woman were to dwell when they were created. It is this sense that most closely approximates the
Hebrew word *eretz* in Genesis 1:2.

Throughout Genesis 1, the term *eretz* is used to denote
"the dry land," as opposed to a body of water, the seas
(1:10). The "seas" do not cover the "land," as would be
the case if the term meant "earth."[32]

Interestingly enough modern Hebrew spoken in Israel
today has preserved the earlier, more localized, meaning of "earth." It has done so, in effect, by coining another word for "world" or "earth" in a global sense. When it
speaks of the "land" of Israel, for example, it uses the
biblical term from Genesis 1. It does not use that term to
refer to the "world at large."[33]

Ibn Ezra (twelfth century) "understood 'the heavens and earth'
in Genesis 1 to be 'the firmament and the dry land,' just as they
are called within the first chapter."[34] Traditionalists cannot
accept this fact since it violates their position that God created
"the waters" *ex nihilo* as an express part of "the earth."[35] But traditionalists must realize that we moderns are post-Copernican—
even more so post-Enlightenment—and we perceive our world
quite differently.

Many traditional commentators feel that the larger context
indicates that the author intended to speak of the universe, or at
least what we call the Solar System, but there was no such
Hebrew word available. They assert that the expression, "the
heavens and the earth," is "a description of the organized universe...."[36] "[T]he heavens and the earth" is a formula that
always designates the totality of the universe in its order and
beauty.[37] Such assertions are simply not true; they result from a
modern worldview.

32.   John Sailhamer, *op. cit.*, p. 49.
33.   *Ibid.*, p. 210.
34.   *Ibid.*, p. 196.
35.   Fields, *op. cit.*, p. 18.
36.   Simpson, *op. cit.*, p. 466.
37.   Blocher, *op. cit.*, p. 64.

These opening seven Hebrew words of chapter 1 comprise then, not an actual creation, but merely an introductory, temporal clause. The *context* of the entire chapter is decisive.[38] *If* verse 1 describes the creation *ex nihilo* of an ordered land-sea-sky, the remainder of the chapter—with its deliberate process of creation so carefully noted—would be quite redundant. *If* "the heavens" were completed in verse 1, then the making of "the firmament" (the sky) in verse 7 seems quite odd, and the whole creative activity in the heavens on Day Fourth is utterly intrusive and repetitious. Likewise, *if* Planet Earth had been created in verse 1, a strange re-creation is taking place when once again the earth is formed in verses 9 and 10.

To continue, verse 2 speaks clearly of chaos, an impossibility if God has just created an orderly world. The overall context exposes the traditional translation as quite contradictory. Verse 1 is looking *forward* to the Creation! Further, as that initial verse looks ahead, so Genesis 2:1 gives a summary title, looking *backward* to the Creation as described in the previous verses: "Thus the heavens and the earth were finished, and all the host of them."

Additionally, verse 2 in the Hebrew can hardly stand by itself as a complete sentence. The nouns precede the verbs, which would be abnormal for finite Hebrew verbs.[39] This also suggests strongly a parenthetical quality for verse 2. Actually,

---

38. Oswald T. Allis in *God Spake by Moses*, (Nutley, NJ: Presbyterian & Reformed Publishing Co., 1976, p. 9) says incorrectly, " 'Create' (*bara'*) is a rare word in the Old Testament [not really; it is found more than 50 times]... It does not necessarily mean creation *out of nothing*...; but this is clearly implied." Sadly, Allis is engaging in wishful thinking. It is *not* "clearly implied"; for implications we look to the context, which appears to deny *creatio ex nihilo* repeatedly.

    E.J. Young and Fields both state (concerning the earlier discussion of $b^ereshith$), in defense of the traditional translation, "In fact, the context favors the absolute state" (Fields, *op. cit.*, p. 156).

    Actually, it is the context that almost *destroys* the case for the LXX/Vulgate/King James interpretation. In reading these two excellent presentations, the student must be constantly on guard for the clever insertion of such "axiomatic" statements that are unproven and undemonstrable.

39. Speiser, *op. cit.*, p. 5, note 2; but see Umberto Cassuto, *A Commentary on the Book of Genesis*, trans. Israel Abrahams, Jerusalem: Magnes Press, 1944, p. 19.

the verbs would be quite superfluous if this verse were a complete sentence, as the traditional versions render.[40] We find here circumstantial clauses urgently calling for a translation such as "...the earth being a desolate chaos...."[41] Thus verse 2 is describing the state of things at the time when God *began* to create something orderly out of preexistent chaos. Most who are familiar with ancient Semitic thought would agree that the darkness (*choshek*) was considered to be a preexistent entity[42]—why not the rest of the chaos also?

Finally, the subject and the main verb of the *opening sentence* of the Bible are found at the beginning of verse 3: "...God said...." Thus we have an introductory temporal clause (verse 1), a parenthetical statement of the existing conditions (verse 2), and the initial creative word (verse 3a)—all in one sentence.[43] So involved an opening sentence may seem awkward to us moderns, but it is quite acceptable to the Bible, both Old and New Testaments. Such sentence structure is termed "periodic." As we have already seen, a similar example would be the opening sentence of the second creation narrative in Genesis 2; it is three-and-a-half verses long.[44] Luke opens his Gospel with a four-verse Greek period! Such an introductory sentence is not at all unusual in the scriptures.[45]

A number of modern Hebrew scholars (both liberal and conservative) hold Genesis 1:1 to be a complete sentence, with *b*e*reshith* in the absolute state, largely because of the more than two millennia of tradition (among the liberals are Gunkel, von Rad, Zimmerli, Eichrodt, Cassuto and Westermann).[46] They consider verse 1 to be *titular*, a headline or summary statement. Verse 2 is then the pre-creation chaos, and verse 3 records God's initial creative effort. And these authors do make a strong case: 2,300 years of versions and transliterations is a formidable objection to overcome. Although this treatise holds otherwise

---

40.   Childs, *op. cit.*, p. 32.
41.   Smith, *op. cit.*, p. 110.
42.   Cf. Job 15:22; 17:12-13: 30:26; 38:9,17,19-20; Jeremiah 33:20; Luke 22:53.
43.   Speiser, *op. cit.*, pp. 11-13.
44.   Cf. Jaki, *op. cit.*, p. 9.
45.   For additional complicated syntactical constructions in the Old Testament, see Hasel, *op. cit.*, p. 166.
46.   See von Rad's explanation, *op. cit.*, p. 47.

about the syntax of these early verses, still the titular hypothesis is quite compatible with the overall thesis maintained herein. As some of these notable liberal scholars have asserted, *creatio ex nihilo* is not a derivative of the traditional translation, even if verse 1 might be a title. Further, as we shall see below, if the titular hypothesis is correct, it would suggest that God was the Creator of verse 2's chaos; this situation is scripturally impossible.

Sailhamer gives three reasons why Genesis 1:1 could hardly be a title. (1) "...[T]itles are not formed that way in Hebrew"; (2) " '[A]nd' at the beginning of the second verse makes it highly unlikely"; (3) "Genesis 1 has a summary title at its conclusion, making it unlikely it would have another at its beginning."[47]

In the light of the foregoing, no student of scripture without a theological ax to grind could consider a creation out of nothing to have taken place in verse 1; to conclude otherwise would render all exegesis of scripture absurd. Let us allow scripture to tell us of *creatio ex nihilo* if it will; doctrine must be derived from the written word, not the reverse. Erroneous reasoning as the result of *a priori* assumptions so often leads a student into *ad hoc* scenarios such as the "gap" or "day-age" theories.[48]

Biblical exegetes are repeatedly faced with certain problems. The greatest of these problems is the historical gap of many centuries between the original writing and the modern reading of the Bible. The cultural and linguistic barriers are immense. The "phenomenon of writing" confronts modern exegetes with a continuing puzzle; that is, the various portions of the Bible were addressed to particular generations, but for centuries have been read by generations not intended (by man) to read them. Thus, as one generation succeeds another, the readers peruse the original "text," knowing ever less about the original "context."[49] Scripture must be investigated contextually.[50] Credible exegesis of the Old Testament does not permit the intrusion of post-Enlightenment categories of thought!

---

47.   *Op. cit.*, pp. 102-3.
48.   See Chapter 8, "Concordistic Theories."
49.   Cf. Gene M. Tucker, *Form Criticism of the Old Testament*, Philadelphia: Fortress Press, 1971, Chapter 1, "The Form Critical Method."
50.   Hyers, *op. cit.*, p. 2.

One of the attributes of God that we learn from other Old Testament scriptures is that *He did not create chaos*. Isaiah 45:18 says of the earth's formation, "...he did not create it a chaos [*tohu*], he formed it to be inhabited!" The succeeding verse adds, "I did not say..., 'Seek me in chaos [*tohu*].'" However, the traditional interpretation of Genesis 1:2 implies that God's initial creation was, crudely, a mess! Examine a literal translation of verse 2: "...and the earth being a *formless waste* and *darkness* being upon the face of the *deep* and the Spirit of God moving over the face of the *waters*...." The five italicized words are all descriptive of chaos. Of all these entities—*tohu, bohu, choshek* (darkness), *tᵉhom* (the deep) and *hamayim* (the waters)—not one is expressly noted in chapter 1 to have been created by God, although numerous other created physical entities are specifically named. Waltke reminds us that "[n]o mention is made anywhere in Scripture that God called the unformed, dark, and watery state of verse 2 into existence."[51] Would God have created confusion?

The famous nineteenth-century liberal scholar, Julius Wellhausen, in attempting to be consistent with his belief in *ex nihilo* creation, suggested just that![52] C.A. Simpson[53] and G. Ch. Aalders[54] more recently agreed, as have many others through the centuries, including Gesenius, the great nineteenth-century Hebrew lexicographer. In their defense, if one accepts the "traditional" rendering of Genesis 1:1, the logical conclusion is that God created the chaos of verse 2. John Calvin, that quite logical Reformer, defended this very interpretation.

Moses simply intends to assert that the world was not perfected at its very commencement, in the manner in

---

51. Bruce K. Waltke, "The Creation Account in Genesis 1:1-3," Part III, *Bibliotheca Sacra*, July 1975, p. 221. However, Psalm 104:6 (*if* it refers to the Creation) might indicate that God had created *tᵉhom*; and Isaiah 45:7 says of the Lord, "I form light and create [*bara'*] darkness [*choshek*]." Apparently, however, the author meant by these statements only that the LORD had restricted the deep and darkness to their assigned times and places. Here *bara'* means "separated," "ordered."

52. Julius Wellhausen, *Die compositioning des Hexateuchs* (3rd ed.) Berlin, 1899, p. 105 (noted in Childs, *op.cit.*, p. 30).

53. Simpson, *op. cit.*, pp. 467f.

54. G. Ch. Aalders, *Genesis*, Bible Student's Commentary, Vol. I, trans. William Heynen, Grand Rapids: Zondervan, 1981, pp. 52f.

which it is now seen, but that it was created an empty chaos of heaven and earth.[55]

All of these credit God with the chaos of verse 2, despite the contradictory fact that verse 1 is in language descriptive of an organized sky-land-sea.[56] E.J. Young avoids this difficult issue by insisting that those five Hebrew words of verse 2 do not refer to chaos, but simply "...it was not habitable, not ready for man."[57] Such exegesis seems quite casuistic. Consider the negative qualities of *tohu wabohu* in Isaiah 34:11 and Jeremiah 4:23 and of *tehom* in Psalm 106:9 and Amos 7:4 (cf. Revelation 21:1). Cyrus H. Gordon says,

> In Genesis 1, the biblical author has sidestepped the embarrassing implication of monotheism, that God is the author of everything, which would make Him the creator of evil as well as good. Instead we read that darkness was in the world before God performed His first creative act: the evoking of light. According to Genesis all of God's creative acts are good; evil is not attributed to Him.[58]

Waltke adds,

> [The *tohu wabohu* of Genesis 1:2] indicates a state of material prior to its creation,...material devoid of order, or without being shaped or formed into something.[59]

All exegetical theories of Genesis 1:2 other than the parenthetic clause are self-contradicting; they contain the seeds of their own invalidation.

The God of the Bible is the very antithesis of chaos. He brings order out of disorder and domesticates the untamed. Consider

55. John Calvin, *Commentaries on the Book of Genesis*, Vol. I, trans. John King, Grand Rapids: Eerdmans, 1948, p. 69.

56. Speiser, *op. cit.*, pp. 12-13; Childs, *op. cit.*, p. 31; Eichrodt, *op. cit.*, Vol. 2, p. 104, note; Edmond Jacob, *Theology of the Old Testament*, trans. Arthur W. Heathcote and Philip J. Allcock, London: Hodder and Stoughton, 1958, p. 144, note.

57. *Op. cit.*, pp. 11-14.

58. Cyrus H. Gordon, "Leviathan: Symbol of Evil," *Biblical Motifs: Origins and Transformations*, ed. Alexander Altmann, Cambridge: Harvard University Press, 1966, p. 1.

59. Waltke, *op. cit.*, Part III, April 1975, pp. 142-43.

some analogies. A sculptor chisels a block of shapeless marble to "create" a work of art;[60] a pioneer clears a forest, cultivates and plants it to "create" a farm; an inventor places together discrete components to "create" a new and useful product; an interior decorator selects and arranges pieces to "create" a lovely home. Such is the nature of God's creativity. *Creatio ex nihilo* is a concept foreign to the Old Testament!

True, the syntactical issue of Genesis 1:1 will still remain controversial: the traditional absolute state ("in the beginning...") as opposed to the construct state ("in the beginning of..."). But because of the great weight of evidence, the total absence of inherent problems, and the overall context of both Genesis 1 and the rest of the Bible, our study will proceed from this point on the assumption that a dependent clause (the construct state) was intended by the biblical author as well as the Spirit of God who inspired its writing.

---

60.   Ramm, *op. cit.*, p. 203.

Chapter 4

Ancient Hebraic Thought and the Concept of "Nothing"

The only other possible Old Testament allusion to "nothing" is found in Job 26:7.

*He stretches out the north over the void,
and hangs the earth upon nothing.*

The King James Version reads, "He stretcheth out the north over the empty place, and hangeth the earth upon nothing." The LXX renders "the north" as "the north wind"—perhaps for a good reason that we are unaware of today. The KJV reads "the empty place" for the final word of the first clause, while the Revised Standard Version renders "the void." Many modern versions render it "empty space."

Actually, the final Hebrew word of that first line is *tohu*, which, as we have already seen, cannot be translated as "nothing" or "void" in modern terms, but rather should be chaos, unformed matter, or the like. Atypically, the New English Bible captures the correct sense, "chaos"; Young's Literal Translation is similar—"desolation."

The final word of the verse, *b*e*limah*, is translated "nothing" in almost all the versions. The New English Bible again is an exception, reading "the void." *B^{e}limah* is a combined word in Hebrew—*b^{e}li*, meaning the negative, "not," and *mah*, "something." But biblical Hebrew cannot intend this to describe "nothing" as we moderns think of nothing. Translators must honor the Hebrew poetic parallelism of *tohu* and *b^{e}limah*; those final words of both lines are required to have something in common. The exegesis of the previous chapter thus holds true for *b^{e}limah* also—chaos, desolation, an uninhabitable place, just as the literal Hebrew says, "not something."

"Hang," Hebrew *talah*, is another of the long list of synonyms that mean the approximation of "create."[1] Recall from the earlier exegesis that the ancient Israelite perceived Earth as "the land" as opposed to "the sea" and "the sky." "The earth" in the second line of Job 26:7 is the Hebrew *'erets*—the land, the ground, founded in the midst of chaotic waters, *t^{e}hom*—not a rotating planet. Note then our modern perception of cosmology written into the RSV, where the translators see the biblical "earth" as a globe, spinning through the largely void Solar System. Other modern translations reveal the same anachronistic worldview. The proper understanding of the biblical "nothing" is found in 1 Corinthians 1:28; its exposition may be seen in the next chapter. Job 26:7 thus does not make a case for a modern cosmology.

Nor does Isaiah 40:23:

who brings princes to nought,
and makes the rulers of the earth as nothing.

"Nought" is the translation of *ayin*, meaning "nothing," or the negative, "not." "Nothing" at the end of the verse is *tohu*, which was discussed above in relation to Job 26:7.

Without a clear understanding of our Western value orientation, we face the twin dangers of ethnocentrism and anachronism. Ethnocentrism is "the judging of all persons in the world in terms of one's own culture on the presumption that, since 'we' are by nature human, so if anyone else is human then they should and must be just as we are...."[2]

---

1. *Theological Dictionary of the Old Testament, op.cit.,* Vol. I, p. 394.
2. Bruce J. Malina, *Christian Origins and Cultural Anthropology: Practical Models for Biblical Interpretation,* Atlanta: John Knox, p. 29; quoted in Ronald A. Simkins, *Creator and Creation,* Peabody, MA: Hendrickson Publishers, 1994, p. 34.

> By assuming that the people of the Bible thought and
> behaved like us, we run the risk of reading into the bib-
> lical texts our own agenda rather than extracting from
> the texts their messages.[3]

We westerners are heirs, not to Hebrew, but to Greek culture, with an additional 2,000 years-plus of human history and
development. We face the problem discussed earlier of the historical and cultural gap. And it is immense.[4] The idea of "nothing" has changed radically. "Nothing" in terms of the zero, the
cypher, is a relatively modern concept. The Babylonians of 2000
B.C. (the place and period out of which came Abram the
Hebrew), even with their most sophisticated sexagesimal numeral system, still did not grasp the idea of the zero for nearly
another 2,000 years.[5] Even then, the zero was known only among
the limited caste of Babylonian astrologers who used their great
mathematical skills to plot and predict from the motions of the
visible planets. The first actual recorded use of the zero in mathematics comes from Ptolemy's *Almagest* in about A.D. 140,[6]
although in earlier centuries various cultures used a blank space
or some distinctive mark to signify a place-value notation (as we
also use the zero). But the concept of "nothing" as found in modern mathematics remained undiscovered for centuries, and it
resisted popular awareness until the western world had experienced a Renaissance.[7]

Before the notion of *creatio ex nihilo* could be proposed and
understood, a philosophical-religious basis had to be established.
This is known to have occurred in the first and second centuries
as a combination of old and new ideas began to interact in the
Middle East. Zoroastrian dualism from the east, Greek philosophy from the west, and Christianity from the center—all con-
spired together to form one of the most powerful and persistent

---

3.   *Ibid.*, Simkins, p. 34.
4.   Ramm, *op. cit.*, pp. 65f, presents a helpful discussion, although he
     includes a number of unsubstantiated statements.
5.   *Encyclopaedia Britannica*, 15th ed.: Vol. 1, p. 1175; Vol. 11, pp. 639f.
6.   *Ibid.*, Vol. 11, p. 640.
7.   Lancelot Hogben, *Mathematics for the Millions*, New York: W.W. Norton,
     1937, Chapter VII, "The Dawn of Nothing, or How Algebra Began,"
     pp. 283f.

heresies during the 2,000 years of Church history: gnosticism.
These new "scientific" teachings excited men's minds, and intelligent, articulate leaders syncretized all they were learning to
propose some complex systems of gnosticism. In the midst of all
this ferment the novel Persian concept of the zero appeared. And,
as far as can be ascertained by this research, the famous gnostic
Basilides first proposed *creatio ex nihilo.*[8]

We learn about Basilides primarily from Hippolytus, the third-
century Bishop of Rome who was later martyred for his faith. An
Alexandrian of the early second century, Basilides had been nurtured in Iranian Zoroastrianism, having been heavily exposed also
to Greek philosophical and Egyptian Christian influences.[9] These
three cultures provided the perfect "mix" for a doctrine of *creatio
ex nihilo.* "Basilides," says Haardt, "in order to give the appearance of having discovered something deeper and truer, extended
his doctrine beyond limits."[10] Bishop Hippolytus describes with
astonishment this novel doctrine of *creatio ex nihilo.*

> **(Time) was, says (Basilides), when there was nothing.
> Not even, however, did that nothing constitute anything
> of existent things;...without any quibbling, it is alto-
> gether nothing....**[11]

Now, for the first time, the Graeco-Roman scholarly world could
conceive of creation out of nothing. Many educated Christians
would have accepted *creatio ex nihilo* immediately because it

---

8.   Edwin Tenney Brewster, *Creation*, Indianapolis: Bobbs-Merrill, 1927,
     p. 53: "But did [the author of Gen. 1] mean by *bara* to create out of noth-
     ing? Unquestionably, by about the beginning of the Christian Era, thanks
     apparently to the great gnostic Bacilides, *bara* had taken on that meaning.
     But in 500 B.C. *bara* meant 'to separate,' 'to cut out,' 'to manufacture.' "

     "The expression *ex nihilo* or *de nihilo* had to be fastened, around 200 A.D.,
     by Christian theologians on the verb *creare* to convey unmistakably a
     process, strict creation, which only God can perform" (Jaki, *op. cit.*, p. 3).

9.   Gilles Quispel, *Gnostic Studies*, I, Istanbul: Nederlands Instituut voor
     het Nabije Oosten, 1974, pp. 103f.

10. Robert Haardt, *Gnosis: Character and Testimony*, trans. J.J. Hendry, Lei-
     den: E.J. Brill, 1971, p. 41.

11. Hippolytus, "The Refutation of All Heresies," VII, viii, *Ante-Nicene
     Fathers*, Vol. V., ed. Alexander Roberts and James Donaldson, Buffalo:
     Christian Literature Publishing Co., 1885, p. 103.

seemed to exalt the true God. Perhaps more important, they accepted *ex nihilo* because its gnostic sources gave it the appearance of being so *scientific*. It is important, however, to remember its heretical origin—important also to perceive in this quotation from Hippolytus that, although the astonished bishop flourished as late as the third century, the concept of "nothing" was quite obviously still foreign to his personal worldview. Incidentally, Neville notes that the pagan Neoplatonists a century later began to adopt *ex nihilo* creation.[12]

As we have seen then, prior to the early second century, even the educated ancients (apart from a select group of Indian and Persian astrologers) could not have imagined what we moderns call "nothing." Therefore, in order to understand the Old Testament worldview, we must practice *Hebraic* thinking: We must conceive a creation narrative without a zero. The Hebraic "nothing" was, rather, chaos—*tohu wabohu, t^{e}hom*, a jungle perhaps, an ocean, or a desert—simply, a place that is uninhabitable, unusable by man. And God in his creativity made a portion of this water-covered planet habitable; that portion is '*erets*, the land. He "ordered" it. When in Genesis 1:4 "...God separated the light from the darkness," He was establishing order between the "good" light and the "evil" darkness. As Jesus stated with great awareness to those arresting Him in Gethsemane, "But this is your hour, and the power of darkness" (Luke 22:53b).

Of all the hundreds of ancient creation myths worldwide (and it may be that there is a solid kernel of truth, albeit distorted, in every one of them), not one depicts *creatio ex nihilo*.[13] Every ancient pagan cosmogony describes a process of formation by which a god (or, gods) created the earth out of preexistent material—not a passive material, but often a body of substance

---

12. Robert C. Neville, *God the Creator*, Chicago: University of Chicago Press, 1968, p. 110.
13. Dwardu Cardona, "Creation and Destruction," *Kronos*, Vol. IV, No. 3, p. 73, "Forum": "In no myth has ancient man ever deluded himself into thinking that the Earth was created out of nothing." Lucretius, the first-century B.C. Roman poet and philosopher, stated, "We shall begin with this principle, nothing is ever gotten out of nothing by divine power" ("On the Nature of Things," Book I, 146, trans. H.A.J. Munro, *Great Books of the Western World*, Vol. 12, Chicago: Encyclopaedia Britannica, 1952, pp. 2-3).

possessing an evil, rebellious personality. Plato and Aristotle saw the resultant orderliness of the world, so they held the Creation to be the work of Reason, some form of Divine Force, the Prime Mover. "Not only was the universe created by a god, it was itself a living creature, and the sun, moon and stars the highest forms of life within it."[14] Unfortunately, these two fourth-century B.C. Greek philosophers have seriously influenced almost every commentary on Genesis 1 for more than two millennia.

The Bible of course differs sharply from other ancient cosmogonies in that it reveals events in Earth's natural history as "...men moved by the Holy Spirit spoke from God" (2 Peter 1:21). Second Peter also asserts, "...we did not follow cleverly devised myths" (1:16a). We today must ascertain that biblical truth in its ancient context to learn what the authors, inspired by God, were trying to tell their contemporaries, *not* their descendants.

Twentieth-century Christians have little idea how extensively modern rationalistic and uniformitarian thought has affected their worldview. Many of us evangelicals assert boldly that we believe the "whole" Bible to be true, all the while viewing it through rationalistic "glasses." We unconsciously try to demythologize the scriptures, questioning the reality of Satan and demonic spirits, miracles, healings, and nearly every other biblical and contemporary manifestation of supernaturalism, scarcely realizing that the Bible had already been demythologized when it was written. We moderns have been tampered with by Aristotle!

As many scholars have pointed out to us deceived westerners, most of the Old Testament was written *in* Hebrew, *by* Hebrews, *to* Hebrews, *within* a Hebrew culture. The Septuagint, which was for centuries the Old Testament for Christians, is Greek, western, the product of a blending of the two cultures. The LXX is very, very different from most of the Hebrew texts found at Qumran as well as the text later declared canonical by the Masoretes. Rashi's is a call back to the original intent of the great majority of the extant manuscripts of the Hebrew Genesis, resulting as well (as we shall see) in a much more plausible exposition as it bears upon modern science, particularly cosmology.

---

14.   W.K.C. Guthrie, *In the Beginning*, Ithaca, NY: Cornell University Press, 1957, pp. 105-107.

This presentation is also a call to creationists to believe *everything* the Bible says about the Creation. Post-Enlightenment reinterpretation of scripture usually leads to error. We must permit the Bible to speak to us!

Not included in the scope of this book is the forming of the animal kingdom, those creatures to whom God gave *nephesh*, life itself. But let us digress momentarily. Scientific creationists today often state that everything God made in Genesis was accomplished by processes that are no longer operative in the earth. It is true of course that the Spirit of God completed his initial creative work in those six days. But Isaiah 48:7 says, "They [new things] are created [*bara'*] now, not long ago...." As may be observed in this verse, a similar creation terminology is used in Isaiah to predict the imminent reestablishment of the Jewish state.

And the same creative (*bara'*) power is available as needed today; for even as Jesus used the Spirit's power nearly 20 centuries ago, we see Him to this day still performing such creative miracles. The physically dead once again are often given God's unique gift of *nephesh*. As J.B. Phillips entitled his book, *Your God Is Too Small*,[15] so creationists should be asked, Is *your* God too small? Creationists tend to be quite defensive of ancient miracles—those recorded in scripture—but are often embarrassed by and even hostile toward contemporary miracles. Only our rationalistic "blinders" prevent us from perceiving that the same personal Spirit and the same natural forces and processes involved in the Genesis Creation *are operative today*. True Christian faith sees God's working in his world much as He has always worked. We moderns are not so far removed from Creation Week after all!

"Jesus Christ is the same yesterday and today and for ever" (Hebrews 13:8).

---

15.   New York: Macmillan, 1953.

Chapter 5

The New Testament and Creatio Ex Nihilo

Although it seems to be difficult to defend *creatio ex nihilo* in the Old Testament, the New Testament does appear to speak forthrightly about a doctrine of creation out of nothing.

But does it? Certainly every student of the Bible has been awaiting a discussion of Romans 4:17 and Hebrews 11:3.

First, Paul tells in Romans 4:17 of the "...God...who...calls into existence the things that do not exist." Then Hebrews 11:3 says, "...the world was created by the word of God, so that what is seen was made out of things which do not appear." What of these apparent biblical affirmations of *creatio ex nihilo*? Is this perhaps an example of "progressive revelation"?

Once again, we must beware of perceiving scripture (these verses having been written in the Greek language and in the thought forms of a generation immersed in a Platonic worldview) through our twentieth-century uniformitarian eyes. The author of the Letter to the Hebrews did not intend what we understand today by "things which do not appear." In recent centuries we have come to understand it to mean nothing—zero! But note carefully: Hebrews 11:3 speaks of "things," not nothings: "...what is seen was made out of *things*...." By that statement our *Old Testament* ancestors would have meant unformed things, confused

things, empty of habitation, wild, desolate, chaotic—yes, even
the Hebrew words of Genesis 1:2—*tohu wabohu, t^ehom*. But by
the time of the New Testament the author of Hebrews spoke in
a Platonic sense of invisible (or, heavenly) things, but *things* nevertheless. A most important point for comprehending the New
Testament concept of creation: Greek Platonism had long since
provided for Jews and (later) Christians the philosophical basis
for distinguishing things visible (earthly) from things invisible
(heavenly). Hebrews 11:3 is not speaking of *ex nihilo* creation,
but rather a creation of physical things *out of* spiritual things.
The author of the Letter to the Hebrews was totally immersed in
a culture (of the educated) that held a Platonic worldview.

As early as the third century B.C. the LXX translators,
already influenced by Alexandrian Platonism, translated the
tohu wabohu of Genesis 1:2, not as "formless chaos" or anything
similar, but rather as "invisible and unordered." The preferred
Greek word *chaos* was available to them, but they understood
tohu wabohu more nearly in Platonic terms. Paul demonstrates
such thinking by the manner in which he spoke of the Creation
in Colossians 1:16: "[F]or in [Christ] all things were created, in
heaven and on earth, *visible and invisible....*" These italicized
words reveal the influence upon Paul of a Platonic worldview.
This Platonic quality of course does not mean that the great
apostle's statement is not quite true; it simply reflects a contemporary style of describing spiritual and physical realities. After
all, Paul grew up in the Diaspora, and he is writing to Greek-
speaking Gentiles.

Second, Paul's reference in Romans 4:17 to God's calling
"into existence the things that do not exist" can be explained by
an analogous quotation from the apostle. He says in 1 Corinthians 1:28, "God chose what is low and despised in the world, even
things that are not, to bring to nothing things that are"—again,
nevertheless, *things*. Paul uses a Greek verb, *katargeo*, which
has many related meanings—the Revised Standard Version translates it ten different ways. Here the RSV renders it "bring to
nothing," while other translations read "make useless" or "nulli-
fy." It can even mean to "destroy." Paul, however, in the same
verse speaks clearly of "things that are not" as well as "things
that are"—again, nevertheless, *things*. A literal interpretation of

these clauses in twentieth-century western terms is extremely awkward, even incomprehensible. Only by studying the statement in its context do we perceive that Paul, who thought in both Greek and Hebraic terms, means that "people and institutions currently held in great esteem will be brought down to being disgraced or confused or destroyed," certainly not to what we consider "nothing" today. We might even say, with the author of Genesis 1, "brought down from order to disorder."[1]

Romans 4:17c says, literally, "...calling the things not being as being." Paul is speaking of the promise to Abraham, the fruit of which (his descendants) did not yet exist, but some day would exist, although certainly not to be created *ex nihilo*. Paul's expression in Romans 4:17 could also be explained analogously by the illustration of a clever mechanic who takes junk parts and builds an acceptable automobile. Modern Americans might say, "He created something out of nothing." No one using this colloquialism could possibly be thinking of *creatio ex nihilo*. Likewise, God takes "nobodies" and makes them "somebodies." And those who think they are "somebodies" God brings down to becoming "nobodies" (as in 1 Corinthians 1:28).

Thus we could state that, on the basis of the foregoing, regardless of how Genesis 1:1 is translated, the sense is still the same, whether derived from the original Hebraic text or the Septuagint/Vulgate/King James tradition. The correct interpretation depends not merely upon the translation, but even more upon understanding the ancients' concept of nothing.

There is a third relevant—and most important—New Testament reference to Creation. Second Peter 3:5 is quite explicit about the meaning of the early verses of Genesis. "By the word of God heavens existed long ago, and an earth formed out of water and by means of water...." The author's choice of "formed" is the perfect participle (as found in Colossians 1:17b), dependent upon the finite verb "existed." It means that the earth had *already* been "framed and possessing existence." Second Peter is definitely not Platonic; the writer *knows* there was preexistent

---

1.   Cf. Isaiah 34:12; 40:23; 1 Corinthians 6:13; 15:24,26; 2 Thessalonians 2:8. Cf. Gerhard Delling, art. in *Theological Dictionary of the New Testament*, Vol. I, ed. Gerhard Kittel, trans. Geoffrey W. Bromiley, Grand Rapids: Eerdmans, 1964, pp. 452-54.

matter; the earth (the land) was "formed out of water," raised up from the ocean depths. This verse is a most perceptive New Testament commentary on Genesis 1:2; it must be dealt with by those who would demand a New Testament doctrine of creation out of nothing. To repeat, those Christians who insist upon *creatio ex nihilo* must explain 2 Peter 3:5 without explaining it away.

Other New Testament scriptures, such as John 1:1; Ephesians 3:9; and Colossians 1:15-17, may be thought to allude to *ex nihilo*, but every one merely refers (as far as Creation is concerned) back to Genesis 1 and 2, the creation out of preexistent chaos.

Such is the New Testament witness to Creation. Again, from Genesis to Revelation the Bible knows nothing of *creatio ex nihilo*.

Chapter 6

The Ancient Commentators

As with all translations, the Greek Septuagint is itself a commentary on Genesis 1:1-3 merely by the way it was translated. We also find some ancient Jewish and Christian references to the Creation apart from the canonical scriptures and the versions. The evidence conforms rather closely to what we have found in the three primary New Testament references.

The late second-century B.C. apocryphal 2 Maccabees contains a mother's admonition to her son: "Look at the heaven and the earth and see everything that is in them, and recognize that God did not make them out of things that existed" (7:28). Some modern commentators feel this verse is the first ancient reference to *creatio ex nihilo*. Such an interpretation is not correct, however, for it serves only to remind us of Paul's later statement in Romans 4:17, which was discussed in the previous chapter. Neither this second-century B.C. Jewish mother nor the scribe who immortalized her courageous speech could have comprehended what we understand today by the concept of nothing. The implication of her statement is that God made the *physical* "heaven and earth," not "out of things that existed," but out of *spiritual* "things" or "ideas"—another obvious example of the contemporary Platonic worldview. The oldest extant copy of 2 Maccabees is written in Greek, although it apparently had been translated from the Hebrew. How the original Jewish author framed the mother's statement cannot be ascertained; however, the initial translator(s) held a Platonic worldview.

The apocryphal Wisdom of Solomon, dating from within a generation of 2 Maccabees, tells of "...your all-powerful hand which created the world out of formless matter" (11:17a). This statement could be understood in the Hebraic sense, conforming to the primary thrust of this book, or, more probably, it reflects the anonymous Jewish author's worldview as influenced by Platonic and Stoic philosophies. Parts of Wisdom are distinctly Hebraic and other parts are strongly influenced by Greek thought. Indeed, the book was written in Greek, probably in Alexandria. Either way the author(s) intended his (their) statement, it underscores all that this presentation has been asserting. Wisdom adds a statement just three verses later:

> But Thou hast arranged all things
> by measure and number and weight (11:20c).

This passage formed a cornerstone of many Roman Catholic commentaries on Genesis 1 through the centuries.

Philo of Alexandria, a Jewish contemporary of Jesus of Nazareth, was so thorougly Hellenized that he conceived, with the Greeks, of the great antiquity (perhaps, eternity) of matter.[1] Of course, at that early date *creatio ex nihilo* would have been foreign to Philo, so he wouldn't have had occasion to speak to the issue.

Following the A.D. 70 destruction of Jerusalem, Rabbi Gamaliel II states that God in Genesis 1 created the earth out of preexistent material that, although not expressly mentioned in scripture, He had created in the first place.[2] The rabbi may have preserved for us a very good description of the worldview of the original author of Genesis 1, although he too would surely have been influenced by Platonism. In either case, he seems to be anticipating Augustine's understanding three centuries later.

---

1.   James Hastings, *The Great Texts of the Bible*, Vol. I, New York: Charles Scribner's Sons, 1911, p. 28.

2.   Georges Vadja, "Notice sommaire sur l'interpretation de Genèse 1:1-3 dans le judaisme post-biblique," *In Principio: Interpretation des Premier Versets de la Genèse*, Paris: Etudes Augustiennes, 1973, pp. 29f (noted in Blocher, *op. cit.*, p. 65).

At some unknown time in the early centuries of this era there appeared an anonymous Jewish writing known as 2 Enoch, or The Book of the Secrets of Enoch. The mysterious author, putting words in the mouth of God, says,

> **Before anything existed at all, from the very beginning, whatever is I created from non-being into being, and from invisible things into the visible... Before any visible things had come into existence...I...moved around in the invisible things... Yet I did not find rest, because everything was not yet created. And I thought up the idea of establishing a foundation, to create a visible creation. And I commanded..., "Let one of the invisible things come out visibly!" (24:2–25:1)[3]**

Here is a prominent example of Platonic thinking—the visible created out of the invisible, precisely as we find it in Romans 4:17; Hebrews 11:3; and 2 Maccabees 7:28. Some students may be impressed with how close Plato came to an Old Testament worldview, yet we observe also how far he missed it. The Greek worldview is perhaps the cleverest ever devised by man, while the Old Testament worldview was inspired by the One who actually did the creating.

A few pertinent references to the Creation appear in the early Church Fathers. The Shepherd of Hermas dates from the first half of the second century. This unknown author describes the "God who dwells in heaven and created the things that are from that which is not...."[4] Again, the Shepherd is thinking in Platonic terms similar to Romans 4 and Hebrews 11 and the creation of "visible" things out of "invisible" things, whose original quality was "that which is not," heavenly rather than earthly.

The near eastern ancients of this period, in keeping with the reigning Platonic worldview, distinguished, not as we do today, between "something" and "nothing," but rather between *types* of "things"—things "visible" and things "invisible."[5] The invisible is

---

3.   James H. Charlesworth, ed., *The Old Testament Pseudepigrapha*, Vol. I, Garden City, NY: Doubleday, 1983, pp. 25-27.

4.   "The Shepherd of Hermas," I, 1, 6. *The Apostolic Fathers*, Vol. 6. trans. Graydon Snyder, Camden: Thomas Nelson, 1968, p. 28.

5.   Cf. Thorlief Boman's discussion of "non-being" in both Greek and Old Testament Hebrew thought, *Hebrew Thought Compared with Greek*, Philadelphia: Westminster Press, 1960, pp. 55-58.

the model, the heavenly ideal, that which is perfect. For modern Jews and Christians the contrast would be between "things earthly" and "things heavenly," as there are a heavenly temple, a heavenly ark of the covenant, and a heavenly altar (Revelation 11:19; 15:5; 9:13), while the Jerusalem temple, the ark and the altar were the earthly "copies." Several centuries of Hellenistic exposure influenced Jewish thinking deeply—the actual religious modifications having been perhaps somewhat limited—but Jewish scholars were most certainly affected metaphysically and philosophically. Jewish (and later, Christian) writings were strongly colored by the dominating Platonic worldview for many centuries.

The Constitutions of the Holy Apostles, dating from the second or third century, says that God "...in the beginning did reduce into order the disordered parts."[6] This valuable Christian teaching depicts tersely that six-day primeval struggle, accurately describing a Hebraic creation out of preexisting, chaotic material. The unknown author(s) certainly grasped the Genesis concept of creation.

Galen, the second-century pagan Greek physician-philosopher, living in Rome, had read the Genesis account of creation: "For [Moses says] that God simply willed the arrangement of matter and it was presently arranged in due order."[7] Galen correctly understands the preexistent matter just as Genesis depicts it. "Arrangement" (and "arranged") is the key word, with no possibility of *ex nihilo*.

The first explicit references to *creatio ex nihilo* in Christian literature are found in the writings of at least one of two contemporary bishops: Theophilus of Antioch, a Jewish Christian whose bishopric began in A.D. 169, and Irenaeus, the bishop of Lyons from A.D. 177. Theophilus contrasts the Stoic and Platonic cosmogonies with his own concept of *ex nihilo*.

Some of the Stoics absolutely deny the existence of God or assert that if God exists he takes thought for no one but himself... Others say that everything happens

---

6.   "Constitutions of the Holy Apostles," Book VII, 34, *Ante-Nicene Fathers, op. cit.*, Vol. VII, p. 472.

7.   Galen, "On the Usefulness of the Parts of the Body," 11, 14, in Robert L. Wilkin, *The Christians as the Romans Saw Them*, New Haven: Yale University Press, 1984, pp. 86-87.

spontaneously, that the universe is uncreated and that nature is eternal; in general they venture to declare that there is no divine providence but that God is only the individual's conscience... Others, on the contrary, hold that the spirit extended through everything is God....

Plato and his followers acknowledge that God is uncreated, the Father and Maker of the universe; next they assume that uncreated matter is also God, and say that matter was coeval with God... But if God is uncreated and matter is uncreated, then according to the Platonists God is not the Maker of the universe, and as far as they are concerned the unique sovereignty of God is not demonstrated. Furthermore, as God is immutable because he is uncreated, if matter is uncreated it must also be immutable, and equal to God....

What would be remarkable if God made the world out of pre-existent matter?... But the power of God is revealed by his making whatever he wishes out of the non-existent, just as the ability to give life and motion belongs to no one but God alone....[8]

Was Bishop Theophilus describing a creation out of nothing? Theophilis does sound somewhat Platonic.

Bishop Irenaeus, however, taught *ex nihilo* creation quite clearly. Theophilus' younger contemporary in far-off Gaul may have found his source in the elder bishop, or, more probably, from Basilides' heretical teachings, including *creatio ex nihilo*, which by this time have been sweeping across the Roman world. Certainly gnosticism was spreading rapidly throughout the Empire at this time—just as Darwinian evolution was to sweep almost everything ahead of it centuries later. In "Against Heresies" Irenaeus has been lashing out at one of the numerous gnostic systems, but in the course of this attack he finds himself agreeing with their newfound doctrine of *ex nihilo* creation:

While men indeed cannot make anything out of nothing, but only out of matter already existing, yet God is in

---

8.   *Theophilus of Antioch: To Autolycus*, trans. Robert M. Grant, Oxford: Clarendon Press, 1970, II, 4.

> this point preeminently superior to men, that He Him-
> self called into being the substance of His creation,
> when previously it had no existence.[9]

Irenaeus provides us with the first certain, extant Christian
espousal of *ex nihilo* creation.

At this point the scene of the debate moved *inside* the
Church. Although the God of the Bible may have been perceived
as being more exalted and almighty by the appropriation of *ex
nihilo*, not all the Fathers would accept it. Some of them were
aware of its suspect origin and, in addition, the new concept of
"nothing" required a radical philosophical adjustment in their
thinking.

The North African Tertullian, following Irenaeus by a single
generation, in his mature years began to consider creation out of
nothing to be orthodoxy. The argument over *ex nihilo* raged
between two obviously brilliant Christian teachers of
Carthage—Tertullian and Hermogenes.[10] We read only one side
of the debate—Tertullian's—so we probably have received a distorted presentation of his opponent's propositions. Tertullian the
lawyer begins with an *ad hominem* attack upon Hermogenes,
which should immediately raise the reader's suspicions about
the quality of the author's argument. The crusty Tertullian then
launches into his typical vitriolic attack with a quite involved
and not always consistent logic.

> ... In every operation...there must be three names men-
> tioned...—the person of the maker, the sort of thing
> which is made, and the material of which it is formed. If
> the material is not mentioned, while the work and the
> maker of the work are both mentioned, it is manifest
> that He made the world out of nothing.[11]

A most illogical argument to be sure! Further, Tertullian's exegesis is poor, for we have already seen that the material out of

---

9.   Irenaeus, "Against Heresies," Book II, x, 4, *Ante-Nicene Fathers, op. cit.,*
     Vol. 1, p. 370.
10. Tertullian, "Against Hermogenes," *ibid.,* Vol. III, pp. 477-502. The subti-
     tle of his treatise is "Containing an argument against his opinion that
     matter is eternal."
11. *Ibid.,* Chapter XX, p. 489.

which God made the dry land is indeed noted in Genesis 1:2 and 2 Peter 3:5. If he knew the scriptures, Hermogenes must surely have reminded his opponent of that fact. Paradoxically, Tertullian proceeds to contradict himself dramatically in his very next chapter, admitting that

> ...scripture has *not* expressly declared that all things were made out of nothing... [italics added].[12]

And there it is! This entire historical presentation could rest on that one mere statement. Tertullian's frank admission is most important to our modern understanding of how *ex nihilo* began to infiltrate the Christian Church. At least Tertullian is honest enough to face what modern exegetes only occasionally do—that creation out of nothing is not mentioned anywhere in scripture. Probably the zero-concept was so novel that Tertullian was as yet unable to think of it as an implicit part of his worldview. Today the idea of nothing is merely assumed in western culture. Stanley Jaki confirms in thorough research what he correctly terms "the post-New Testament formulation of the idea of 'creation out of nothing.' "[13]

So the new concept of *creatio ex nihilo* took many of the Church Fathers by storm. The great Augustine (A.D. 400), however, was hesitant to accept it. He must have known the pagan sources of *ex nihilo*, having for years been a keen student of philosophy. His writings indicate his own years-long struggle, and Augustine's final position is similar to that proposed in this book: "Although the world has been made of some material, that very same material must have been made out of nothing."[14] Augustine was thinking of "material" for the initial Creation that had a *pre*-biblical origin—*ex nihilo*—*before* Genesis! In spite of Augustine's ignorance of the laws of thermodynamics, gravity, and other natural phenomena, he was probably as close to correct as he could be, given the limits of fifth-century scientific knowledge and a worldview rooted in Neoplatonism.

---

12. *Ibid.*, Chapter XXI, p. 489.
13. *Op. cit.*, p. 6.
14. Augustine, "De Genesi contra Manichaeos," Book I, vi; (noted in White, *op. cit.*, pp. 5, 26).

Perhaps the most telling evidence from the early Church is the fact that *ex nihilo* creation is almost totally absent from the dozens of creeds and creedal statements that were published by various Fathers of the Church and by several ecumenical councils. A number of creeds include a creationist statement such as "...Maker of all things visible and invisible...," but this merely reveals the prevailing Greek worldview.

The only clear exception is from the third-century author we might expect, Tertullian. He included three creedal statements in his extant writings, but in only one of the three was *ex nihilo* noted. Perhaps Tertullian had only recently heard of the concept when he wrote *The Prescriptions against the Heretics*, which project forced him to make a clear creedal statement (against the gnostics). In his creed, Tertullian said,

> ...[T]he Creator of the world, who produced everything from nothing through his Word, sent forth before all things; that this Word is called his Son....[15]

How interesting and informative it is, not that Tertullian included *ex nihilo* in his third and final extant creedal statement, but that he omitted it from the first two creeds (*On the Virgin's Veil* and *Against Praxeas*)! Obviously Tertullian added this doctrine to his personal faith quite late in his career.

The Roman Church did not even include *ex nihilo* creation in the extensive *Canons and Decrees of the Council of Trent* (1546–64). Only in the First Vatican Council (1870) was it decreed that "...God...created out of nothing."[16] And, as Church historians are all aware, that wasn't the only error of Vatican I. However, the nineteenth-century Catholic scholar, John Henry Newman, declared with great insight, "Holy Scripture...speaks of a process of formation out of chaos which occupied six days...."[17] The Orthodox Confession of the Eastern Church had earlier (1643) included *ex nihilo*.[18] So we see that this doctrine was obviously centuries in its establishment.

15. *Early Latin Theology*, The Library of Christian Classics, Philadelphia: Westminster Press, 1956, p. 40. Cf. Philip Schaff, *The Creeds of Christendom*, Vol. II, Grand Rapids: Baker, reprinted 1983, pp. 11-73.
16. Schaff, *ibid.*, p. 239.
17. Jaki, *op. cit.*, p. 233.
18. *Ibid.*, pp. 290-300.

The early third-century Church Father, Origen, "...held that God's creative activity is without beginning or end, and that an infinity of worlds has preceded this."[19] Within this same writing, however, Origen told of a current Alexandrian creed that included this syncretistic statement: "...God...who, when nothing was, brought all things into being...."[20] Origen's "On the Principles" is extant only in a very poor Latin translation by Rufinus (late fourth century); the original Greek is impossible to restore. This third-century Egyptian creed may have reflected the new doctrine of *ex nihilo*; after all, Alexandria is where *ex nihilo* creation had been first proclaimed a century earlier. Origen certainly would not have held it. Like the quite Hellenized Philo before him, Origen held to a number of pagan Greek concepts; so influential was the Platonic worldview that Origen's lifelong work included the attempt to syncretize Christianity with Platonism. Thus Origen was three centuries later condemned as a heretic by the Second Council of Constantinople.

But even the rabbis of the same period often held similar Hellenistic views. The *Genesis Rabba*, a fifth-century Palestinian writing, also speaks of earlier worlds created and destroyed by God. In fact, some of the Midrashic commentaries on the Creation are so fanciful that they hardly deserve to be termed mythological.[21] The idea of other, prior worlds is a common human heritage. When a pagan mythology tells of a destruction of previous worlds, however, it includes the Flood as one of those destructions and the subsequent world order as a re-creation. A present-day Bible student would not conceive of the Flood in those terms. Creation to our modern minds is quite different from any of the ancient views, biblical or non-biblical.

Caedmon, the uneducated herdsman of seventh-century Britain, shared his vision of Genesis and related narratives, all set to music. The Venerable Bede recorded Caedmon's Anglo-Saxon verse. The simple herdsman's vision of creation was quite biblical. According to the singing Caedmon, God had long since

---

19. Brewster, *op. cit.*, p. 96. Origen's view is expounded in his "On the Principles," *Ante-Nicene Fathers*, Vol. IV, *op. cit.*

20. Schaff, *op. cit.*, p. 22.

21. Robert Graves and Raphael Patai, *Hebrew Myths, the Book of Genesis*, Garden City, NY: Doubleday, 1964, pp. 34f.

created the primeval earth, but it was not yet formed ready for habitation. The six days of Genesis 1 describes the subsequent ordering of the earth as we know it. Caedmon therefore in his heavenly vision pictured a preexistent earth, created earlier by God but as yet unfit for habitation by man until the Genesis creation, a picture quite similar to that of Augustine[22] and quite compatible with scripture. Caedmon's vision reveals a Spirit-breathed quality.

Throughout the Patristic Era and the Middle Ages Christian writers expressed divergent beliefs. Most believed in *creatio ex nihilo*; a few chose a creation out of existing matter.[23] The rediscovery of the fourth-century B.C. Aristotle by the medieval Scholastics brought a resurgence of the concept of prior worlds into the Church. Some Christian writers even adopted the idea of the eternity of matter as they tried to "baptize" Aristotle into the faith; but Thomas Aquinas, foremost of the Scholastics, wouldn't accept it. Departing from Aristotle at this point, Aquinas (and most of his contemporary schoolmen) opted strongly for *ex nihilo*.[24]

At the time of the Reformation, the Protestant Church largely freed itself from its dependency on the Greek and Latin translations of the Bible and returned to a serious study of the original Hebrew. By that time, however, the interpretation of Genesis 1 and 2 in the Greek Bible had already become a lasting part of the Church's tradition—and it was to remain an essential part of that tradition for centuries to come. Even in the works of the great Reformers and exegetes (Luther and Calvin, for example), there was little fundamental questioning of the old view. Although these men were highly skilled Hebrew scholars, for the most part, the Hebrew text was interpreted in light of the creation traditions which had been established by the Greek Bible.[25]

---

22. Fields, *op. cit.*, pp. 29-30.
23. Brewster, *op. cit.*, p. 96; Jaki, *op. cit.*, chapters three and four.
24. Haber, *op. cit.*, p. 26.
25. Sailhamer, *op. cit.*, p. 191.

And so the doctrine of *creatio ex nihilo* arrived in the modern Church fully clothed—hallowed, unalterable.

Remaining for centuries in the quiet backwater of biblical scholarship was the eleventh-century Rashi's call to return to the ancient Hebraic understanding of Genesis 1:1-3. Even contemporary liberal commentators are quite divided on Rashi's exposition. Regardless of proper exegesis, the vast majority of Bible students still honestly feel that any interpretation of Genesis 1 other than creation from nothing would demean the Almighty God. John Pearson, the well-read seventeenth-century English bishop, states the case for all who protest against the idea of the preexistence of matter.

> **For if some real and material being must be presupposed by indispensable necessity, without which God could not cause any thing to be, then is not he independent in his actions, nor of infinite power and absolute activity, which is contrary to the divine perfection... So doth it contradict his all sufficiency.**[26]

It is noted forcefully however that the bishop appeals, not to scripture, but to human logic and religious piety. The present work is an appeal to scripture.

26.   John Pearson, *An Exposition of the Creed*, rev. W.S. Dobson, New York: D. Appleton, 1844, p. 81.

Chapter 7

Scientism

Some readers nurtured in evolutionary thought might describe this treatise as "anti-science." Such a pejorative epithet is inappropriate; it is, rather, "anti-scientistic."

Scientism is the attempt to extend currently popular scientific theories into other cultural disciplines. Scientism's zealots in *every* generation imagine that somehow "man" is being replaced by "modern Man"; improved education and up-to-date scientific knowledge are releasing us from superstitious bondage. Such efforts to "reform" other disciplines through "modern science" are quite ancient. The pastoral Israelites settling in the Promised Land learned "agricultural science" from their pagan Canaanite neighbors—and paid a terrible price in the loss of God's protection (see the Book of Judges). Many scholars do not perceive this historical continuum.

The discipline with which we are now concerned is theology. Scientism invades the Church in any generation in which currently held scientific theories appear to conflict with biblical Christianity. Christian leaders who are embarrassed by certain "unscientific" aspects of biblical Christianity's unique, scandalous faith will then attempt to syncretize the two disciplines with unbridled enthusiasm. Such creative efforts toward bridge-building by philosophers and theologians have, throughout Church history, seemed to fascinate Christian intellectuals, but the end result is always an attenuation of revealed truth.

Gnosticism spawned the first major scientistic attempt within Christendom. Already incipient in the Graeco-Roman world before the Church's birth at Pentecost, gnosticism clearly portrayed itself as superior science. "The very nature of Gnosticism...suggests a very strong prevailing spirit of scientism."[1] Gnostics were an intellectual elite; they claimed to have been "enlightened"—and thus they destroyed for early Church use a perfectly good biblical word.[2] Even those Christian leaders who rejected this powerful heresy were deeply affected by it philosophically; gnosticism clearly captured the pagan spirit of the second and third centuries. There was a good basis for Irenaeus' statement that Simon of Samaria founded gnosticism:[3] like Simon, its teachers attempted to combine three claims—esoteric knowledge, a "scientific" understanding of reality, and the power of the Christians' Holy Spirit.

Bringing with him the mathematics of the Magi and their zero-concept, the gnostic Basilides of Alexandria must have been an impressive teacher. *Creatio ex nihilo* was novel, and, as the idea percolated within the worldview of Platonism and, very shortly, Neoplatonism, it seemed so scientific! Basilides unwittingly gave the Church a doctrine that, to the human mind, might make her Creator appear yet more unique and all-powerful. Although *ex nihilo's* near-total adoption required many centuries, the final result was inevitable.

During its two millennia, Church history displays three prominent *scientistic* errors that arose under the guise of "modern science." All have been so powerful as to be nearly impossible to dislodge. In the second through the fifth centuries, as we have seen, it was gnosticism with its superior "science," bringing among its many errors the teaching of *creatio ex nihilo*. In recent years the prominent liberal theologian Paul Tillich was called a "gnostic."[4] Modern liberalism in the Church is indeed highly scientistic and somewhat gnostic: Many liberal scholars have

---

1.   G. Van Groningen, *First Century Gnosticism*, Leiden: E.J. Brill, 1967, p. 18. Van Groningen's work has some serious weaknesses, yet he carefully documents gnosticism's "scientistic" basis.

2.   John 1:9; Ephesians 1:18; Hebrews 6:4; 10:32.

3.   Acts 8:9-14. Irenaeus, "Against Heresies," Book I, 27:4; *Early Christian Fathers*, Philadelphia: Westminster Press, 1953, p. 368.

4.   Van Groningen, *op. cit.*, p. 186.

attempted to discover a "Jesus of history" as distinct from a "Christ of faith," and they continue to search for an imaginary "God's word" within "the word." Liberalism further syncretizes the Bible and contemporary scientific theory to formulate an implausible "theistic evolution," a synthetic cosmogony alien to both Bible and science.

During the medieval centuries, Aristotelianism, with its more earthly concept of concrete reality, supplanted the traditional Neoplatonism amid a similar breathtaking excitement in the Roman Catholic scholarly world—again, as the result of scientism. Aristotelianism had filtered through Byzantine scholars to the Arabs, and thence to the western Church's Scholastics, most notably Thomas Aquinas. Within a brief time this ancient pagan philosophy utterly dominated the science of the western Church's scholars and the secular elite. Galileo's seventeenth-century affliction was actually Aristotelian science in the Italian universities. The Roman Church has yet to remove Aristotelianism from its Thomistic theology; as recently as a century-and-a-half ago the University of Salamanca in Roman Catholic Spain was still teaching the dying remnants of Aristotelian geocentrism.

Calvinism too has its philosophical roots in Aristotle; in his massive biblical commentary John Calvin skipped hurriedly (six brief paragraphs in 22 sizable volumes) through the supernatural "gifts of the Spirit" in 1 Corinthians 12 and deliberately omitted the highly supernatural Book of Revelation.[5] Although John Calvin vehemently protested Aristotelian philosophy in the Roman Church, his personal worldview (as with other intellectuals of his time) was still largely informed by Aristotelian science. Calvin seriously tried to divest himself of Aristotelian philosophy (what we today call "science"), but religion and science are so eternally intertwined that he was unable to extricate the one from the other. Thus Calvin's quite logical Reformed faith could be termed a somewhat-westernized biblical system.

Third, the nineteenth century dawned upon a Protestant Church in turmoil, fighting a losing battle over the same issue of antisupernaturalism. The antisupernaturalism of the Enlightenment gave birth to *two* rebellious children in the Church.

---

5.   John Calvin, *Commentary on the Epistles of Paul the Apostle to the Corinthians*, trans. John Pringle, Grand Rapids: Baker, reprinted 1979.

One of the two offspring, modern liberalism, influenced by the excitement of rationalism, promptly denied the biblical record of miracles. Deism became the religion of many of the elite.

In the other cradle, educated evangelicals increasingly suffered great anguish, attempting to retain their biblical faith while accepting what "modern science" was telling them. Tragically some Christian leaders began acceding to this new scientism, which denied the existence of miracles—not quite becoming totally rationalistic, but inconsistently affirming the *biblical* miracles while denying *contemporary* miracles! It is called dispensationalism;[6] during the nineteenth century this type of anti-supernaturalism spread quickly among some Christian leaders of Reformed persuasion (largely because of John Calvin's roots in Aristotelian science).

Today dispensationalism is stronger than ever in the Church; the average Christian layman has been victimized by this strange inconsistency as well.[7] Dispensationalist thinking now permeates denominations that have never even heard such a word. Thus twentieth-century creationists of antisupernaturalistic persuasion are logically required to insist—with no scriptural basis—that God's creative work of Genesis 1 was accomplished under physical laws that no longer operate. Scientistic antisupernaturalism afflicts not only creation science, but also the broader Church of Jesus Christ wherever it has been affected by western culture.

Why hadn't the distinctive tenets of modern dispensationalism been taught centuries earlier? Simply, it was because the western world had not yet experienced the Enlightenment. Enlightenment thinking (or, rather, a *reaction* to Enlightenment thinking) forms the basis for the novel aspects of dispensationalism in the Church. Dispensationalists are not as committed to

---

6.   Not to be confused with the strictly limited *biblical* concept of two dispensations, so vital to Reformed theology, e.g., 2 Corinthians 3:7-11; Ephesians 1:9-10; Hebrews 9–10.

7.   For a powerful critique of dispensationalism, see John Gerstner, *Wrongly Dividing the Word of Truth: A Critique of Dispensationalism*, Brentwood, TN: Wolgemuth and Hyatt, 1991. However, Gerstner holds uncritically to his own Calvinistic interpretation of scripture.

biblical inerrancy as they usually claim. Again let us remind ourselves that "Jesus Christ is the same yesterday and today and for ever" (Hebrews 13:8).

We should note carefully that all three philosophies—gnosticism, Aristotelianism, and dispensationalism—have been unbiblical intrusions into the Church by the world, each one arising right on schedule, following the secular triumph of "modern science." Scientistic heresies are almost impossible to dislodge; all three mentioned above remain firmly entrenched, and their adherents tend to become quite emotional when opposed. We do well to remember the words of Westermann, quoted earlier: "We have some extremely deeply rooted notions regarding the creation of the world and of man which...do not come from the text of the Bible, but from the history of its interpretation."[8]

Those primarily responsible for reading the Bible through the lens of contemporary worldviews have, for the most part, been the Bible's own friends.[9]

We are warned of this danger by no less than the British scientist (and evolutionist) Arthur Peacocke, "Theology should never marry the science of the day; because if she does, she'll be a widow tomorrow."[10]

As George H. Tausch said, "Man's capacity for self-deception is unlimited." Scientism, with its erroneous apriorism, continues to cripple man's quest for truth.

8.   Westermann, *op. cit.*, p. 1.
9.   Sailhamer, *op. cit.*, p. 166.
10.   Don B. DeYoung, "Origins: Spontaneous or Supernatural," *Creation Perspectives,* May 1997, pp. 3-4.

Chapter 8

Concordistic Theories

As we have just observed, countless writers have tried for centuries to reconcile the Bible with what they have been perceiving in the natural world around them. Origen and Augustine—indeed, many of the Church Fathers—wrestled with the problem; the medieval Scholastics dealt with it by determinedly conflating contradictory philosophies; devout Christians of scientific bent during the past three centuries have agonized over the seeming contradictions between Genesis 1 and the reigning scientific theories. This is an especially severe problem currently in the English-speaking world. Christians who think of the biblical creation narratives as being in conflict with the "real" natural history of the world have often attempted to re-interpret scripture to bring "theology" in line with "geology." Each one who has succumbed to the scientistic temptation to force a portion of Genesis 1 to mean anything other than its clear intent does so in order to achieve "concord," a harmony with conclusions derived from the *perceived* natural data. He has accepted a concordistic theory. Stanley Jaki says that, for Genesis 1, concordism is "its greatest peril."[1]

I have to confess to such attempts in my early years as a Christian. I felt quite justified in doing so. After all, I was defending

---

1.   *Op. cit.*, p. 31.

God! Nor had I yet discovered that the whole Bible is really true: It actually is God's word!

When we examine the "days" of Genesis 1, literally—"And there was evening and there was morning, day one....And there was evening and there was morning, day second..."—all reasonable exegesis indicates that in each usage the author is clearly referring to what we today would describe as one full rotation of the Earth. Henry Morris states that God "defined the word 'day' the very first time He used it. 'God called the light Day, and the darkness He called Night. And the evening and the morning were the first day' (Genesis 1:5)."[2] Any other interpretation of the "day" is totally invalid. But this obvious interpretation violates *modern* cosmogonies. So some Christians develop or adopt concordistic theories in order to resolve the perceived contradictions. As we examine these various attempts at harmonization, we must remember that they have all been developed as the result of the rise of contemporary "science."

A number of the Church Fathers authored their own interpretations of Genesis 1, but all, including the authoritative Basil, fell into concordism simply because they were wedded to the mandatory Platonic worldview and a Ptolemaic cosmology. The fourth-century Eusebius even declared that Moses had been Plato's teacher![3] Greek philosophy seems to have forced nearly every educated Christian into making an attempt to explain the Creation so his intelligent Greek brethren could understand it. Every attempt collapsed upon its *a prioris*. Regardless of the hexaemeron, the six-day creation of Genesis 1, most of the Fathers believed that God had created primeval matter in an instant. The medieval Scholastics fared no better, except that the rules of the game were now dominated by Aristotelian philosophy. Most of them, however, did retain the *ex nihilo* tradition.

A newer concordistic approach to creation is the restitution hypothesis, popularly known as the gap theory. Attributed to Martin Luther[4] as well as the early seventeenth-century Episcopius[5]

2.   "The Literal Week of Creation," *Back to Genesis*, May 1998: Institute for Creation Research: El Cajon, CA.

3.   Jaki, *op. cit.*, p. 81.

4.   Brewster, *op. cit.*, p. 152. Luther, however, accepted a six-day creation and a 6,000-year history for the world.

5.   Delitzsch, *op. cit.*, p. 79.

(but without specific references cited for either), the theory later seemed to be required in order to explain extremely distant stars as well as the fossils that were being uncovered in growing numbers. The first clear citation of the gap theory appeared about 1776,[6] but it was not popularized until the early nineteenth century.

In 1814 a Scottish minister named Thomas Chalmers became caught up in the intellectual ferment concerning prehistoric time scales. He also wanted to believe what his King James Bible appeared to be telling him. Although Chalmers was a superb scholar-scientist-minister, he too was apparently unaware of the medieval Jewish commentaries that shed the light he needed on Genesis. Nor did he analyze carefully the original Hebrew of Genesis 1:1-3 as, of course, many of the linguistic tools we possess today were unavailable. The great Glasgow clergyman also chose to accept uncritically what the gentlemen-scientists of the early nineteenth century were saying about an "old" Earth. Emerging uniformitarianism was already creating quite a stir among Christian students. Chalmers tried to marry his strong biblicism to a desire to be a "modern" pastor and scholar.

So he suggested a compromise—an *ad hoc* proposal—which placed a "gap" of millions (or later, billions) of years between Genesis 1:1 and 1:2. The King James Version reads, "In the beginning God created the heaven and the earth." Chalmers proposed that this "event" was succeeded by a time gap of many millennia. Then, a few thousand years ago, God took up the tools of creation once again, and verse 2 and the rest of the Bible follow consecutively.

My own opinion, as published in 1814, is that it (Genesis 1:1) forms no part of the first day—but refers to a period of indefinite antiquity when God created the worlds out of nothing. The commencement of the first day's work I hold to be the moving of God's Spirit upon the face of the waters. We can allow geology the amplest time...without infringing even on the literalities of the Mosaic record...."[7]

---

6.   Ramm, *op. cit.*, p. 196, note. Ramm details the development of the gap theory, pp. 196f.

7.   William Hanna, *Posthumous Works of Thomas Chalmers*, Vol. I, New York: Harper, 1849, p. 1.

This compromise was embraced by the sectarian J.N. Darby, one of the early elders of the Plymouth Brethren, and was popularized during the latter half of the nineteenth century by G.H. Pember and by the early twentieth-century Scofield Reference Bible.

> **It is thus clear that the second verse of Genesis describes the earth as a ruin; but there is no hint of the time which elapsed between creation and this ruin. Age after age may have rolled away, and it was probably during their course that the strata of the earth's crust were gradually developed. Hence we see that geological attacks upon the Scriptures are altogether wide of the mark, are a mere beating of the air. There is room for any length of time between the first and second verses of the Bible. And again; since we have no inspired account of the geological formations, we are at liberty to believe that they were developed just in the order in which we find them. The whole process took place in preadamite times, in connection, perhaps, with another race of beings, and, consequently, it does not at present concern us.[8]**

While the world of biblical and scientific creationist scholarship largely ignores Chalmers' gap theory, his proposal has enjoyed a continuing popularity among some fundamentalist Christians.[9]

> **The inclusion of this theory in the Scofield Bible is most unfortunate, for it has led so many into believing a theory which was tailored to harmonize science in its present fluid form and the Bible in its immutable form.[10]**

Most biblical commentators will not even mention the restitution hypothesis; if they do, it receives scant but scornful notice. An example is a mere footnote by Skinner: "The view that verse 1 describes an earlier creation of heaven and earth, which were

8.   Pember, *op. cit.*, p. 28.
9.   See, e.g., R.O. Corvin, *Home Bible Study Course*, Charlotte: PTL Club, 1976, Vol. I, p. 1; Vol. 5, p. 1; LeBaron W. Kinney, *Acres of Rubies*, New York: Loizeaux Brothers, 1942, pp. 157-59.
10.   Fields, *op. cit.*, p. 43.

reduced to chaos and then refashioned, needs no refutation."[11] Skinner is saying that the gap theory has no basis in scripture.

The restitution hypothesis is an *ad hoc* explanation. Such improvisations necessarily appear whenever one or more of our basic assumptions is/are incorrect. The problem is two-sided. The first erroneous assumption leading to the gap theory is biblical traditionalism instead of careful exegesis. The other side of the coin is uniformitarianism which, if accepted uncritically, nullifies much of the Old Testament, a significant amount of the world's ancient literature and a great deal of Earth's geologic testimony.

If one accepts either or both of these erroneous assumptions, then he is required by the conflicting evidence to begin fabricating an *ad hoc* explanation—a growing house of cards—in order to deal with his inconsistencies. He will also find it necessary to resort to seeming human logic, not to the totality of scripture and not to the full natural evidence. Those principles that we consider axiomatic must be allowed to be challenged until they are firmly established, emended or disproven.

The gap theory was formulated, as we have seen, because of an uncritical acceptance of two doubtful premises, a biblical traditionalism and the uniformitarian hypothesis. First, the correct exegesis of Genesis 1:1-3 utterly voids the gap theory: a billion-year gap in the middle of a sentence is incredible. Even assuming the traditional, Septuagintal translation, the Bible contains not a shred of evidence for the gap theory. Second, there is the uniformitarian hypothesis requiring long ages, an idea that has made the gap theory appear necessary to some Christians. This is not the place to deal with the mountains of evidence that challenge the doctrine of uniformitarianism. Let us merely note that this philosophy has long been assumed but never demonstrated.

Thus the gap theory was unnecessary. Still worse, some of its proponents have asserted—again, according to a characteristic nineteenth-century pietistic logic—that the angels' Fall took

---

11.   Skinner, *op. cit.*, p. 14, note. Several commentators who discuss the restitution hypothesis demonstrate its utter impossibility, e.g., Dillman, Stigers, Allis. Hyers, *op. cit.*, p. 39, calls it "bizarre." Every Christian who has considered the gap theory to be plausible should read Fields' *Unformed and Unfilled, op. cit.*, for a complete and devastating critique.

place during this "hiatus" between verses 1 and 2. The chaos of verse 2 is explained as the result of the angelic rebellion and casting down to Earth. Although the Bible gives us no hint of such a placement for the heavenly warfare, Genesis 6:2 may be a better potential "dating" for that "event." The pseudepigraphal Book of Enoch 6:6 says that this rebellion took place during the time of Jared (Genesis 5:15-20). Yet there is one note of honesty to be found in the gap theory. Of all the concordistic theories, it is one that takes seriously this fact: verse 1 is written in language descriptive of an organized cosmos, while verse 2 describes a chaotic earth. But of course the gap theory, requiring hairline-thin scriptural distinctions, is exegetically impossible.

A similar concordistic theory appeared in 1784. Francois Xavier Burtin proposed that the fossils demonstrated the ruins of the period he called "the chaos" *prior* to Day One of Genesis.[12] A more modern commentator, Merrill Unger, has proposed, in the middle of a carefully reasoned exegesis, the same hypothesis of at least one prior earth-age, destroyed by God, says Unger soberly, because of sin: "Thus Genesis 1:1, 2 evidently describes not the primeval creation *ex nihilo*, celebrated by the angels (Job 38:7; Isaiah 45:18), but the much later refashioning of a judgment-ridden earth in preparation for a new order of creation—man."[13] Unger is determined to posit a re-creation whether or not the biblical context or science demands it. He is so close to the correct exposition of Genesis 1, but he does not realize how much he has been affected by modern rationalistic thinking. He need not portray a pre-biblical destruction of which the Bible says nothing and which geology and paleontology do not require. To his credit, however, Unger is attempting to swallow courageously the bitter pill of the preexistent chaos of Genesis 1:2.

A most persuasive and very modern concordistic theory suggests that the seven-day sequence of Genesis 1:1–2:4 is merely a "literary framework" to glorify God as Creator, never to describe a literal calendar of the Creation. Variations of the literary

---

12. Haber, *op. cit.*, p. 152.
13. Merrill F. Unger, "Rethinking the Genesis Account of Creation," *op. cit.*, p. 28. E.J. Young (*op. cit.*) and Fields (*op. cit.*) both deal convincingly with interpretations such as Unger's, but they nowhere refute the unique thesis forming the basis of the present work.

framework hypothesis have been proposed, and several of them are eloquent, but every one begins with man's wisdom and forces it upon the word of God. Such reinterpretations are a modern phenomenon; the ancients knew better.

Christianity Today stated editorially that Augustine held to a form of the literary framework hypothesis,[14] but this assertion has been thoroughly refuted by David C.C. Watson.[15] Actually, Augustine agreed with other Patristic writers that God created the heavens and the earth in a moment, and perhaps He did, but, as noted earlier, *prior to Genesis 1*.[16] Augustine believed in the literal six-day creation of Genesis 1. We must remember also that Augustine's worldview had been strongly influenced by Neoplatonism, with all its scientific limitations, and he tended to spiritualize the Old Testament, as did the apostle Paul, in his preaching and writing (although Augustine accepted Genesis 1 literally). To this day, many preachers will quite often allegorize Old Testament passages, finding gems of exposition that the original authors never dreamed of. Augustine "meditated" in his *Confessions*[17] and, in *The City of God*, tended to allegorize Genesis 1,[18] not because of any uniformitarian worldview, but because he had been immersed in Greek philosophy for years before his conversion. To the ancient Greek scholars, God's work is timeless.

Henry Morris describes the novel literary framework theory in his *Scientific Creationism*:

> **The particular "framework" in which these ideas are developed varies according to the particular expositor. Some speak of Genesis as "allegorical," others as "liturgical," others as "poetic," others as "supra-historical." All agree, however, in rejecting it as "scientific" or**

---

14. *Christianity Today, op. cit.*, p. 24.

15. *Bible-Science Newsletter*, Vol. 22, No. 5, May, 1984, pp. 1f.

16. "He who dwells in eternity created all things in a single instance." *Realencyklopaedie fuer protestantische Theologie und Kirche*, 3rd edition, Vol. 17, Leipzig: J.C. Hinrichsche Verlag, 1896, p. 695, quoted in Sailhamer, *op. cit.*, p. 206.

17. Books, XI, XII, XIII, noted by Watson, *op. cit.*, p. 2.

18. Gerhard F. Hasel, "The 'Days' of Creation in Genesis 1: Literal 'Days' Or Figurative 'Periods/Epochs' Of Time?", *Origins*, Loma Linda, CA: Geoscience Research Institute, Vol. 21, No. 1, p. 7.

"historical." They concur that Genesis teaches the fact
of "creation" and the "fall," but deny that it has anything
to say concerning the method. They hope to retain
whatever theological significance it may have while, at
the same time, avoiding scientific embarrassment.[19]

As Bert Thompson notes, "The framework hypothesis contends
that the treatment of creation in Genesis was *logical*, not *chronological*."[20] The literary framework theory, like all other attempts
at harmonization, is based upon an uncritical acceptance of uniformitarianism, which demands long ages. It also perceives Genesis 1 as Hebrew poetry.[21] The chapter further has a "chiastic," or
"palindromic" feature, with the first three days' activities somewhat paralleled by the next three days. So the interpreter with
a "framework" mind-set uses this pattern to look, not for history,
but for the "theological intent" of the author. The literary framework theory thus treats the narrative, not as (the German) *his-
torie*, but rather as *geschichte*, or folk history. Its meaning then
becomes as subjective as the interpreter chooses to imagine it.

Concerning the significance of the chiastic quality of Genesis 1, this is no more than an interesting coincidence: *all four* of
the resurrection narratives in the Gospels also betray chiasmus.
Do we then treat these New Testament stories as folk history?
Hasel rightly disputes the basic assumptions of all variations of
the literary framework theory.

> **Compared to the hymns in the Bible, the creation ac-
> count is not a hymn; compared to the parables in the
> Bible, the creation account is not a parable; compared
> to the poetry in the Bible, the creation account is not a
> poem; compared to cultic liturgy, the creation account
> is not a cultic liturgy. Compared to various kinds of lit-
> erary forms, the creation account is not a metaphor, a
> story, a parable, poetry, or the like.[22]**

---

19.   Henry M. Morris, *Scientific Creationism*, San Diego: Creation-Life Pub-
       lishers, 1974, p. 244; quoted in Bert Thompson, *Creation Compromises*,
       Montgomery, AL: Apologetics Press, Inc., 1995, p. 215.

20.   *Ibid.*, p. 215.

21.   For a statement on Old Testament poetry, see Chapter 10, Question 4,
       "What Did God Intend by Genesis 1:1-3?"

22.   Gerhard F. Hasel, *Origins*, Vol. 21, No. 1, p. 19.

Barely more than a generation old, the framework hypothesis was early challenged by G. Ch. Aalders. As noted by E.J. Young, Aalders asked two questions of anyone who proposes the literary framework.

> (1) In the text of Genesis itself, he affirmed, there is not a single allusion to suggest that the days are to be regarded as a form or mere manner of representation and hence of no significance for the essential knowledge of the divine creative activity. (2) In Exodus 20:11 the activity of God is presented to man as a pattern, and this fact presupposes that there was a reality in the activity of God which man is to follow. How could man be held accountable for working six days if God himself had not actually worked for six days? To the best of the present writer's knowledge no one has ever answered these two considerations of Aalders.[23]

Finally, the literary framework hypothesis seems too esoteric to be a reasonable theory of interpretation, reminding us somewhat of the modern "metaphysical" reinterpretations of scripture, as in Christian Science, Unity School of Christianity and so many other New Age cults. In order to understand a "metaphysical" interpretation of the scriptures, one must first have access to a glossary of "redefined" biblical words and phrases. The remainder of the Book of Genesis is quite clear to the average reader, but the literary framework requires that the reader of the first chapter possess considerable prior arcane knowledge and definitions. Thus the literary framework theory violates the principles of biblical hermeneutics.

In another popular theory today called the "day-age hypothesis," each of the six days of creation becomes as long an "era" as modern rational man chooses to make it.

The day-age hypothesis must deal first with the word *day*—*yom* in Hebrew. The word must be understood "figuratively," we are told. Although some biblical usages of *yom* were clearly intended to express *limited* periods of time, the day-age interpretation here is utterly invalid. Genesis 1 paints a clear picture, without question as to what the scripture means: "And there was

---

23. *Op. cit.*, p. 45.

evening and there was morning, day one,...day second,...day third, etc." (literal translation). "God called the light Day, and the darkness he called Night. And there was evening and there was morning, one day." Only by a willful attempt to twist the scripture could an exegete find anything but one earth-calendar-day, based upon Earth's rotation (not necessarily upon the sun, which is not put in its place until the fourth day), in each of those sentences. Marcus Dods long ago dealt decisively with such a practice.

> **The Bible needs no defense such as false constructions of its language bring to its aid. They are its worst friends who distort its words that they may yield a meaning more in accordance with scientific truth. If, for example, the word "day" in these chapters does not mean a period of twenty-four hours, the interpretation [all exegesis] of scripture is hopeless.**[24]

If any version of the day-age hypothesis is correct, then Genesis 1 must be incorrect! Its proponents may not legitimately claim to believe "the whole Bible."

Those Christians who would change "day" into "age" are not doing their homework in the Hebrew lexicons. A lexical study of *yom* demonstrates biblically that it *never* means a long, indeterminate age. But commentators promoting the day-age hypothesis do not reveal that fatal information when they tell us that *yom* must be interpreted figuratively.[25] Hasel states categorically that "[n]one of the lexicographers have departed from the meaning of the word 'day' as a literal day of 24 hours for Genesis 1."[26] It is a rare professor of Hebrew who finds anything but a normal day in the *yom* of Genesis 1.

Yet Christian writers opt for the day-age hypothesis quite often. *Christianity Today* presented an impassioned editorial appeal to impress a longer—much longer—meaning upon the word "day."[27] The editor would convince his readers that such is

---

24. Dods, *The Book of Genesis*, The Expositor's Bible, New York: A.C. Armstrong & Son, 1903, p. 4.

25. Fields, *op. cit.*, details the evidence disproving the day-age interpretation, pp. 168f. Every creationist should read this book.

26. Origins, *op. cit.*, p. 22.

27. *Op. cit.*, pp. 22f.

the way most evangelical scholars interpret Genesis 1. In logic, this would be termed "special pleading."[28]

The literary framework enthusiast N.H. Ridderbos asks, "Are we to take literally the representation that for every great work (or two works) of creation He used a day? It is open to serious doubt whether the author of Genesis 1...actually meant to say that."[29] What is Ridderbos' textual basis for his "serious doubt"? His exegesis is open to serious doubt!

The Living Bible's paraphrasers deliberately committed a most grievous error in their footnote to Genesis 1:8 (and elsewhere): "Literally, 'There was evening and there was morning, a second day (or, "period of time").' "[30] Again, do they have a shred of lexical evidence for inserting the optional "period of time"? Those words were clearly intended arbitrarily to legitimize the day-age hypothesis; the footnotes are a disgrace to the word of God.

Even so strong a biblical inerrantist as Gleason Archer yields to cultural pressure, giving the yom of Genesis 1 an indeterminate definition; he also favors the pre-biblical ruin-and-re-creation model.[31] Archer needs to know that his attempts at harmonization are simply unnecessary and potentially harmful.

Obviously one who suggests such a forced, *ad hoc* meaning upon the days of Genesis 1 must already have accepted uncritically the idea of very ancient life upon the earth. In fact, gradualistic thinking is so deeply imbedded in his concept of origins that he would require scripture to be emended to fit his understanding of natural science.

Among their writings one will *never* find statements such as: "after years of study in the Hebrew text, and after comparing many grammars and lexicons as well as all of scriptural usage, we have finally come to the conclusion that the days of Genesis 1 must be interpreted,

28. For another detailed response see E.J. Young, *op. cit.*, pp. 43f. Young comments pointedly: "The basic reason why Moses used the device of six days was that creation occurred in six days" (p. 82, note).

29. N.H. Ridderbos, *Is There a Conflict between Genesis 1 and Natural Science?*, Grand Rapids: Eerdmans, 1957, p. 31.

30. *The Living Bible*, Wheaton, IL: Tyndale House, 1971, p. 1.

31. Archer, *Encyclopedia of Bible Difficulties*, Grand Rapids: Zondervan, 1982, pp. 58-65.

on the basis of its linguistic, grammatical, and syntactical features, as long periods of time, rather than normal, 24-hour days" (italics added).[32]

Whenever *yom* is used with a numeral in the Old Testament (as in Genesis 1), it *always* (150 times) refers to a literal earth-day.[33] This from a conservative commentator. Now, from a liberal scholar, Cuthbert A. Simpson:

> There can be no question but that by *Day* the author meant just what we mean—the time required for one revolution [*sic*] of the earth on its axis. Had he meant an aeon he would certainly, in view of his fondness for great numbers, have stated the number of millenniums each period embraced. While this might have made his account of creation less irreconcilable with modern science, it would have involved a lessening of God's greatness, one sign of which was his power to do so much in one day.[34]

The day-age hypothesis derives then, not from careful Bible study, but from the *scientistic* attempt to harmonize Genesis with current scientific theory. This is often true even of one who claims to hold to biblical inerrancy. He perceives geological data through uniformitarian eyes. The universal, enormous geologic signatures of the Flood remain misinterpreted. He will not question his basic cosmogonic assumptions. E.J. Young says of such a concordistic view,

> What strikes one immediately...is the low estimate of the Bible which it entails. Whenever science and the Bible are in conflict, it is always the Bible that, in one manner or another, must give way. We are not told that science should correct its answers in the light of Scripture... Yet this is really surprising, for the answers which scientists have provided have frequently changed with

---

32. Fields, *op. cit.*, p. 166.
33. Hasel, *Origins, op. cit.*, p. 26.
34. Cuthbert A. Simpson, "The Book of Genesis," *The Interpreter's Bible*, New York, Nashville: Abingdon Press, 1952, p. 471.

the passing of time. The "authoritative" answers of pre-Copernican scientists are no longer acceptable; nor, for that matter, are many of the views of twenty-five years ago.[35]

Astronomer Hugh Ross eloquently attacks the traditional creationist position with a day-age proposal, which is beguiling countless Christians because of his regular exposure on the Trinity Broadcasting Network. The greater portion of his argument is based upon astronomy, *all of which is resolved in this book.*

Ross accepts uncritically many conclusions of atheistic evolutionists about life on this earth—their faulty datings, their denials of the clear evidences for the worldwide Flood, their ignoring of examples of rapid building of coral and rapid deposition of varves, their inbred aversion to catastrophism. In short, Ross looks at Earth's history through western culture's uniformitarian glasses. God is exceedingly able to accomplish massive changes in this earth in a startingly brief time.[36]

Don B. DeYoung, also an astronomer, has written a devastating review of Ross' *Creation and Time* in the *Creation Research Society Quarterly.*[37] Every Christian who has been impressed with Ross' dating scheme *must* search out and read this book review.

Hugh Ross desperately wishes his scientific brethren to accept Jesus Christ, a most commendable desire. But does he realize that what he perceives as the embarrassing Creation-Flood scenario of the Bible is not nearly as scandalous as the message of the Cross? In our evangelistic efforts to win our peers for the Kingdom, we must trust the power of the Holy Spirit to work in mankind's hearts. Young-Earth creationists too must allow new converts to hold to their uniformitarian, evolutionist worldview "as long as they can" while the Spirit of Truth performs his sweet work in their hearts, in his time, just as He accomplished in my own evolutionist heart more than 30 years ago.

---

35. E.J. Young, *op. cit.,* p. 53.
36. See Hugh Ross, *The Creator and the Cosmos,* Colorado Springs: NavPress, 1993; *Creation and Time, ibid.,* 1994.
37. *CRSQ,* Vol. 31, No. 4, March 1995, pp. 248-249. Cf. also the review by Danny R. Faulkner, *CRSQ,* Vol. 32, No. 1, June 1995, pp. 43-44.

Although Ross displays a precious faith in Jesus Christ, he does not understand how fallible human logic is, how susceptible to peer pressure we all are, especially intellectuals, who betray exceptional gullibility to rational-sounding anti-theistic schemes. In attempting to throw his fellow Christians a lifeline, Hugh Ross has instead thrown them an anchor. As this work has been stressing, we Christians must learn to "think biblically."

Once a concordistic creationist begins harmonizing the creation narrative with "modern science," he just might open the door for the next rationalistic reinterpretation. The "days" of Genesis 1 are obviously out of order, he thinks; so, to begin with, we must reverse days three and four. After all, the sun was necessary for photosynthesis of the third day's green plants. This and other such conjectures inevitably follow the first concordistic attempt. From that point theistic evolutionary thinking is but one gentle step.

Actually, "the last word" on the "days" of Genesis 1 has been spoken by Gerhard F. Hasel, writing in *Origins*.[38] Hasel exhaustively examines *yom* from various aspects—semantic, linguistic, syntactical, historical and grammatical—and finds that in Genesis 1 it can only mean one earth-day, based upon the Earth's rotation. Every Christian who finds anything else owes himself the duty of reading Hasel's definitive article.[39]

A recent novel concordistic attempt has been John Sailhamer's *Genesis Unbound*. As an Old Testament specialist, much of his scholarship is excellent. But again, Sailhamer begins with the assumption of long ages during which the Earth was quickly populated with many new life-forms. This "period" he includes totally *within* verse 1, a slight variation on the ruin-and-re-creation theory. A quick mental run through the six days' activities shows us that Sailhamer is required to put out brush

---

38. *Op. cit.*, p. 30. For additional important biblical and scientific evidence, see also Ken Ham, "Do the Days Really Matter?" *Back to Genesis*, Institute for Creation Research, Sept. 1990. Cf. Sailhamer, *op. cit.*, p. 243-45.

39. The most eloquent attempt (that I have seen) to justify the day-age theory is found in Hugh Ross' newsletter, *Facts & Faith*: Otto J. Helwig, "How Long an Evening and Morning?" Vol. 9, No. 3, 1995. Still, its logic is quite strained and the arguments remind us of those in Hugh Schonfield's *The Passover Plot* (New York: B. Geis Assoc., 1966), exhibiting great scholarship but proving nothing.

fires all along that road. He repeatedly does violence to the text. It is one of the more strained harmonizations—quite awkward. A single illustration from the Bible's initial verse will suffice: *reshit*, "beginning," he says, "always refers to an extended, yet indeterminate duration of time—*not* a specific moment."[40] Has Sailhamer stretched the facts? Let us examine other uses of *reshit*: "...from *the beginning* of the year to the end..." (Deuteronomy 11:12); "In *the beginning* of the reign of..." (Jeremiah 26:1); "Like the *first fruit* on the fig tree" (Hosea 9:10). No example could be found that might possibly be "an extended, yet indeterminate duration of time."

Sailhamer continues:

> **When my children ask me where the dinosaurs fit into the biblical account of creation, I tell them they were created, lived, and became extinct during "the beginning."**[41]

Sailhamer appears to be making a desperate attempt to harmonize Genesis 1 with contemporary views of the age of the Earth by comparing *bᵉreshith* with other biblical examples. The reader can see how Sailhamer has abused the process of exegesis. If only Sailhamer were not committed by tradition to *creatio ex nihilo* as well as long ages, most of his exposition would drop into place in a simple, logical explanation, and nothing would be forced.

Quoting the chauvinistic medieval rabbis, Sailhamer insists that God created the universe in Genesis 1:1; then the rest of the chapter, he says, is the creation of the land promised to Abraham, the land of Israel, which he says is also the Garden of Eden.[42]

Sailhamer gives his "interpretive" translation of the Bible's first verse.

> **Long ago God created the world. He created the sun, the moon, and the stars, as well as all the creatures which inhabit the earth. He created all of them out of nothing—**

---

40. *Op. cit.*, p. 38.
41. *Ibid.*, p. 105.
42. *Ibid.*, pp. 46f, 68f.

not in a single instant of time, but over a vast period of time.[43]

As Anatole France said, "Man shows no greater talent than in his ability to deceive himself."

An additional *ad hoc* theory is the "titular" hypothesis—Genesis 1:1 is a "title" for the rest of the narrative; yet it too betrays the authenticity of scripture. Already noted earlier (see Chapter 3, "Exegesis of Genesis 1:1-3") is the group of commentators who desire to retain the traditional translation, but who realize they must deal with the inherent contradiction of the chaos. So they state frankly that they feel God created *tohu wabohu*—in spite of Genesis' silence and Isaiah's clear testimony to the contrary. This is a characteristic traditional interpretation. Again we find an attempt at honesty with the basic scripture, while violating the larger biblical context. John Diodati, a Reformed theologian living in Calvin's Geneva, gave his (and Calvin's) opinion in 1543:

> **God giving the world its first being, began with the creation of the two general parts of it, and then went to the particulars... The lower and elementall part of the universe, here indifferently called earth, waters, and abysse, because it was a confused masse of all the Elements.**[44]

As already noted, some prominent modern scholars are also to be found in this camp,[45] despite Childs' assertion:

---

43.   *Ibid.,* p. 99
44.   John Diodati, *Pious Annotations upon the Holy Bible,* London: Nicholas Fussell, 1543, p. 3.
45.   E.g., E.J. Young, *op. cit.,* says (p. 95): "The material from which the sun, moon and stars were made was created, i.e., brought into existence, at the absolute beginning [verse 1]. On the fourth day God made of this primary material the sun and moon and stars... On the third day the creation of our globe was completed, although the primal material of the globe was brought into existence at the absolute beginning... Although the earth (i.e., in its original form) was created in the beginning, nevertheless, on Day three God made the earth." Young is obviously picking his way through a labyrinth of exegetical problems. Attempting to retain his axiomatic *ex nihilo,* he thus mars seriously an otherwise excellent presentation.

> It is rather generally acknowledged that the suggestion
> of God's first creating a chaos is a logical contradiction
> and must be rejected.[46]

Further, in Isaiah 45:18 the prophet asserts categorically, "He did not create it a *tohu!*"

To attribute the creation of the chaos of *tohu wabohu* in Genesis 1:2 to the God of the Bible is a serious error. In fact, the Hebrew words of verses 1 and 2—"create" (*bara'*) and "chaos" (*tohu wabohu*)—are mutually exclusive and should not be used together, unless antithetically, as in Genesis 1:1-2 and Isaiah 45:18. Chaos throughout the Old Testament has an evil quality. Loretz says that chaos and creation are two absolute opposites. Creation, he states, consists of the ordering of chaos.[47] Loretz is correct; that is precisely the biblical relationship of chaos and creation. Again it must be stated that in spite of the fact that a number of modern scholars—conservative and liberal—have credited God with the creation of the chaos, it is highly unwarranted by the biblical context.[48] Von Rad insists, "To be sure, the notion of a created chaos is itself a contradiction."[49] God is credited with creating everything else in Genesis 1, but not one of the five physical entities of verse 2, the "chaos" verse, is depicted as coming from his hand.

Further, if God were creating "the heavens and the earth" in verse 1, then the author should have noted that activity as belonging to Day One; simple logic tells us that. The titular hypothesis is as unlikely as all the other *ad hoc* constructions.

For several generations liberal Bible scholars on the Continent have provided the Christian world with some excellent Old Testament studies by dealing honestly with the scriptures exactly as they have found them—and in proper context. They are able to do this because most of them are evolutionists who make no pretense of accepting biblical inerrancy. Continental scholars largely went through the harmony struggles several generations

---

46. Childs, *op. cit.*, p. 30.
47. O. Loretz, *Schöpfung und Mythos*, Stuttgart: 1968, pp. 83f, noted in Hasel (*The Bible Translator*, op. cit., p. 157), who as a traditionalist is quite unhappy with Loretz' proper exegesis.
48. Cf. Waltke, *op. cit.*, Part III, pp. 216-28.
49. Von Rad, *op. cit.*, p. 46.

ago. In the English-speaking world, however, commentators to this day often seem to have a deeply-rooted urge to harmonize the Bible with the perceived natural world about them, thus burdening Christendom with some bizarre attempts at concord.

This has caused a most serious problem concerning Bible translation. The King James translators *usually* tried to produce the English equivalents of the Hebrew and Greek whether they understood them or not. Modern Bible translators into English often allow their worldview to intrude, determining that their English translations be required to make sense to their very western concepts of reality. So we may accept, for example, the liberal German Gerhard von Rad's fine scholarship without adopting his personal worldview. It is my opinion that von Rad is less dangerous to our faith than those seductive English-speaking commentators and translators who are the great harmonizers.

Indeed, Davis A. Young and Pattle P.T. Pun, two science teachers in Christian colleges, both claiming to be avowed Christians as well as avowed theistic evolutionists, frankly acknowledge that Genesis 1 clearly speaks of six earth-days.[50] They are to be commended for at least this much integrity even though they firmly hold to an evolutionary position. However, both Young and Pun later contradict themselves with their own implausible harmonizations.

If the reader still holds to a concordistic theory, consider: Would you have even sought for an alternative explanation for some aspect of Genesis 1 had you not first accepted—without proof—the uniformitarian hypothesis? Challenge uniformitarianism and you will discover that we Christians *do not need a concordistic theory* to explain the observed evidence in the heavens or the earth!

We are happy where science confirms biblical statements, but contradictions cause us no consternation. To be sure, some such contradictions may be the result of improper biblical interpretation. If this is so, then the erroneous interpretations should be corrected. But let it

---

50.   Davis A. Young, *Creation and the Flood,* Grand Rapids: Baker, 1977, pp. 44, 172. Pattle P.T. Pun, "A Theory of Progressive Creationism," *Journal of the American Scientific Affiliation*, March 1987.

never be forgotten: science is changing and the Bible is not. Therefore, what may be a contradiction now, may be completely resolved as science progresses. If we do not allow for the progress of science, we, too, may someday find ourselves left with neat harmonizations which no longer harmonize! Such a position cannot be legitimately criticized as "sticking one's head in the sand." It is not ignoring "the facts"—particularly ones dealing with dating—as any knowledge of scientific estimations of the earth's age over the past one hundred years will show. Harmonizers ignore this.[51]

Now, I ask the reader to observe carefully a few personal notes. A most important point, the first contributes toward the authenticity of the entire book. Is the present thesis to be perceived as merely another in a long line of concordistic theories, attempting once again to bridge a chasm between theology and geology? Not so! I was years ago aware of the Hebraic understanding of Genesis 1:1-3 because of a seminary course entitled, "Hebrew Exegesis of the Creation Narratives." The exegesis truly surprised me. My interest in creationism developed some years later. Never since those seminary studies have I felt the need to search out a concordistic theory to explain away the obvious intent of the Bible's opening chapter. My personal experience has been one of distress over most creationists' stubborn adherence to the traditional, Septuagintal exposition and forced interpretations of Genesis 1:1-3 by otherwise competent scholars. Every concordistic theory, including *creatio ex nihilo*, begins with a certain worldview, and then requires the Bible to fit. The present thesis, conversely, begins with the Hebrew scriptures, exegetes them in the simplest, most obvious manner, and then forces the reader to emend his biblical interpretation of Creation—even his worldview, if necessary.

As I have studied the various concordistic theories, I have marvelled at the human mind's inclination "to persuade itself." Then I recall my own experience of having many years ago convinced myself that theistic evolution could be harmonized with Genesis 1.

---

51.   Fields, *op. cit.*, p. 46.

Attending a conference of the International Council on Biblical Inerrancy, I was horrified to discover that a sizable number of the participants (probably a majority) held to the gap, the literary framework, or the day-age hypothesis. The Holy Spirit is the Spirit of Truth; such Christians should at the least admit that they are inerrantists concerning all but the first three chapters of the Bible. Honesty and integrity demand no less than this. Stanley Jaki describes pointedly the "two-thousand-year-old plague, which is concordism."[52]

By this time my iconoclasm has surely succeeded in alienating every camp. Like the gentle young man who chose to identify with both sides during the American Civil War—he wore a blue shirt and gray trousers, and thus was shot by both armies— I must have irritated every reader at some point. However, this book has not been written to gather Establishment bouquets, whether from liberals or from creationists. I have been seeking only Truth, which effort should hold a value in itself, trusting that the search has been fruitful. I trust too that the reader who has held to one or another of the concordistic theories is thankful to have been relieved of some of his lingering uneasiness by these revelations. To discover that neither the Bible nor science needs to be forced should be quite liberating to a Christian. But please continue—there are more offensive revelations to come.

Probably the greatest handicap to overcome in perceiving God's creative activity in Genesis 1 is one's own worldview. If a researcher's personal perception of reality has been conditioned largely by rationalistic concepts, he will experience extreme difficulty in imagining the rapidity of a full-blown six-day Creation. We read of God's parting the Red Sea, stopping the sun for Joshua, and striking a Syrian army blind for Elisha; but for most Christians these are "long ago and far away." Thinking Christians can hardly believe that Almighty God could and would do in one day what an entire nation of humans might require a decade to accomplish—or probably not be able to accomplish at all.

But if a researcher has become accustomed to a personal, continuing experience of the miraculous, the literal six-day Creation seems rather reasonable to his mind. My own experience of God's creative power is based at least partially upon empirical

---

52.   *Op. cit.*, p. 299.

data. I have seen God restore perfect hearing to an ear that was totally deaf for 46 years, and another for 54 years—each within an instant. I have a friend who was born without eyeballs, but who at seven months received perfect eyes in a moment as the result of her mother's faith. I know of a man who suffered a compound fracture in his leg which, following immediate prayer, suddenly snapped into place, totally healed. There are numerous modern accounts of food being multiplied when the need was there. An impoverished pastor-friend prayed with his wife that God would repair her decayed teeth; suddenly the sensation of tiny hammer-blows began in her mouth, and 20 minutes later the pastor's wife had a perfect set of teeth. Cancerous tumors healed instantly, new hearts replacing diseased hearts, split-second deliverance of cystic fibrosis, many dozens of healings occurring simultaneously, blind eyes replaced by perfect eyes— such miracles appear occasionally in western culture, but are rather commonplace in third-world nations unfettered by rationalistic *a prioris*.

The list of such modern miracles is endless, so imagining this all-powerful Creator's six-day accomplishment is not difficult for me in the least. The suddenly miraculous is very much a part of my personal worldview, yet it does not at all negate my appreciation for the orderliness of God's natural laws. I describe these contemporary miracles solely for the purpose of helping us all to develop a biblical worldview that can include the spectacular rapidity of the Genesis hexaemeron. This presentation does not demand a *deus ex machina* beyond what the Bible clearly describes. Scientific writers, like all other authors, are incapable of writing with total objectivity; our compositions are deeply affected by both our experiences and our *lack* of experiences. Christians and non-Christians alike have a capacity for convincing themselves of almost any scheme of logic, usually depending upon their own personal perceptions of reality. So concordistic theories will abound as long as Christian writers fail to appreciate fully the awesome power of the working Creator and Sustainer.

Again it must be repeated, the historical evidences for the origins of our universe, our earth, and life upon the earth simply do not demand any interpretation of the first chapter of Genesis other than what a simple, straightforward reading of the

Hebrew text would give—exactly as an Old Testament Israelite would have understood it. As Jaki says, "For the ancient Hebrews all that Genesis 1 stated was real."[53]

---

53.   *Op. cit.*, p. 270.

Chapter 9

From Chaos to Cosmos

"The theological thought of chapter 1 moves not so much between the poles of nothingness and creation as between the poles of chaos and cosmos."[1] "Thus the text is interested in the gift of *form*, rather than the gift of *being*."[2] Von Rad and Blocher have just described the basic thesis of this work.

Commentators who hold to the *creatio ex nihilo* position in Genesis 1:1 sometimes declare that those who disagree have a problem: What is to be done about the chaos of verse 2?[3] There is no problem with the chaos, for therein lies the answer. The pre-Genesis scene so concisely pictured by the biblical author is that of primordial, wild ocean waters convulsing beneath a darkened, moisture-laden sky—a lonely, chaotic desolation, chosen by God to be formed into something with order, beauty, light and physical life.

Every western mind then asks the question, "But where did that chaos come from?" Simply, the Bible doesn't say.[4] The author of Genesis 1 is unconcerned about so rationalistic a question. We westerners derive such questions from fourth-century B.C. Greece.

1.   Von Rad, *op. cit.*, p. 49.
2.   Blocher, *op.cit.*, p. 66.
3.   E.g., Hasel, *The Bible Translator*, *op. cit.*, p. 164.
4.   Cf. Waltke, *op. cit.*, Part IV, p. 338.

> To the Greek the origin of matter was a pertinent and even pressing question. This is evidently not so with the [author of Genesis 1]. If he thought of the question at all, he was content to leave it unanswered. It is more likely that it never entered his mind; he did not answer it because he was not aware of it as a question.[5]

What the Bible does portray so briefly in Genesis 1:1-2 is anticipatory of the God of order "seizing" this co-existent protyle and forming a habitable land mass, using the chaotic matter itself as the stuff of creation. Further exposition of this "seizing" is found largely in Job, Psalms, Isaiah, and Jeremiah.

The remainder of the first chapter (Genesis 1:3ff) then describes the *process* of creation, the sequence of the various events. Eight major acts were compressed into those initial six days. The first four days were preparation and provision for the living beings; the final two days involved the actual creation of the animal kingdom and God's gift of *nephesh*, life itself.

Tohu wabohu, that unformed chaos, to which are added the darkness, *choshek*, and the watery deep, *tehom*—all are understood in Job, Psalms and several of the Prophets to have been dominated by entities that are at enmity with God. They are controlled by the "powers" resisting God's power.[6] God represents order, light, life, love, creation. The chaotic deep represents disorder, darkness, destruction, death. The bathic sea, the wild ocean waters, is that which was contained by God in the Creation.

---

5. W.R. Lane, *op. cit.*, p. 73.

6. Hermann Gunkel in 1895 published his landmark *Schöpfung und Chaos in Urzeit and Endzeit* (Göttingen: Vanderhoeck and Ruprecht, 1895), depicting the cosmogonic warfare. Although flawed by typical late-nineteenth-century rationalistic logic, Gunkel's work contains a great deal of sound scholarship, which should not be ignored. In recent years additional articles and books—many inspired by the archaeological finds at Ugarit—have been written about the theomachy. The Ugaritic literature has helped to moderate Gunkel's excesses.

   For the student interested in pursuing the subject further, see Mary K. Wakeman, *God's Battle with the Monster*, Leiden: E.J. Brill, 1973; Gordon, "Leviathan: Symbol of Evil," *op. cit.*; Nicholas K. Kiessling, "Antecedents of the Medieval Dragon in Sacred History," *Journal of Biblical Literature*, LXXXIX, 1970, pp. 167-77; Bernhard W. Anderson, *Creation versus Chaos*, New York: Association Press, 1967; Marvin H. Pope, *Job*, and Mitchell J. Dahood, *Psalms I, II, III*, Anchor Bible, *op. cit.*

Parts of the Old Testament other than Genesis tell of that containment. "He gathered the waters of the sea as in a bottle; he put the deeps in storehouses" (Psalm 33:7). "The waters stood above the mountains. At thy rebuke they fled..." (Psalm 104:6b-7). "...he assigned to the sea its limit, so that the waters might not transgress his command, when he marked out the foundations of the earth" (Proverbs 8:29). "He...pushed the oceans back to let dry land appear" (Psalm 24:2, paraphrased in *The Living Bible*). The scene is one of warfare.[7]

The warfare of Creation Week is not a struggle between equals. God is clearly superior, but Evil incarnate resists at every turn, as it does to this day. The Bible pictures a "leashing" of the primordial waters that there might be land habitable by God's special creation in his own image, Man. God speaks through the prophet in Jeremiah 5:22b of how He restricted the threatening deep that completely surrounded the dry land: "I placed the sand as a bound for the sea, a perpetual barrier which it cannot pass; though the waves toss, they cannot prevail, though they roar, they cannot pass over it." Psalm 104:9 continues the same thought: "Thou didst set a bound which they should not pass, so that they might not again cover the earth."

The English word that most accurately describes this forceful action of God's Spirit upon the darkness and the waters is *muzzle*, as one would muzzle a wild dog. Job 7:12 asks, in recalling the ancient tradition, "Am I the sea, or a sea monster, that you muzzle me?"[8] Job 38:8-11 describes an all-powerful God telling of his titanic feat of muzzling, not destroying, the rebellious powers:

> *Or who shut in the sea with doors,*
> *when it burst forth from the womb;*
> *when I made clouds its garment,*
> *and thick darkness its swaddling band,*
> *and prescribed bounds for it,*

---

7. Cardona, in "Creation and Destruction," (*op. cit.*, p. 73) says, "[*Bara'*] has the etymological meaning of 'forcing into shape.' The word also contains a connotation of violence."

8. Mitchell J. Dahood, "Mišmār 'Muzzle' in Job 7:12," *Journal of Biblical Literature and Exegesis*, 80, 1961, pp. 271-72. Cf. Pope, Job, Anchor Bible, *op. cit.*, pp. 60-61.

and set bars and doors,
and said, "Thus far shall you come, and no farther,
and here shall your proud waves be stayed"?

Based upon the Ugaritic (a Semitic dialect similar to Hebrew), the Masoretic text of Psalm 68:22 is correctly emended to read, "I stifled the serpent; I muzzled the deep sea."[9] The apocryphal Prayer of Manasseh addresses God "...who hast shackled [muzzled] the sea by thy word of command, who hast confined the deep..." (verse 3). It is quite interesting to note in Mark 4:39a that Jesus of Nazareth, recalling those primeval events in which He Himself had participated several thousand years earlier, spoke authoritatively when confronted once again by the darkness and wild waters of the Sea of Galilee: "[H]e...rebuked the wind, and spake to the sea [literally], 'Be still! Be muzzled!' " (Greek *pephimoso*) This expression was characteristic also of the various ancient Mesopotamian and Canaanite literatures; Albright translates a Ugaritic inscription, "I muzzled Tannin [the dragon]...."[10]

Significant too is the watery source of five apocalyptic beasts, "four great beasts" of Daniel 7:3 who "came up out of the sea," and Revelation's beast who was seen "...rising out of the sea..." (13:1a). In apocalyptic symbolism the sea usually represents the peoples of the world (at enmity with God), e.g., Revelation 17:15. The LXX translators rendered *tehom* as *abyssos*, later to be found in the New Testament as the abyss, the abode of the unrighteous dead. For a Hebrew Old Testament precedent, see Psalm 71:20, where *tehom* in the plural has just such a meaning.[11]

Job 26:12-13 continues in even more shocking (to the modern mind) language the portrayal of the battle of Creation: "By his power he stilled the sea; by his understanding he smote Rahab...his hand pierced the fleeing serpent." And so Isaiah, "Was it not thou that didst cut Rahab in pieces, that didst pierce the dragon?" (51:9b) The ancient rabbis called Rahab "the Angel of the Sea."[12] The coiled, evasive serpent—in the Bible variously

---

9.   Dahood, *JBLE, op. cit.*, pp. 271-72.

10.   William F. Albright, *Bulletin of the American Schools of Oriental Research*, No. 84, 1941, p. 16, quoted in Heidel, *op. cit.*, p. 106.

11.   Cf. Howard Wallace, "Leviathan and the Beast in Revelation," *The Biblical Archaeologist*, Vol. XI, No. 3, Sept. 1948, pp. 66-67.

12.   Ginzberg, *op. cit.*, Vol. I, p. 156.

given the appellatives Rahab, Leviathan and the dragon—is the personification of, or analogous to, the evil that has been restricted by God in the Creation. The evil forces resisting the Creator are consistently linked to the wild ocean waters.[13,14] In fact, the Old Testament descriptions of God's struggle and victory over Rahab-Leviathan-dragon-t^ehom-darkness, except where used in a clearly variant metaphorical sense, always refer back to the Creation.[15]

Waltke claims that these Old Testament poetic references, so similar to the seven-headed monster of the ancient Near Eastern creation myths, merely "served as a helpful metaphor to describe Yahweh's creative activity"[16] for the authors of Job, Psalms and Isaiah. In other words, Waltke is suggesting that strict monotheists could never have believed those stories literally, as did all their pagan neighbors. Such myths, he claims, were "borrowed imagery," used only poetically, and therefore not to be taken seriously.

Yet Waltke (and other conservative scholars who claim to accept biblical inerrancy) should be asked if he believes that the Old Testament re-telling of the seven-headed dragon theomachies is "borrowed imagery," while he views the more up-to-date seven-headed dragon of Revelation 12:3 with considerably more acceptance? Such conclusions reflect inconsistent exegesis, once again probably attributable to our modern rationalistic worldview.

> [W]e must take seriously the metaphorical character of the biblical references to creation. They should not simply be dismissed as convenient figures of speech or hollow tropes, as if they were historicized "useful fictions." They are not mere illustrations. As metaphors, they

---

13. Wakeman, *op. cit.*, p. 102: The sea (*yam*) "is found parallel to...Rahab, Leviathan and the *tannin* [dragon] as well as to *t^ehom*." Additional Old Testament references to the anti-creation serpent/waters are Job 3:8; 9:13; 41:1f; Psalm 89:9-10; 93:3-4; 104:25-26; Habakkuk 3:8-15.

14. Jacob, *op .cit.*, p. 141: "It is not without reason that the Israelites did not become a seafaring people and that they always showed a kind of instinctive horror of the sea and its dangers."

15. Wakeman, *op. cit.*, p. 3.

16. Waltke, Part I, *op. cit.*, p. 34.

were used to convey significant analogies, and we must interpret them as such in order to understand their meanings.[17]

There are certain variant metaphorical uses of Rahab, the dragon/serpent, in the Old Testament. These allegorical nicknames are always carefully noted as referring to the earthly enemies of God and his people (e.g., Psalm 40:4 ["the proud"]; 87:4; Isaiah 30:7; Jeremiah 51:34; Ezekiel 29:3; 32:2). We find such a variant use of "the dragon" even as late as the pseudepigraphal Psalms of Solomon (2:29) in the first century B.C., where the author speaks disparagingly of the Roman conqueror of Palestine, Pompey. Early Christian polemics maintain this same imagery concerning their earthly enemies.[18] However, such instances of variant metaphors are easily perceived by their contexts. And, of course, we also have specific personages, Rahab the harlot of Jericho and Leviathan of Job 41, whose given names are coincidentally identical. All other Old Testament references to Rahab, Leviathan and the dragon/serpent speak specifically of the archenemy of God's Creation. The biblical writers possessed a strong anti-mythological bias, giving us all the more reason for dealing with this material more than casually.

Israel's earthly battles are viewed in scripture as similar metaphors: God's victory over chaos.[19] Whenever Israel won a battle, particularly if the LORD's hand had been obvious, it was perceived as a creation metaphor (e.g., Exodus 15; Psalm 74; Isaiah 51:12-13). "Creation is the paradigm of redemption."[20]

The Old Testament monster also is multi-headed: "You shattered the heads of the *dragon* on the waters; you crushed the heads of Leviathan" (Psalm 74:13b-14a).[21] Ancient Mesopotamian and Canaanite myths all tell us that this anti-creation dragon's heads total seven.

---

17.   Simkins, *op. cit.*, p. 89.

18.   Kiessling, *op. cit.*, pp. 172f.

19.   Simkins, *op. cit.*, pp. 107-117.

20.   *Ibid.*, p. 117.

21.   See Wakeman, *op. cit.*, pp. 63, 68, note 5, where "dragons" or "sea monsters" [*tanninim*] is to be emended to the singular. The plural of the Masoretic text violates the original Hebrew parallelism. Cf. Kittel, *Biblia Hebraica, op. cit.*, p. 1040, note to v. 13.

From Ugarit comes this inscription: "When thou shalt smite Lotan, the fleeing serpent, (And) shalt put an end to the tortuous serpent, Shalyat of the seven heads...."[22] Revelation confirms the ancient memory with its seven-headed dragon (12:3) and seven-headed "beast rising out of the sea" (13:1). Both Testaments speak clearly of incarnate Evil having been decisively defeated by God and being merely restricted for the present; but both anticipate the final destruction and disposition of Earth's ancient enemy at a future time.[23]

Leviathan...is a monster who sums up cosmic evil and was vanquished by God of old and will be annihilated by God once and for all in the end of days.[24]

Isaiah 27:1 foretells this eschatological event:

In that day the Lord with his hard and great and strong sword will punish Leviathan the fleeing serpent, Leviathan the twisting serpent, and he will slay the dragon that is in the sea.

John of Patmos knew very well the Old Testament imagery of the multi-headed beast of $t^e hom$; thus Revelation concludes the ages-long theomachy with those gentle statements of ultimate, total triumph: "And the sea gave up the dead in it..." (20:13), "and the sea was no more" (21:1c).

The "personality" of the evil chaos is evident in scripture. Indeed, the Hebrew $t^e hom$—"the deep"—appears to be a proper name; as with any proper name there is rarely a definite article before it. Thus an appropriate translation would be "Deep" rather than "the deep."[25] There is no word or concept in biblical Hebrew for a personal or impersonal "nature."

We must not transfer uncritically our accustomed ways of thinking to Israel. We must, rather, face the exacting

---

22. Heidel, *op. cit.*, p. 107.
23. Apparently the future elimination of the dragon/waters was common currency in first-century Judaism, appearing also in the pseudepigraphal Testament of Levi 4:1 and Assumption of Moses 10:6.
24. Cyrus H. Gordon, "Leviathan: Symbol of Evil," *op. cit.*, p. 9. Cf. G.C.D. Howley, F.F. Bruce, H.L. Ellison, eds., *The New Laymen's Bible Commentary*, Grand Rapids: Zondervan, 1979, p. 135.
25. Wakeman, *op. cit.*, p. 89.

> demand of thinking ourselves into ideas, in a "view of
> life", which are unfamiliar to us... This can easily be
> shown in the case of the concept "nature", a concept
> which has become so indispensable to us but of which
> Israel was quite definitely unaware. Indeed, if we use
> the term in the interpretation of Old Testament texts,
> then we falsify something that was quite specific to
> Israel's view.[26]

To the ancient Israelite *all* sources of power, life and growth are
spiritual, personal. Nothing "just happens"; there is spiritual
activity—good or evil—behind every earthly event. Read Job 1
and 2 with this in mind. Water itself is not that which is evil, but
rather the malevolent spiritual power controlling the seas.
Indeed, water in the creation narrative of Genesis 2 is the very
basis for fertility. The ocean and the fresh water are contrasted,
one misused by a hostile spiritual power and the other provided
by a caring God as a life-giving necessity.

"And God saw that it was good" contrasts the nature of the
newly formed earth with the evil chaos that had formerly been
reigning unchained. The Hebrew word for "good" has a broader
range than its English translation: "very good" could well be chosen to capture the fullness of intent.[27] In fact, Genesis 1:31 looks
back at the Creation, describing it in much stronger terms, "And
God saw everything that he had made, and behold, it was very
good...." So, if we use "very good" above, then perhaps a better
phrase in verse 31 would be "extremely good."

Because God's "holiness" is aligned against the evil powers
of chaos, there is actually a severe struggle occurring. God is
always superior, but the evil powers never cease their striving.
The natural events that were occurring as the Creation's third
day was taking place must have been awesome. Ocean bottoms
apparently were heaving up to expose the ground, probably a
single land mass ("Pangaea"), for there is no biblical indication
of separate continents until "...the earth was divided" (Genesis
10:25; 1 Chronicles 1:19). As already noted, such a usage of *'erets*
normally meant "the land," "the ground." Thus the scripture, if

---

26.   Gerhard von Rad, *Wisdom in Israel*, Nashville: Abingdon, 1972, p. 71.
27.   Ridderbos, *op. cit.*, p. 66; Speiser, *op. cit.*, p. 5.

Genesis 10:25 does indeed refer to the breakup of an actual "Pangaea," casually anticipates a catastrophic variation on the modern theory of plate tectonics. In the massive upheaval described so concisely in Genesis 1:9-10, God was forming a place fit for habitation by his physical creations, both animal and plant life.

God firmly took charge in this spiritual warfare, with his Spirit "sweeping" across the rebellious waters and driving back the darkness with his gift of light.[28] When God who is Spirit speaks the word, no other power can prevent the results from occurring in the physical realm. The consummation of the opening round of the struggle perhaps has been noted quietly in verse 5: "...and the darkness he called Night." Historically, when one person forcibly took authority over another, the victor normally seized the opportunity to "name" the vanquished.[29] The naming simply means that God had now established his authority over the darkness, although the darkness was still permitted a limited nocturnal sovereignty.

> In Hebrew as in Babylonian thought, name is inextricably bound up with existence. Nothing exists unless it has a name. "Whatever has come to be has already been named" (Eccl. 6:10a). Its essence is concentrated in its name (cf. Gen. 27:36). Hence the act of creation is not complete until all creatures have received a name (Gen. 2:18-23). The Creator of the heavenly host, in bringing them into being, calls them all by name (Isaiah 40:26). Personal existence is regarded as continuing posthumously in the name which is perpetuated by a man's descendants. To cut off a name, therefore, is to end the existence of its bearer....
>
> ...The name in the OT is the essence of personality, the expression of innermost being....
>
> ...A change of name accompanies a change in character... That which is called by Yahweh's name is his

---

28. Jesus consistently portrayed the darkness as evil: "But this is your hour, and the power of darkness" (Luke 22:53b); "And cast the worthless servant into the outer darkness; there men will weep and gnash their teeth" (Matthew 25:30).

29. Cf. E.J. Young, *op. cit.*, p. 35, note. See also 2 Kings 24:17.

possession and therefore comes under both his authority and his protection.[30]

*To him who conquers I will give some of the hidden
manna, and I will give him a white stone, with a new
name written on the stone which no one knows except
him who receives it* (Revelation 2:17b).

God's first act of creation was to form light. Light is essential if Good is to prevail. In the Bible, light and darkness are separate, distinct entities[31]—in this present age intermingled—each
one allowed to rule over its designated segment of the daily cycle
as depicted in Jeremiah 33:20: "Thus says the LORD: If you can
break my covenant with the day and my covenant with the night,
so that day and night will not come at their appointed time...."
"Darkness" is *not* merely the absence of light.

*He has described a circle upon the face of the waters
    at the boundary between light and darkness* (Job
    26:10).

And when I waited for light, darkness came (Job
    30:26b).

Or have you seen the gates of deep darkness? (Job
    38:17b)

*Where is the way to the dwelling of light,
    and where is the place of darkness,
that you may take it to its territory
    and that you may discern the paths to its home?*
    (Job 38:19-20)

And night shall be no more (Revelation 22:5a).

Darkness is as much a biblical entity as light.

"Order" and "history" belong together. God creates history; He begins by working through "evening and morning, one
day." Thus the Bible, from its very beginning, assumes a plan,
a purpose, to history. Karl Barth says, "The aim of creation is

---

30. *The Interpreter's Dictionary of the Bible,* Vol. 3, New York: Abingdon
     Press, 1962, pp. 501-502.
31. Childs, *op. cit.,* p. 33.

history."[32] Chaos is non-historical; cosmos implies history. History, according to the Bible, is going somewhere.

And God keeps it going somewhere. The ancient Israelite perceived God's *sustaining* hand in the twice-daily tides, annual seasonal and river changes, and each new day, new moon, new year. The earth is organized, but requires the Divine Sustainer. The chaos is not yet destroyed, only contained, co-existing with the order and life impressed upon the earth by God. The tension remains yet. Though the waters try to inundate, to regain their former supremacy, God is the Sustainer who prevents such a disaster, "...upholding the universe by his word of power" (Hebrews 1:3a). Each morning He calls back the darkness (*choshek*); at every high tide He calls back *t^{e}hom*. Von Rad notes tersely, "The cosmos stands permanently in need of this supporting Creator's will."[33] Jacob, Anderson and Stuhlmueller describe the situation well.

> This direct intervention of God in nature is not only a proof of the lordship with which He makes use of all the elements; it sometimes takes the form of a veritable struggle, because in spite of its perfection, Creation is unceasingly menaced by two forces which have not been created by Yahweh but have simply been subjected to Him, namely darkness and the sea, residues of the chaos which existed before Creation. Darkness is a power hostile to Yahweh, whose essence is light... The sea constitutes a still graver menace... The vast domain of waters was...only more or less neutralized by being confined within certain limits assigned to them... But the water, though driven back, has only one desire, to return and take up again the place it originally occupied.[34]

> The raging, unruly waters of chaos symbolize the powers which threaten to destroy the meaningfulness of history, as though—to recall Jeremiah's vision—the

---

32. Karl Barth, *Church Dogmatics*, Vol. III, part I, Edinburgh: T. & T. Clark, 1958, p. 33.

33. Von Rad, *op. cit.*, p. 49; Bernhard W. Anderson, "The Earth Is the Lord's," *Interpretation*, Vol. IX, 1955, pp. 10-14, provides a grand statement about God the Sustainer.

34. Jacob, *op. cit.*, p. 140.

world ever has the possibility of returning to chaos
(Jeremiah 4:23-26).[35]

> Yet, if creation is an historical event, contrariwise, histo-
> ry is a continuation of this creative power of God. [Isaiah
> and Jeremiah] use such terms as ['*asah* and *yatsar*] in
> describing God's intervention in Hebrew history.
> Through the events of history, therefore, Yahweh is
> forming, making or creating history... At each moment
> of time, darkness must be dispelled and the raging
> waters of the abyss kept in their place by the creative
> word of God.[36]

Since God is the Creator, He retains the right to allow the
earth to revert to its former state, which He accomplished temporarily in the Flood simply by removing his sustaining power.
"The waters above" thereupon collapsed upon the earth during a
40-day period,[37] this catastrophe occurring simultaneously as
"...all the fountains of the great deep burst forth..." (Genesis
7:11). These worldwide eruptions didn't "just happen": God
ordered them! *Baqa'* ("burst forth") in the present usage (simple
passive form) means "a breaking forth (in order to liberate)
caused by something or someone." These simultaneous events
were probably what occasioned what we see in the geologic record
as the deepest layer of buried fossils, arbitrarily designated
"Cambrian Period" on the uniformitarian geologic time scale.
Evolutionists call the Cambrian "a sudden explosion of life," but
this is not true; rather, it was a sudden explosion of *death*, caused
by the initial stages of the Flood. The entire Creation, so beauti-
ful and good in the beginning, sank to a much lower level of existence. Entropy increased with a vengeance, and sin-ridden man
became the saddest specimen in all of God's handiwork.

God had declared man to be his deputy immediately upon
the latter's creation in Genesis 1:26f. Man's responsibility was to

---

35. Anderson, *Creation versus Chaos, op. cit.*, p. 132.

36. Stuhlmueller, *op. cit.*, pp. 435, 465.

37. A similar event occurred on a much smaller scale when "...the Lord
     brought back the waters of the sea" to inundate the Egyptians pursuing
     Israel (Exodus 15:19).

"...fill the earth and subdue it." In his edenic setting man was assigned to be God's agent for overseeing, for good, "...every living thing that moves upon the earth." After the Fall the image of God was marred by sin and death. Man has since tried to set himself up as sovereign, which in his sinful condition is only presumption. Being unable to effect this attempt at sovereignty, man usually finds himself tragically adding to the world's disorder in the ages-long war between Good and Evil. A commentary on the Book of Revelation describes the situation well.

> **There is a kind of reversal in [Revelation's] bowls of judgment of the process of creation, beginning with the earth, the sea, the sun, and ending with the general chaos of the whole ordered system of the world. The highly colored apocalyptic language thus represents a deep truth—that when men defy God, they are turning the world back into chaos.[38]**

> **Sin involves the danger of undermining the integrity of the Creation and of leading to a return of chaos.[39]**

The natural principle involved here is called "entropy," a result of the Second Law of Thermodynamics.

Albert Einstein declared that entropy is the premier law of all science,[40] as the apostle Paul confirms in Romans 8:20-22: "For the creation was subjected to futility...the creation itself will be set free from its bondage to decay...." The apostle proclaimed a principle in harmony with the Second Law of Thermodynamics 18 centuries before "natural" man could formalize it.

Wherever the gospel is preached and heeded, however, increased "order" inevitably results. God's Spirit still today slows

---

38.   Herbert H. Wernecke, *The Book of Revelation Speaks to Us*, Philadelphia: Westminster Press, 1954, p. 130. Other reversals of the creation pattern have been noted elsewhere in scripture. Cf. Michael Fishbane, "Jeremiah IV 23-26 and Job III 3-13: A Recovered Use of the Creation Pattern," *Vetus Testamentum*, Vol. XXI, 1971, pp. 151-67.

39.   Jacob, *op.cit.*, p. 141.

40.   Jeremy Rifkin, with Ted Howard, *Entropy: a New World View*, New York: Viking Press, 1980, p. 6.

and even miraculously reverses the world's natural entropy as Christians pray and believe Him.

> **The spiritual plane is not governed by the ironclad dictates of the Entropy Law... While the Entropy Law governs the world of time, space, and matter, it is, in turn, governed by the primordial spiritual force that conceived it.**[41]

Just as the Israelites' clothing did not wear out in 40 years in the wilderness (Deuteronomy 8:4), so is the final verse of the Gospel of Mark true to this day: "And they went forth and preached everywhere, while the Lord worked with them and confirmed the message by the [miracles] that attended it" (16:20). Miracles are often dramatic, abrupt reversals of the world's natural entropy. In biblical language, they are demonstrations of God's "saving" actions. "Creation and salvation are almost identical terms in the Old Testament."[42] Nations, communities, families and individuals that are led by the Spirit of God soon begin to witness noticeable slowings of entropy's "normal" rate of degeneration; increased prosperity and all its benefits ensue. The reverse is true also: note how many areas of Russia are actually in worse condition for having been enchained by Soviet godlessness than they were before the Communist Revolution.

For all his frantic efforts, unspiritual, natural man is more of a pawn in this universal struggle than he will admit. His primary responsibility in this age is to choose sides—and to lead others to choose sides—for the final conflict.

The Bible pictures *three* stages in this cosmic warfare between order and chaos for control of the Earth. The first picture we see is that scene in Genesis 1:2 where chaos has full sway. Verse 3 initiates what we could call the present age, where order and chaos exist side by side, temporary supremacy going now to one and now to the other in a centuries-long pattern of continuing warfare, although the decisive battle has long since been fought at Calvary. This age, beginning at Genesis 1:3,

---

41.   *Ibid.*, p. 8. This statement, if understood as referring to the God of the Bible, is correct, in spite of the fact that the authors are caught up in New Age occultism.

42.   Boman, *op. cit.*, p. 182.

encompasses nearly all of scripture. The third, the fulfillment stage, is described in the final two chapters of the Bible: "Then I saw a new heaven and a new earth; for the first heaven and the first earth had passed away, and the sea was no more" (Revelation 21:1). That last clause is more than an afterthought; it depicts a new earth where chaos is utterly nonexistent. Amos 7:4 predicts the final struggle in characteristic Old Testament prophetic language: "...the Lord God was calling for a judgment by fire, and it devoured the great deep [t^ehom]." "And there shall be continuous day" (Zechariah 14:7a); "And night shall be no more" (Revelation 22:5a). The chaos (*tohu wabohu*, t^ehom) and darkness (*choshek*) are eliminated upon the conclusion of the war; the victory of Good is complete, and Evil is no longer merely chained but permanently cast into the flames.

Note once again that this new earth is not *creatio ex nihilo*. According to 2 Peter 3:5f, *fire* is God's primary instrument for destroying the present earth, but the new earth will be, in modern terms, the same earth—reformed, renewed, re-created—no longer oppressed by the old serpent-enemy, Satan. The Bible, as we can see, has a sublime, overarching view of Earth's history, far more awesome and worship-inspiring than the pagan evolutionary philosophies of origins.

"Thus the heavens and the earth were finished, and all the host of them" (Genesis 2:1). So the scripture sums up the initial accomplishment, God's work of creation, from chaos to cosmos.

Chapter 10

Questions

1.   Is This Dualism?

It is almost a Sunday school cliché that the Bible is not dualistic.[1] We are told that the Babylonian Genesis is dualistic, with the "good" Marduk vanquishing the "evil" Tiamat and using her body as the raw material for creation. Zoroastrianism may be dualistic; Taoism too may be dualistic, but not the Bible. So we are told.

This is not true. The presence and power of personal evil are so obvious in scripture that one could wonder how such an erroneous teaching developed. Certainly the Bible is dualistic! Spiritual warfare swirls about us.[2] The warfare transcends Earth's history. Creation was enveloped in warfare. The struggle continues to this day and will culminate in the ultimate victory of Good and Earth's final, once-for-all re-creation.

Finegan says, "Dualism usually makes the creation evil...."[3] Not so! Finegan is referring to some of the *gnostic* systems that considered spirit good and matter evil. Platonic philosophy and

---

1.   E.g., Hastings, *op. cit.*, p. 6.
2.   For an impressive exposition of biblical dualism, see Donald Grey Barnhouse, *The Invisible War*, Grand Rapids: Zondervan, 1965. An entire volume is devoted to the subject. See also Henry M. Morris, *The Long War Against God*, Grand Rapids: Baker Book House, 1989.
3.   Jack Finegan, *In the Beginning*, New York: Harper & Bros., 1962, p. 15.

Iranian Zoroastrianism encouraged such a dichotomy. But Martin Luther, in his call to the Church to return to biblical Christianity, bitterly attacked this horizontal division; he made the division vertical, and rightly so. Biblical dualism faces the fact that some *spiritual* entities are good and some are evil; some *physical* entities are good and others evil. Johannine theology provides excellent New Testament confirmation of Old Testament spiritual warfare. Biblical dualism describes the good God seizing chaotic matter that had been under control of an evil spiritual power and forcibly forming it into a wholesome creation. The Bible further insists on another distinctly dualistic conception: that which is material can never become spiritual (see 1 Corinthians 15:50).

Is this dualism? It certainly is.

Gnostic studies define dualism as spiritual versus material, considering that which is spiritual as "good" and that which is physical, material, as "evil." But the God of the Bible cares deeply about the material: He is now in the process of redeeming this physical earth.

Scientists today almost by definition live with a non-spiritual worldview. A great leap of faith is usually required for a scientist—even one who is a creationist—to recognize the dominance of spiritual forces in this created universe. "The whole world is in the power of the evil one" (1 John 5:19b)—indeed, the entire biblical worldview can hardly be harmonized with the day-to-day scientific approach. A scientist who happens to be a Christian normally functions as if the physical were autonomous, his Sunday pronouncements notwithstanding. Admitting a loving, spiritual Creator is sometimes difficult for scientists trained in rationalistic philosophies; but accepting the activity of evil spiritual forces during the process of creation is perhaps more than even many creation scientists can receive, in spite of the biblical testimony.

Dualistic pagan religions make their gods "anthropomorphic." The whole pantheon engages in sexual activity, warfare, love, hate, jealousy, ambition, etc. Biblical commentators tend to be repelled by anthropomorphic behavior among the Old Testament "host of heaven," so they often attempt to allegorize, demythologize or simply ignore such biblical references. Yet the

Bible speaks clearly of those "angels that did not keep their own position" (Jude 6), but "took to wife such of them as they chose" (Genesis 6:2), producing giants in the earth (Genesis 6:4). Almighty God walks (Genesis 3:8), talks (1 Kings 22:20), has arms (Job 40:9), nostrils (Psalm 18:15), and feelings (Exodus 20:5; Leviticus 26:30); He loves (Hosea 11) and hates (Proverbs 6:16), and yes, even conducts warfare (Judges 4:15; Isaiah 42:13; Revelation 12:7). God acted still more anthropomorphically and created man in his own image, which means that "the man looks like God" (Genesis 1:27).[4] Indeed, verse 27 does mean precisely that.

> **The words *image* and *likeness* reinforce one another: there is no "and" between the phrases, and Scripture does not use them as technically distinct expressions, as some theologians have done, whereby the "image" is man's indelible constitution as a rational and morally responsible being, and the "likeness" is that spiritual accord with the will of God which was lost at the Fall... After the Fall, man is still said to be in God's image (Genesis 9:6) and likeness (James 3:9)....[5]**

We westerners love to spiritualize biblical statements that seem too anthropomorphic. Scripture is clear: Adam looked like God! Further, Adam "...became the father of a son in his own likeness, after his image, and named him Seth" (Genesis 5:3). We *must* stop "westernizing" the word of God!

Many of us Christians—a bit like the ancient gnostics—perceive a God who is too distant, too impotent, too uninvolved.[6] Yet the God of the Bible condescended to create a world He could become involved in, and a man enough like Himself that God could perceive Himself in a father role. Against the charge of "anthropomorphism!" we could assert that the greatest anthropomorphism of all is, as the angel Gabriel announced to young Mary, "The Holy Spirit will come upon you, and the power of the

---

4.   Cf. G. Ch. Aalders, *op. cit.*, p. 71.
5.   Derek Kidner, Genesis, *An Introduction and Commentary*, Downers Grove, IL: InterVarsity Press, 1967, pp. 50-51.
6.   See, e.g., J.B. Phillips, *Your God Is Too Small, op. cit.*

Most High will overshadow you..." (Luke 1:35), and God became Man in Jesus of Nazareth!

Almighty God even became *weary* during Creation Week, in spite of some attempts to generalize from Isaiah 40:28. Nearly all modern commentators tell how the Lord God created "effortlessly," speaking only the word, and it was accomplished.[7] Again, the biblical evidence suggests otherwise. Effortless creation is another modern myth.[8]

Prior to the eighteenth-century Enlightenment, writers, artists and sculptors portrayed God on the seventh day of creation as *tired*. Medieval and Renaissance sculpture has been described by White:

> The furrows of thought on the Creator's brow show that in this work he is obliged to contrive; the knotted muscles upon his arms show that he is obliged to toil; naturally, then, the sculptors and painters of the mediaeval and early modern period frequently represented him as the writers whose conceptions they embodied had done—as, on the seventh day, weary after thought and toil, enjoying well-earned repose and the plaudits of the hosts of heaven.[9]

> The Almighty...is shown as seated in almost the exact attitude of the "Weary Mercury" of classic sculpture—bent, and with a very marked expression of fatigue upon his countenance and in the whole disposition of his body.[10]

Again, effortless creation is a *modern* myth. The Spirit's exertion must have been great as He swept "over the face of the waters." The physical violence as the dry land was being lifted would have been incredibly spectacular. The stubbornness of the waters (more than simple inertia) was not easy to overcome. The

---

7.   E.J. Skinner, *op. cit*, p. 15; S.R. Driver, *The Book of Genesis*, London: Methuen, 1904, p. 5, note; Dillman, *op. cit.*, p. 60; Spurrell, *op. cit.*, p. 3; Ridderbos, *op. cit.*, p. 30.

8.   Cardona, *Kronos*, Vol. IV, *op. cit.*, p. 74.

9.   White, *op. cit.*, Vol. I, p. 1.

10. *Ibid.*, p. 3, note.

four (or five) chaotic entities noted in Genesis 1:2 imply a mighty resistance to God's efforts.

Our Creator was quite serious when, as scripture says, He rested on the seventh day. Yet many modern scholars treat that first sabbath as a mere literary device for man's instruction.[11] This is ironic in view of the fact that conservative writers often interpret the remainder of this creation narrative quite literally. Although Genesis 1 does not mention specific effort or struggle by the Spirit of God, one cannot argue from silence that the acts of creation were accomplished without exertion; a number of other scriptures confirm the great effort.

The biblical keys to understanding God's personal sabbath are found, first, in Genesis 2:2b: "He rested on the seventh day from all his work which he had done"; second, in the poetic references to creation, replete with allusions to violence, noted in the previous chapter; third, the clear statement of Exodus 20:11, where it is said that "...in six days the LORD made heaven and earth, the sea, and all that is in them, and rested the seventh day; therefore the LORD blessed the sabbath day and hallowed it"; and fourth, we note God's own words in Exodus 31:17: "It is a sign for ever between me and the people of Israel that in six days the LORD made heaven and earth, and on the seventh day he rested, *and was refreshed.*" The Bible is to be interpreted quite literally unless otherwise implied by the context!

Still there is more. A working Father is complemented by a working Son.

> *Jesus said to them, "My food is to do the will of him who sent me, and to accomplish his work." ... "My Father is working still, and I am working." ... "We must work the works of him who sent me, while it is day; night comes, when no one can work"* (John 4:34; 5:17b; 9:4).

The Holy Spirit, the third Person of the Trinity, is the "executive arm" of the Godhead, and the One whose workings are most visible to man.

Genesis 1 might have revealed itself in its pristine purity had more attention been given to the presentation of

11.   E.g., Arthur S. Peake, *A Commentary on the Bible*, London: T.C. & E.C. Jack, 1931, p. 135.

God there as a worker, however supereminent. Like any worker, God too started from a piled-up material necessary for construction.[12]

Further, a working man was created to represent and rule on behalf of and in the power of the working God.

And God blessed them, and God said to them, "Be fruitful and multiply, and fill the earth and subdue it; and have dominion over the fish of the sea and over the birds of the air and over every living thing that moves upon the earth" (Genesis 1:28).

For we are his workmanship, created in Christ Jesus for good works, which God prepared beforehand, that we should walk in them (Ephesians 2:10).

Therefore, my beloved, as you have always obeyed, so now...work out your own salvation with fear and trembling; for God is at work in you, both to will and to work for his good pleasure (Philippians 2:12-13).

The point is that God is more actively involved in this universe, in this earth, in this human race, than our rationalistic minds can appreciate. He was involved in the struggle of creation, is still involved in his continuing work as Sustainer, as well as in the culminating battles that are even now shaking the earth and the heavens. The presence of powerful evil, the horrible death of his own Son, the deteriorating condition of the human race—all indicate that God is prepared to suffer losses in order to win the war. He grieves every moment He loses a soul who has chosen death rather than life. Portions of Job, Psalms and Isaiah fairly reek with allusions to violent spiritual warfare; and, of course, the New Testament portrays great violence in both spiritual and material realms. The immanent God is powerfully involved in his creation!

It is hoped that this entire presentation will enable the reader to perceive the great sweep of Earth's violent history from Creation to Culmination—the majesty, the purposefulness, the agony, the pathos, and the victory of its loving, persevering Creator. Biblical dualism is highly visible from beginning to end.

---

12.   Jaki, *op. cit.*, p. 294.

2. What Is Genesis' Relationship to Pagan Cosmogonies?

We have already noted most of the Old Testament's poetic references to creation. They reflect many similarities to neighboring pagan cosmogonies that have been uncovered by archaeologists since the mid-nineteenth century. In addition to the Genesis narratives, Rahab/Leviathan—the serpent—suggests a common pool of traditions throughout the ancient Middle East.[1] Heidel insists that one cannot fully understand Hebrew history without studying the literature of the nations surrounding Israel.[2] Briefly, the Mesopotamian creation epics abound in apparent parallels to Genesis 1, as well as other Old Testament passages. For a century after the first Mesopotamian mythological cosmogony was discovered, liberal Bible scholars were pointing out the "obvious" dependence of Genesis upon its Mesopotamian "ancestor."

In recent years, however, scholars have, with more wisdom, noted the impressive *differences* between the two. Dahood observes that the Hebrew *tᵉhom* is equivalent to *thm* of Ugaritic, a very early northwest Semitic dialect quite similar to Hebrew. *Tᵉhom* therefore "does not derive directly from Babylonian sources, as urged by several generations of scholars."[3] The biblical narrative is prior. Heidel too is satisfied that earlier scholars were wrong.[4] Sarna says it well: "The [biblical] Creation account is non-mythological... The outstanding peculiarity of the biblical account is the complete absence of mythology in the classical pagan sense of the term."[5] "A straightforward reading of Genesis 1 and 2 gives every impression that the events happened just as they are described. It is intended to be read both realistically and literally."[6]

Although most of Genesis 1 is strictly prose, a word should be added about Old Testament poetry, which includes nearly half

---

1. Cassuto, *op. cit.* pp. 8f.
2. Heidel, *op. cit.*, p. 5.
3. Dahood, *Psalms III*, Anchor Bible, *op. cit.*, p. 36. Cf. Fishbane, *op. cit.*, p. 159.
4. Heidel, *op. cit.*, pp. 82f.
5. Sarna, *op. cit.*, p. 9. Cf. Stigers, *op. cit.*, p. 48; also Sailhamer, *op. cit.*, p. 81.
6. *Ibid.*, Sailhamer, p. 237.

of the Old Testament and almost all of the remaining Old Testament references to the Creation. Biblical poetry too has a quality quite different from what we moderns would expect. We think of modern poetry as being quite subjective, and it is. But the poetry of the Old Testament, particularly as found in the Prophets, is far more objective than the poetry of our contemporaries. Job, Psalms and the Prophets reflect distinctive poetic styles intended to communicate rather clearly to their contemporaries. Job 38 is an exquisite poetic celebration of God's Creation, telling us a great deal about the subject. Biblical poetry is non-mythological, in spite of two centuries of liberal pronouncements to the contrary. For example, to speak of the "poetic" structure of Joshua 10, referring to "the long day," proves nothing. Poetry or prose, Joshua 10 speaks of an actual, natural event that armchair scientists have futilely tried to demythologize for generations. The biblical references to the Creation picture, in the idiom of their time, the original, God-revealed primeval history of Earth.

How then do we explain the similarities of Genesis 1 to the widespread Canaanite and Mesopotamian creation myths?

Young responds to the question correctly: "The so-called cosmogonies of the various peoples of antiquity are in reality deformations of the originally revealed truth of creation."[7] Pagan religion always leads to mythological thinking.[8] Somewhere in great antiquity Man, apart from the true God, began to confuse Creator with creation, forming a mythological synthesis. Similar to the Bible these myths may be, yet the differences are vital. Pagan cosmogonies are ultimately dependent upon Earth's actual natural history, correctly recorded in Genesis.

A century ago the University of Chicago's Ira M. Price suggested the proper relationship between Genesis' creation narratives and the many other similar ancient creation myths.

Their common elements seem to point to a time when the human race occupied a common home and held a

---

7.   E.J. Young, *op. cit.*, p. 82, note.

8.   The modern pagan religion known as secular humanism, for example, is replete with half-truths, or precisely what a future generation might call "myths."

common faith..., each handing on from age to age records concerning the early history of the race... One ancient religion did not borrow these universal traditions from another, but each possessed primitively these traditions in their original form. The Genesis record is the purest, the least colored by extravagances, and the nearest to what we must conceive to have been the original form of these accounts.[9]

Unger adds,

The Genesis account is not only the purest, but everywhere bears the unmistakable impress of divine inspiration when compared with the extravagances and corruptions of other accounts. The Bible narrative, we may conclude, represents the original form these traditions must have assumed.[10]

Even liberal scholars are impressed with the striking independence of the biblical narratives. Commenting on the Canaanite, Egyptian and Mesopotamian influences, Tucker adds with astonishment,

But in view of Israel's location near the crossroads of the civilizations of the ancient world and her relatively weak political and cultural position, it is surprising that the influence was not even more significant![11]

Modern studies have solidly underscored the truth that Israel's unique faith and scriptures were not "religion," but developed rather as the result of direct intervention and revelation by the Spirit of God.

The fact that pagan cosmogonies appear to have some relationship to the correct description of the Creation should not offend our piety. Satan consistently displays the counterfeit, the

---

9.   Ira M. Price, Ovid R. Sellers, E. Leslie Carson, *The Monuments and the Old Testament*, Philadelphia: The Judson Press, 1958 (first published in 1899, revised in 1925 and 1958), p. 127.

10.   Merrill F. Unger, *Archaeology and the Old Testament*, Grand Rapids: Zondervan, 1954, p. 37. Cf. Heidel, *op. cit.*, pp. 71-118.

11.   *Op. cit.*, p. 22.

half-truth. Nor should our piety be offended by the Old Testament's allusions to preexistent matter. The first chapter of Genesis varies from pagan cosmogonies in many respects, but
creation out of nothing is not one of them.

Most pagan cosmogonies perceive creator and creation as
virtually identical. The Roman Pliny (first century A.D.) says,
"The world...is sacred, eternal... It is the work of nature, and
itself constitutes nature."[12] Among the Canaanites and their
Semitic neighbors, only the father of gods, El, a name we also
find in the Old Testament, was not necessarily identical with the
creation. The Canaanite El was probably a declension of the original Creator God of Noah and his sons, but El had been "semi-
retired" from the effective activities of the pagan pantheons.[13]

Matter, according to the Bible, is not an absolute; it is distinct from and subservient to God.[14] Scripture makes no mention
of a past eternity of matter, although Revelation seems to depict
the future eternity of matter.

The ancient Greeks pondered much about such concepts.
But speculation of this type is foreign to scripture.

**The Old Testament Jews were probably among the least
speculative people known to history. The concrete
earthiness with which they speak of sacred things can
sometimes shock us. But there is a wisdom in [the opening words of Genesis] for which other races of men
sought in vain.**[15]

---

12. *The Natural History of Pliny*, trans. John Bostock and H.T. Riley, London:
     George Bell & Sons, 1893, pp. 13-15.

13. Simkins, *op. cit.*, p. 87.

14. John Calvin, quoted in Eugene M. Klaaren, *Religious Origins of Modern
     Science*, Grand Rapids: Eerdmans, 1977, p. 43, gives a devastating cri-
     tique of paganism's confusion of Creator and creation: "As if the universe,
     which was founded as a spectacle of God's glory, were its own creator!"

     For a philosophical discussion of "creator-created," see Neville, *op. cit.*,
     pp. 94ff.

15. Bruce Vawter, *A Path Through Genesis*, London: Sheed & Ward, 1957,
     p. 37. However, Jewish scholarship following the dispersion of A.D. 70
     began to take on highly speculative qualities, as occasionally reflected in
     the Mishnah and the Talmud.

3. Which Earth?

When we deal with the question of the age of the Earth, the inquiry is painfully enlarged by asking a further question: Which earth?

This may sound foolish, but to any of the ancients it would have been an all-important question. The peoples of antiquity around the globe thought in terms of cycles of world destructions and re-creations. We have noted Origen's cyclical view, which of course tended to conform to already ancient Greek and Egyptian traditions. Second Peter 3:3-13 provides possible hints of three "earths" or "worlds." Even secular catastrophists point to several biblical stories that, although localized in their viewpoints, might well have been describing worldwide cataclysms. Patten *et al.* suggest a number of catastrophes in addition to the Flood, among which are included the tower of Babel, Sodom and Gomorrah, the Exodus and the long day of Joshua.[1] If indeed these events were global in scope, the ancients would have considered every one to be the end of one "earth" or "earth-age" and the beginning of another.

There are innumerable allusions to these catastrophes in very ancient literature worldwide. And our planet does bear enormous scars that speak eloquently of such violent upheavals. No other event in ancient history is so well-attested as the Flood, both by literature and by geology.

Uniformitarianism in Earth's natural history has apparently, however, been the rule since Isaiah's time; neither the Bible nor any other human history records a subsequent catastrophe of global proportions. There have been no further "new earths." Scripture of course promises the one more—and final—cosmic destruction and "new earth" to come.

The *pre-Flood* earth—what the ancient Greeks called the "Golden Age"—was uniformly warmer and much more hospitable, as both Bible and paleontology amply confirm.[2] The earth *as we know it* is primarily the post-Flood re-creation, geologically quite recent, with subsequent convulsions such as the

---

1. Patten, Hatch and Steinhauer, *The Long Day of Joshua and Six Other Catastrophes*, Seattle: Pacific Meridian, 1973.

2. Whitcomb & Morris, *op. cit.*, present the biblical and paleontological evidences for the warmth of the Adam-to-Noah age, pp. 239f.

splitting apart of the continents (recorded in Genesis 10:25 and 1 Chronicles 1:19), well-attested by modern geology, the strange natural events during Joshua's generation and the eighth-century B.C. upheavals described in Isaiah 24; 38:8; and perhaps Amos 1:1 and Zechariah 14:5.

Because of its violent natural history, guided by the hand of God, Earth's age is confused and quite difficult to ascertain. Some measurements of age would be valid only as far into the past as the most recent global catastrophe. Additional geological yardsticks would have been affected by the division of the continents, by ancient mountain range deformations and by the Flood with its massive volcanic upheavals. Still further into the past, the Creation catastrophe would provide the *terminus a quo* for certain determinations. Other measurements, such as stellar distances, computed in multi-millions of light-years, would be utterly unaffected by cosmic "accidents" occurring within the relatively small confines of our Solar System.[3] Thus old-Earth and young-Earth proponents hurl valid age measurements at each other, leading to an unresolved conflict with apparently solid evidences appearing on both sides of the controversy. Our catastrophic history simply has had varying effects upon Earth's measurements of age.

Earlier there was mentioned the marginal concern about radiometric dating, in particular the uranium-thorium-lead, potassium-argon and rubidium-strontium dating techniques. Although some serious questions about these methods have already been noted, this work renders moot much of the creationist argument against these types of radiometric dating, because the proper exegesis of Genesis 1:1-3 allows for such very old dates in some of Earth's stones, if not in its bones.

Uniformitarians traditionally have denied the recent global convulsions that are so obviously part of the geological record, although today increasing numbers are realizing how untenable is that position in the face of the earth's mute testimony. It is good to see a slow awakening to the truth, although catastrophic evidences are usually considered by evolutionists to

---

3.   Patten, *The Biblical Flood and the Ice Epoch*, Seattle: Pacific Meridian, 1966, suggests "galactogenesis," a cosmic calendar that conforms somewhat to the present findings. See pp. 295f.

be local, rarely if ever worldwide, or, if global, then very ancient geologically.

The point to be stressed is that the entire earth has repeatedly—including during Creation—suffered enormous shocks. These catastrophic events have affected our time measurements variously. Perhaps those scientists who are interested in paleochronology will begin to ask the question any ancient would have asked: Which earth are we talking about?—the chaos before the Creation?—or the comfortable world of Adam and his successors?—or the badly scarred and severely degraded earth of Noah's descendants?—or the earth subsequent to the divided continents?

The question is troublesome. Which earth indeed!

4. What Did God Intend by Genesis 1:1-3?

The initial chapter of Genesis bears another distinctive quality that has not yet been noted. It should be observed first that some of the narrative portions of the Old Testament are written in non-chronological order (e.g., Genesis 2).[1] The precise order of events is often not a concern of the biblical writer. Genesis 1, on the other hand, is a revelation from God that bears all the marks of precise, deliberate sequence, with a unique concern (among the ancient Hebrews) for "time" in a language whose "tenses" are based upon the state of an action, not time of occurrence. Von Rad describes that first chapter eloquently.

> **Nothing is here by chance; everything must be considered carefully, deliberately, and precisely....What is said here is intended to hold true entirely and exactly as it stands. There is no trace of the hymnic element in the language, nor is anything said that needs to be understood symbolically or whose deeper meaning has be deciphered... These sentences cannot easily be over-interpreted theologically! Indeed, to us the danger appears greater that the expositor will fall short of discovering the concentrated doctrinal context.[2]**

God is speaking clearly and distinctly in chapter 1. If this narrative is exegeted properly—and in its simplest understanding—it will be discovered that He provides a wealth of wisdom to every generation of mankind.

But let us limit our present concern to the first three verses. It has already been ascertained what the author meant by these opening lines, that the Creation began with preexistent material. Now we need to ask further, What did *God* intend by those verses?

It may be found elsewhere in scripture that God sometimes adds a subsequent, "ultimate" meaning to particular

---

1. E.J. Young, *op. cit.*, pp. 47-48.
2. Von Rad, *op. cit.*, pp. 47-48. Heidel, *op. cit.*, insists however that Genesis 1:27-28 "are poetry pure and simple. The whole chapter is written in a solemn tone and in dignified prose...which easily glides over into poetry" (p. 93, note). While the earlier portion of his assertion may be true, Heidel's final six words strain our credulity.

scriptures.[3] Did He perhaps attach further meaning to Genesis
1:1-3 for latter-day readers? Until we examined more carefully
the creation references of Romans 4:17 and Hebrews 11:3, God
appeared to have added *ex nihilo* in the New Testament. This
possibility should have been reconsidered already by the reader
who is not bound by religious tradition. The doctrine of creation
has been clearly demonstrated *not* to be an example of what is
called progressive revelation. In the New Testament, particularly 2 Peter and Revelation, creation still means what it meant in
the Old Testament. For the apostle Paul and, especially, the
author of Hebrews, a somewhat Platonic worldview has been
added.

The Bible fairly shouts that God is consistent. If He is going
to alter his course or accomplish a unique work, God always
alerts his servants the prophets (Amos 3:7). Otherwise He does
not vary, "for I the Lord do not change" (Malachi 3:6a). To illus-
trate, let us examine his pattern concerning creative miracles all
through the scripture. Every formation of life recorded in Genesis 1 and 2 was just that—a creative miracle. The LORD is not
limited by the First Law of Thermodynamics (conservation of
energy). Most Christians believe that Almighty God has the
power to create out of nothing at any time He desires. The biblical record provides consistent evidence, however, that He does
not. We all believe He *could* create out of nothing, but He doesn't;
this is characteristic of God's "self-limitation." All creative miracles in the Bible begin with at least a "seed."

In Genesis 2:7 the LORD God formed man from the ground;
in verses 21 and 22 He took one of the man's ribs to "build up"
the woman. The Sidonian widow offered Elijah only a handful of
meal and a little oil, yet the food lasted for more than two years

---

3.   Cf. Conrad E. L'Heureux, "Understanding the Old Testament Prophe-
      cies," *The Bible Today*, Vol. 23, No. 1, Jan. 1985, pp. 56-57; Ridderbos, *op.
      cit.*, p. 18. E.g., Matthew 2:15b: "This was to fulfil what the Lord had spo-
      ken by the prophet, 'Out of Egypt have I called my son.'" That New Tes-
      tament verse refers to the angelic instruction to Joseph to return home
      from Egypt with his infant son Jesus. But as we look back to Hosea 11:1b,
      we find that the original statement referred to Israel's exodus out of
      Egypt under Moses. God gave Hosea's statement additional, "ultimate"
      meaning in the New Testament. Such a "dual fulfillment" is found occa-
      sionally in biblical prophecy.

(1 Kings 17:16). Elisha prayed for the widow of his student-prophet and God multiplied her tiny supply of oil (2 Kings 4:1-7). Note that in each case God began to create with something "in hand."

Jesus of Nazareth never performed a creative miracle out of nothing. He placed mud or spit on damaged eyeballs to produce two complete eyes. He created wine out of water. He fed 5,000 with five loaves of bread and two fish. In Matthew 15:30-31 people with missing hands or feet found to their joy that new limbs had grown out of the stumps. God's miracles always seem to have some material to begin with. Not that the Almighty Creator *needs* material, but rather, He appears to have chosen to limit Himself so that He regularly creates in such a manner. So consistent a *modus operandi* indicates the process by which God in Genesis 1 created the Earth and its occupants as well. The very laws under which He operates today are the same laws operative in the Creation of Genesis 1.

The Book of Isaiah, for example, portrays the predicted re-establishment of the nation of Judah following the Babylonian exile in specific terms of *creation*. The author repeatedly relates the formation of the heavens and the earth to the coming re-creation of the Jewish nation, using *bara'*, *'asah* and *yatsar* freely and interchangeably. Thus creation identical in terms and concept appears in both Genesis and Isaiah. "This historical act of re-creating Israel unveils God's power in creating the universe out of primal chaos."[4] The final two chapters of Revelation also speak of re-creation in much the same manner.

> God's creative activity is thus not limited to the genesis of the world, *as it is for us*, but creation is a collective concept which expresses all the positive saving actions of God at all times... [italics added].[5]

Boman recognizes clearly our most unbiblical western misunderstanding of God's power and our *un*scriptural limitation of his creativity to a six-day period some millennia ago.[6]

---

4.   Stuhlmueller, *op. cit.*, p. 451.

5.   Boman, *op. cit.*, p. 173.

6.   See, e.g., Whitcomb and Morris, *op. cit.*, pp. 222-27.

What did God intend by the opening sentences of Genesis? He intended exactly what the human author said: Everything— dry land, plant and animal life, man himself—was created out of something already existing, even as God's creativity continues to operate today. There was, and is, at least a "seed" already in existence.

Of the reader who yet clings to *ex nihilo* creation, the question is now asked, What will you have lost by releasing this traditional tenet? You have not lost the belief in biblical inerrancy, if indeed you have held this view. You have not lost your faith in the one holy and all-powerful God. You have not lost anything of lasting spiritual value. He is still to be worshiped as Earth's Almighty Creator, Sustainer and Redeemer. You have merely changed your mind, because of the overwhelming evidence, about a questionable point of doctrine. You have lost nothing more.

5.   When Did the "Creation" Occur?

Surely every Christian who holds such a belief would like to conserve his theological "axiom" that God created the universe *ex nihilo*. Agreeing with the early fifth-century Augustine, my own personal opinion is that God did just that—*but prior to Genesis 1:1*! I think so, but that is all. I am not nearly as certain of *creatio ex nihilo* as I am certain of those doctrines that the Bible clearly enunciates. Theological speculation—which is what *ex nihilo* creation was in the second century—can lead one astray...dangerously.

The questioning reader, now having noted my own (Augustinian) opinion of an original *pre-biblical* creation out of nothing, might wonder then why this book was written. First, and most important, I am convinced that the Bible speaks of a recent creation out of existing matter; Christians can better understand the mighty biblical acts of God with that knowledge. And second, there are ample scientific evidences of the very ancient lifeless Earth and universe, which contradiction leads to serious disagreements among creationists and loss of credibility in the scientific world. This work simply brings together data relating to the age of the Earth from the two broad disciplines, with the delightful result that they are found to be in basic accord.

It was noted earlier that the correct translation of Genesis 1:1-3 is the key to the entire thesis. Sailhamer, who is a firm believer in *ex nihilo* creation, makes an important admission.

> **If the translation of Genesis 1:1 is changed to something such as, "When God created the heavens and the earth, the earth was formless and void," the loss of the concept of "creation from nothing" is immediate and transparent.[1]**

Sailhamer is absolutely correct.

The "fallout" from this correct translation of Genesis 1:1-3 could affect the dating of the primeval earth quite seriously. If God began his Creation with preexistent material, then we have no *biblical* limitation on how old was the "chaos" when God began to create (order) the universe, if indeed we could measure chaos in historical terms.

---

1.   *Op. cit.*, p. 250.

Could the preexistent universe have been billions of years old—prior to Genesis' creation narrative? Countless stars, in terms of light years, are indeed that far away. Because the correct exegesis of the first three verses potentially allows for such an extended, earlier time period, "billions of years" would *not* be an unscriptural statement! Thus the sorest point between old-Earth and young-Earth creationists is resolved by the proper exegesis of these three verses. The problem of the huge distances of most stars is promptly settled.

Note that on Day Fourth all the stars were necessarily moved around in the heavens. More probably, the violence in the heavens was affecting only the bodies within the Solar System— perhaps not even all of them. But the entire universe would have *appeared* different from the viewpoint of a spectator on the Earth as, of course, that is the perspective of Genesis 1. And now we are thinking like ancient Israelites! Therefore our study should prove helpful to scientists and Bible students alike, serving to relieve unnecessary tensions and disagreements.

Revelation 21 and 22 raise a sobering question. Since those two chapters suggest a *future* eternity of matter, what does that say to our theories of origins? Do these final scriptures imply a *past* eternity of matter as well? Does all this mean that matter is eternal, as many ancient religions depict it? Or even as some contemporary atheistic evolutionists would have it? Not at all! Marcus Dods says of Genesis 1, "The writer merely desires to refer the origin of the known world, *the heaven and the earth,* to God; and he does not consider the question of the eternity of matter."[2]

Therefore, *when* did the "Creation" occur?

Biblical chronology unconditionally indicates that the Creation described in Genesis occurred only a few thousand years ago. The entire half-billion-year-plus uniformitarian geologic column is telescoped by the Bible to within those six-to-ten millennia. Although Genesis begins with this recent Creation, the Bible does speak elsewhere of several earlier "events."

> *The Lord created* [wisdom] *at the beginning of his work, the first of his acts of old....at the first, before the beginning of the earth. When there were no depths...before he had made the earth...* (Proverbs 8:22f).

---

2. Dods, *The Book of Genesis,* Edinburgh: T. & T. Clark, 1911, p. 1.

All the host of heaven (angels) was created prior to Genesis 1, "For in [Christ] all things were created, in heaven and on earth, visible and invisible..." (Colossians 1:16). "All things were made through him" (John 1:3a). "...when [God] laid the foundation of the earth...all the sons of God [the heavenly host] shouted for joy" (Job 38:4a,7b). According to a well-attested variant text, Revelation 13:8 tells us that "the book of life of the Lamb that was slain" contains names that were "written before the foundation of the world" (cf. Ephesians 1:4).

Of these prior "events" we are told in scripture, but of the origins of chaotic Earth, of *t^{e}hom, choshek* and *tohu wabohu,* we are told nothing.[3] Even the angels' Fall is not definitely placed, although it may have been recorded in a later context (Genesis 6:2) for good reason; the pseudepigraphal Book of Jubilees and Book of Enoch both seem to confirm this view.

One might ask, logically, how then a proposed *creatio ex nihilo*—whenever it took place—became controlled by rebellious powers, since according to Isaiah God did not create a chaos?

First, Isaiah refers only to the Creation of Genesis 1 as not being a chaos (uninhabitable); the author never speaks of an earlier, hypothetical creation out of nothing. Second, we have no biblical evidence for describing or dating these proposed pre-Adamic "events," so such rationalistic ponderings about the chaos are

---

3.   The eleventh-century Rashi makes an interesting observation about *t^{e}hom.*

And if you should say that (the verse) comes to teach that these (heaven and earth) were created first, and that its interpretation is: In the beginning of every thing (first of all) He created these...—in that case (if you insist that the passage indicated the order of Creation), you should be astonished at yourself, for indeed, the waters came first,...and as yet Scripture had not revealed, when the creation of the waters took place. (From) this you learn that the waters came before the earth [the dry land]... Scripture does not teach us anything about the order of the earlier or later (acts of creation) (Rashi, *op. cit.,* pp. 2-3).

As noted earlier, Psalm 104:6a might be referring to the Creation-event: "Thou didst cover [the earth] with *t^{e}hom* as with a garment." Some feel, however, that this verse refers to the Flood.

Charles notes a later rabbinic tradition: "...seven things created before the world,...Torah, Repentance, the Garden of Eden, Gehenna, the Throne of Glory, the Temple, and the Messiah..." (R.H. Charles, *Pseudepigrapha,* Oxford: Clarendon Press, 1913, p. 562, note).

perhaps only a modern "busyness." Time is tied to matter and order; an angelic "rebellion" would have occurred, not in time, but in eternity; its results are felt in time. One can perceive easily why some very modern commentators have posited a pre-Genesis angelic Fall. But the presence in the world of pre-creation Evil has no necessary identity with the (later?) Fall of the angels. The question is probably unanswerable on this side of heaven. This work avoids speculation about such matters where the Bible could speak but remains silent.

Scientific conjectures are safer. For example, if the big-bang theory could overcome its *scientific* challenges, that date for the "original" Creation might have been ten billion or more years ago. But, without some crucial emendation, even the big bang could not accommodate creation out of nothing! Recent "evidences" for the big bang are seriously compromised by many inexact measurements, faulty enough to void the research, in spite of a prominent media blitz to the contrary.[4] In addition, the big-bang theory requires incredible amounts of "cold dark matter"—an *ad hoc* fabrication for which there is only hypothetical evidence.

Perhaps somewhat more promising is the newer concept of the "inflationary universe." The already traditional big-bang theory cannot explain what might have happened during the first moment of creation, specifically, the initial second. A new unified field theory, drawing together all the basic forces of the universe, fits elegantly into a creationist scenario of creation *ex nihilo*—10 to 20 billion years ago!—and quite compatibly with the primary thesis of this book. The model of the inflationary universe seems to agree

> ...with the generally accepted description of the observed universe for all times after the first 10^{-30} second... According to the inflationary model, the universe had a brief period of rapid inflation, or expansion... In the course of this stupendous growth spurt all the matter and energy in the universe could have been created from virtually nothing.[5]

---

4. *Creation Research Society Quarterly*, Vol. 29, Sept. 1992, p. 102; Vol. 30, Dec. 1993, p. 123; Vol. 31, March 1994, pp. 216-17.

5. Alan H. Guth & Paul J. Steinhardt, "The Inflationary Universe," *Scientific American*, Vol. 250, No. 5, May 1984, p. 116.

The model of the inflationary universe not only appears to explain and predict accurately some of the characteristics of the universe, but it also leads to those startling final words: "...all the matter and energy in the universe could have been created from virtually nothing." Guth and Steinhardt conclude their article with this bold statement:

> The inflationary model of the universe provides a possible mechanism by which the observed universe could have evolved from an infinitesimal region. It is then tempting to go one step further and speculate that *the entire universe evolved from literally nothing* [italics added].[6]

Could this explain how it all began?

Russian cosmologists had originated the inflationary model, and, along with others, had tinkered with the concept, ever improving it. More recently, Andrei Linde, a Russian now on the faculty of Stanford University, has proposed his newer "chaotic inflation" scenario. Incorporating what is valid of the big bang, he suggests repeated big bangs within the overall context of the inflationary universe.[7] Again, the key is his theory's ability to explain many features of our observable world, something the big bang alone cannot do. Whether or not this theory is plausible will remain for future research to ascertain, but it certainly harmonizes quite well with all that has been said about the Creation in this book. And, of course, it's all done with mathematics, without practical demonstration.

The Second Law of Thermodynamics—entropy—also strongly suggests some sort of initial creation. The world is "running down"; thus logic would appear to require that it have had a beginning. And, because the universe is yet far from equilibrium, it must have been organized in a possibly measurable past—cosmologically speaking. This *seems* to be appropriate, but that is all.

Dating the recent formation of the earth (and the heavens) from the preexisting material noted in Genesis 1:2 is as far back

---

6. *Ibid.*, p. 128.
7. "The Self-Reproducing Inflationary Universe," *Scientific American*, Nov. 1994, pp. 48-55.

as we can proceed biblically without stumbling in the darkness. Perhaps Bishop Ussher was not correct about the date of the Creation, but he was much closer than attorney Charles Lyell's arbitrary uniformitarianism. Because of the serious discrepancies between the ancient manuscripts and versions, Creation Week is often estimated biblically to have occurred six to eight thousand years ago. Some creationists feel compelled to add several more millennia. That opinion seems reasonable; the great variation of centuries between the chronologies of the ancient versions of Genesis appears to make it a possibility. The only plausible figures for life on the earth—scripturally—are in the thousands, certainly not millions of years. The mounting natural evidence in our own generation, combined with the correct exegesis of Genesis 1, makes so recent a dating no longer appear ridiculous to the open-minded inquirer.

One simple illustration concerns the question of the age of life on the earth. The Lompoc, California, diatomaceous earth beds are organic deposits of a type that is said to be building at the rate of one to five centimeters per thousand years.[8] These figures for the deposition of the thick diatomite deposits are then extrapolated to many millions of years by uniformitarian logic, and this intimidating "evidence" is presented to prove the concept of long ages for life on the earth.[9] Herein is seen an example of old-Earth advocates' only strong argument for very ancient life—sedimentary deposits containing once-living organisms in extremely thick strata. Implicit within this argument is also to be found gradualism's greatest weakness—its basic, unquestioned *assumption* that these deposits have always accumulated at rates not very much different from those which are current. The *rate*, or *varying rates*, of processes is the controversial point.

It is fortunate for scientific inquiry that diatomaceous earth has commercial value, for in 1976 in the quarry at Lompoc workers uncovered an 80-foot-long baleen whale—*standing on its tail.*[10]

8. Arthur N. Strahler, *Physical Geology*, New York: Harper & Row, 1981, p. 243.

9. Daniel Wonderly, "Non-radiometric Data Relevant to the Question of Age," *Journal of the American Scientific Affiliation*, Vol. 27, No. 4, Dec. 1975, p. 147; D. Young, *op. cit.*, pp. 78f.

10. *Chemical & Engineering News*, Oct. 11, 1976, p. 40.

Obviously the whale and the diatomite were all thrust into that pit catastrophically, and in minutes instead of millennia. Actually, the whale had once been lying on its side: the entire deposit had then been turned violently into its present position 90 degrees from its original orientation. Suddenly the burden of proof shifts. This single striking discovery of "a whale on its tail" renders utterly invalid any uniformitarian use of the Lompoc beds as evidence for ages older than biblical chronology allows, and it certainly strengthens the case for Flood geology. Surely also this discovery should initiate some caution among old-Earth adherents as they retroject current rates of all other organic depositions into the "prehistoric" past. Apart from the commercial value of the Lompoc diatomite, these beds would continue to be used improperly as evidence for an old Earth.

Why do such depositions of homogeneous sediments show up around the Earth? Sedimentologist Guy Berthault has demonstrated in extensive experiments at Colorado State University how this widespread phenomenon might have occurred in a brief time during the Flood. Berthault's research has filled an important gap in creationist studies.[11]

Gradualists today will generally admit to "local" catastrophes, such as earthquakes, volcanism, and, of course, a more widespread Ice Age. But the "glasses" they wear cannot seem to admit the possibility of worldwide catastrophes, at least in recent millennia. Indeed, the scope of such a global event as the Flood would have been so enormous as to be incredible to the modern geologist or paleontologist who, perhaps, cannot see the forest for the trees.

To underscore the dating problem of "Creation," we quote Sailhamer again:

> **If the translation of Genesis 1:1 is changed to something such as, "When God created the heavens and the earth, the earth was formless and void," the loss of the concept of "creation from nothing" is immediate and transparent.[12]**

---

11. Guy Berthault, "Experiments on Stratification," *Proceedings of the Third International Conference on Creationism*, ed. Robert E. Walsh, Pittsburgh: Creation Science Fellowship, Inc., 1994, pp. 103-109.

12. *Op. cit.*, p. 250.

Therefore, the Creation of Genesis 1 is dated (approximately) by straightforward biblical chronology, while a proposed "original" creation of the preexistent chaos may have occurred perhaps *billions of years earlier*. Whether we like it or not, this is the clear result of proper exegesis. Sailhamer's grudging confirmation is especially meaningful.

6. Is There a Conflict Between Theology and Geology?

It has often been proclaimed during the past two centuries that science and religion do not belong together. Gunkel states the case.

> The conflict between theology and geology is eliminated when both stay within their boundaries. Religion has to leave it to science to speak about the creation of the world and man as best as it can. But natural science, if it observes its boundaries, should neither affirm nor deny the dogma about creation.[1]

Gunkel is in error. Science and religion have always been synthesized in human culture, as is still the case.

Galileo is a good case in point. Modern worshipers at the altar of "science" would have us believe that Galileo tried to demonstrate the astronomical fact that the Solar System is heliocentric, and that the Roman Inquisition opposed the march of scientific truth. This accusation against the Roman Catholic Church is far removed from reality. Yet such we have all learned from our history and science textbooks.

Actually, Galileo's seventeenth-century confirmation of heliocentricity by the use of his telescope was at first welcomed by the Church at Rome, in particular the Jesuit astronomers. However, the science faculty at the University of Bologna was severely critical of this sarcastic rebel. The disagreement over heliocentricity was between a scientist and the scientific community. Finally, in order to bring the explosive issue to a resolution, Pope Urban VIII asked for a position paper from the science faculty at the University. The paper was totally geocentric and filled with distortions, appealing to "scientific" tradition, to Aristotle and, interestingly, to religious tradition.[2]

> Urban VIII and his court may be considered much less the oppressors of science than the first bewildered

---

1. Hermann Gunkel, *Genesis*, Göttingen: Vanderhoeck & Ruprecht, 6th ed., 1964, p. 131 (trans. from the German). Cf. also Von Rad, *op. cit.*; Hyers, *op. cit.*; *et al.*

2. Jerry Bergman, "The Establishment of a Heliocentric View of the Universe," *Journal of the American Scientific Affiliation*, Vol. 33, No. 4, pp. 225-30.

casualties of the scientific age... The original challenge
went far back in time. [Galileo] had become a danger
when he started writing in Italian [rather than Latin, the
language of science] and when he decided to bypass the
universities and vested intellectual authority and reveal
his mind to enlightened public opinion.[3]

It has been known for a long time that a major part of
the Church intellectuals were on the side of Galileo,
while the clearest opposition to him came from secular
ideas.[4]

Galileo was condemned by the Inquisition not so much for
teaching error as for reneging on an earlier pledge to the Church
not to speak so brashly and publicly of his revolutionary
insights. "He realized at last that the authorities were not interested in truth but only in authority."[5] Churchmen of many per-
suasions spoke bitterly of Galileo later, but not until the science
faculty at the University and the Jesuit astronomers had deliberately made his case "religious," and the ecclesiastics were provoked into perceiving that his teachings might be threatening
the authority of the Roman Church. Seventeenth-century secular scientists thoroughly enjoyed their ability to generate such
civil and ecclesiastical recriminations, as some in the university
communities still do to this day. Galileo's tragedy is not one of
Church versus science, but rather the religious traditionalism of
scientists who typically resent revolutionary ideas.[6] His experience has a distinctly modern ring to it.

The seventeenth century, in retrospect, almost opened the
floodgates for creationism. Western man was slowly learning the
historical and scientific methods. Honest historians of science
have long recognized that these important advances were due
almost exclusively to scholars immersed in Lutheran and
Reformed theology or the Pietistic Revival of the late seventeenth
century. In spite of the devastation of Europe's Thirty Years' War,

---

3.   Georgio de Santillana, *The Crime of Galileo*, Chicago: University of
      Chicago Press, 1955, p. 204.

4.   *Ibid.*, p. xii.

5.   *Ibid.*, p. 257.

6.   Bergman, *op. cit.*, pp. 225f.

this became the century of the giants of Christian historical and scientific scholarship. Contemporaneous with the occultists Bacon, Leibnitz and Descartes, there were Kepler, Galileo, Newton, Burnet, Whiston, Arnold and countless other scientist-philosophers, most of whom *took the Bible seriously*, who were slowly learning how to discover God's truths in the heavens above and the earth beneath. Building upon one another's researches and philosophizings, these devout pioneers seemed headed in the right direction.

However, the traditional concept of a "tranquil" Flood was standing in the path of a scientific understanding of Earth's early history. A careful exegesis of Genesis 7:11,19-20; 8:3,5; and Matthew 24:39a would have pointed to the titanic wave action of the Flood. Genesis 8:5a says, quite literally, "And the waters were going and diminishing until the tenth month...." Jesus made a pertinent statement, recorded in Matthew 24:39: "[A]nd they did not know until the flood came and swept them all away...." An awareness of these seven-and-a-half months of enormous (and probably intermittent) surging breakers would have led seventeenth-century scholars to the correct perception of the stratigraphy of Earth's huge sedimentary deposits.

They also were unaware of the ancient Jewish records that told of the volcanic eruptions and conflagrations accompanying the Flood. The very high pre-Flood concentration of oxygen in the atmosphere (more than 30 percent) would have created a veritable tinderbox of flammable materials worldwide. Assuming that the Deluge was due exclusively to a tranquil rainfall rather than the more destructive "fountains of the great deep" bursting forth—the varied strata, with the fossils they contained, bewildered seventeenth-century scientists (and nearly all since) concerning the cause of their deposition and the resultant true age of life on the earth.[7] Apparently it never occurred to them to ponder why the rain ended after 40 days, while the survivors remained in the ark for more than a year.

---

7. The Old Testament writers were quite aware that the greater danger to the earth during the Deluge came, not from the skies, but from the seas. See, e.g., Job 7:12; 26:12; 38:8-11; Psalm 68:22; 104:6-9; Prov. 8:29; Isaiah 27:1; Jer. 5:22.

Still, sooner or later their Christian descendants should have produced a viable creation model, one that would fit both the biblical testimony and the growing natural evidence. William Buckland, an early nineteenth-century clergyman-geologist, accurately perceived the catastrophic nature of the Deluge; but he apparently overlooked some important scriptural details of Genesis 7 and 8. To this day students of the philosophy of science still miss the truth:

> **It required another scholarly clergyman, the Revd John Fleming,…to call into question the closeness of correspondence between the Mosaic testimony and the geological and paleontological evidence. Moses left word of a gentle strand of water rising placidly for 40 days, with the flood leaving no trace except a rainbow. This was hardly the account of a violent and transient storm.**[8]

The Christians who studied geology could not answer this objection effectively, leading even Buckland into forsaking Flood geology.[9] Such a common misinterpretation of the Genesis Flood has ruled to this day. Careful biblical exegesis and rabbinical studies would have indicated that the global fires and seven-and-a-half months of violent onslaught of waves many hundreds of feet high must have caused incalculably more damage than 40 days of rainfall alone. Buckland's biblical beliefs were thus increasingly perceived as a handicap to understanding. Witnessing a growing rationalistic antisupernaturalism, the eighteenth and early nineteenth centuries began closing the door on creationism. The scientific study of origins was thereby dealt a crippling and nearly permanent blow by antisupernaturalism's stifling apriorism.

As recently as 150 years ago, most of Europe's scholars generally regarded the hundreds of Flood legends of antiquity as historical, and they viewed the geological strata as evidences of that Flood. But Lyell's and Darwin's hypotheses—untested and unproven—promptly caused catastrophism to be banished from universities, libraries and scientific journals.

---

8.   Hallam, *op. cit.*, p. 43.
9.   *Ibid.*, p. 51.

Rationalism's restrictive rules had led inexorably to the philosophies of uniformitarianism and evolutionism, the latter a regression back to ancient religious beliefs. Those two pagan concepts, now dressed in modern technical clothing, are both quite religious; they are contemporary religious dogma, statements of faith. Uniformitarianism and evolutionism are built only upon highly selective data; they are little more than modern mythological constructions, guided by and themselves expressing the underlying religious beliefs and desires of their worshipers. Uniformitarianism and evolutionism are the contemporary humanist's perception of reality, containing modern distortions of truth much as we find distortions in ancient pagan cosmologies around the world.

The modern religion of secular humanism resembles its ancient pagan precursors in that all religions are evolutionary. In fact, only the Judaeo-Christian biblical record is *non*-evolutionary, even as Judge William R. Overton correctly noted in his infamous decision in the 1982 Arkansas Creation Science trial. *All* religion is evolutionary. Left to his own devices, man can never discover who he is, where he came from, or where he is going. He will always reason his way into an evolutionary trap. Though his denials may be loud, the reality remains that the humanist's evolutionary worldview is his religion—and is thus holy, untouchable.

Today a scientist may safely challenge any dogma except the two that are sacred, uniformitarianism and evolutionism. If a scientist, writing alone, dares to confront either of those two doctrines, he may expect the full pressure of the modern Inquisition. Secular catastrophists as well as creationists have in this generation been calling attention to contradictory data, although their contributions remain largely scorned or unacknowledged. Because of the sheer weight of evidence—catastrophic burials, mass extinctions of life, etc.—uniformitarianism in the sense Hutton, Lyell and Darwin wrote of it has in recent years come under moderate attack, particularly by Goldschmidt's "hopeful monster" theory and its up-to-date stepchild, Stephen Jay Gould's "punctuated equilibrium."[10] But these incredible *ad hoc*

---

10.   "The hopeful monster" theory had its origin in ancient mythology and
        Greek philosophy, such as the sixth-century B.C. Anaximander (W.K.C.
        Guthrie, *op. cit.*, p. 32f), although Goldschmidt and his successors were
        probably at first unaware of their pagan precursors.

hypotheses would constitute mere hiccups in the vast uniformitarian time scheme; the basic half-billion-year-plus geologic column remains sacrosanct to this day.

Although most scientists speak scornfully about such a possibility, Immanuel Velikovsky *et al.* have written persuasively on
the subject of historical catastrophism, adducing extensive biblical, mythological, historical and geological evidence. Writing
prior to the Space Age, Velikovsky compiled a truly remarkable
(even if not recognized) record of many dozens of explicit and
implicit predictions about the nature of the Solar System.[11]
Although Velikovsky's reconstructions of Earth's recent history
may be riddled with errors, and his "catastrophic evolution" may
merely resemble Goldschmidt's and Gould's theories, still his
confirmed prior descriptions of the Solar System can be denied
only by those who are willfully blind. See especially his books,
Worlds in Collision and *Earth in Upheaval.*[12] For a similar albeit
creationist position, see Donald W. Patten in the Bibliography.

Establishment science has attempted to discredit totally
Velikovsky's work, but a number of British scholars have been
critiquing his work in a more responsible manner. My plea for
this present research is that it be handled as the British
researchers have done in examining Velikovsky's writings. One
vitally important result in the United Kingdom has been the
most impressive work of David Rohl.

An Egyptologist by profession, Rohl reexamined critically
the traditional bases for ancient Egyptian chronology. Using the
monuments themselves, he demonstrated clearly that all but one
of the four conventional pillars of near eastern chronology—each
of them in ancient Egypt—were in egregious error, and always
by a century or more. Velikovsky's revised dates Rohl also found
to be in error.

The most gratifying results for a Christian are the clear
demonstrations by Rohl of repeated harmonizations of Old Testament events with the Egyptian archaeological record. In the

---

11.   Cf., e.g., Thomas Ferté, "A Record of Success," *Pensée*, Special Issue,
      Vol. II, No. 2, May 1972, pp. 1-15, 23.
12.   Immanuel Velikovsky, *Worlds in Collision, Earth in Upheaval*, Garden
      City, NY: Doubleday & Co., 1950 and 1955.

process, Rohl discovered the Old Testament to contain a remarkably accurate record of ancient Levantine events and personages. After more than a generation of liberal "proofs" that biblical chronology is "in error," Rohl's work brings the Bible and near eastern chronology once again into most agreeable synchronism. Some Egyptologists who have the courage to reexamine their traditional dating system are beginning to admit grudgingly that Rohl just may be at least partly correct.[13]

Peer pressure among scientists weaves a suffocating blanket of repression, effectively retarding the progress of science through the ages. A cursory study of the history of science—to this day—demonstrates this truth, which has been witnessed once again in our very generation on the subject of Alfred Wegener's theory of continental drift (plate tectonics). American geologist Frank B. Taylor proposed the theory independently. Hallam's *Great Geological Controversies* eloquently and in detail presents the furor concerning a theory that has grown prominently in recent years, although it may now be waning in popularity; certainly Wegener's theory of plate tectonics is by no means proven nor totally accepted in the world of science. Perhaps Wegener and Taylor were wrong about this theory, but it didn't deserve the vicious response it received.

> **...In the early 1950's continental drift was taken seriously by very few. The minute number of staunch adherents tended to be dismissed as cranks... A large number of people were either noncommittal or had a sneaking sympathy with the ideas of Wegener and du Toit, but considered it professionally wise to keep fairly quiet about it. (p. 148)... One of Wegener's strongest critics, R.T. Chamberlin,...quoted with evident approval an overheard remark...in 1926. "If we are to believe Wegener's hypothesis we must forget everything which has been learned in the last seventy years and start all**

---

13.   David Rohl, *A Test of Time: The Bible—from Myth to History*, Vol. One, London: Century Ltd., Random House, 1995. For an alternative neo-Velikovskian synchronism between biblical and Egyptian chronologies, see E.J. Sweeney, *The Genesis of Israel and Egypt*, London: Janus Publishing, 1997.

over again." [p. 151]... The American paleontologist G. G. Simpson noted in 1943 the near unanimity of paleontologists against Wegener's ideas... "The known past and present distribution of land mammals cannot be explained by the hypothesis of drifting continents." Bailey Willis was even more outspoken than Simpson. "...My reason refuses to consider 'continental drift' possible... The geology upon which protagonists of the theory rest assumptions is as antiquated as pre-Curie physics... Thus the theory of continental drift is a fairy tale..." [pp. 135-36].[14]

In nearly all matters the human mind has a strong tendency to judge in the light of its own experience, knowledge and prejudices rather than on the evidence presented. Thus new ideas are judged in the light of prevailing beliefs. If the ideas are too revolutionary, that is to say, if they depart too far from reigning theories and cannot be fitted into the current body of knowledge, they will not be acceptable. When discoveries are made before their time they are almost certain to be ignored or meet with opposition which is too strong to overcome, so in most instances they might as well not have been made.[15]

Alfred Wegener was neither geologist nor paleontologist. His formal training was in astronomy and meteorology, perhaps explaining why the present work had to be written by a non-specialist.

The Space Age is slowly demolishing any so-called evidence for uniformitarianism in Earth's ancient history. More than 120 "hypervelocity impact craters" caused by meteoritic impacts on the Earth have been located by satellite.[16] So the knowledge

---

14. Anthony Hallam, *Great Geological Controversies*, Oxford and New York: Oxford University Press, 1983, pp. 110f.

15. W.J.B. Beveridge, *The Art of Scientific Investigation*, London: Heinemann, 1950, p. 152.

16. Benny Joseph Peiser, "Catastrophism and Anthropology," *Chronology and Catastrophism Review*, Special Issue, The Society for Interdisciplinary Studies, July 1994, pp. 130-34.

explosion of our generation has been most kind to the creationist viewpoint. It is sparking a revolution that deeply offends the religiosity of many evolutionary scientists. Evolutionists thus seem less anxious to respond to creationists with the facts than they are exercised by the "religious" effort of trying to stamp out creationism. Their attacks are largely *ad hominem*, or they set up straw men to demolish, both of which are prominent characteristics of religious bigotry.

Christians often marvel at the explosive hostility of secular humanists to the teachings of creationism and the Flood. Such incredible hostility is not based upon scientific consideration whatsoever, but rather upon emotional and religious feelings. First, if God is the Creator, then we all owe Him our allegiance, and sinful human nature utterly rejects that call to obedience. Second, if there was a worldwide Flood, that event would speak of God's judgment upon sin, and this too is unacceptable to sinful humanity. These two points also explain why a new Christian—whose sin has just been dealt with—no longer senses that deep hostility to God's judgment and thus is much more open-minded scientifically.

The biblical faith is unique. It is *not* religion. In fact, religion is perceived as a major problem throughout the narrative portions of the Bible. "Religion" is normally man's attempt to find a god (or gods) and to discover how to control it (or them). In the scriptures we observe precisely the opposite. We perceive the one true God who cannot be found by man (Isaiah 45:15a; 55:8-9) and who thus cannot be controlled, but rather who has chosen to reveal Himself to man (1 Corinthians 1:21). He is the Creator, a highly moral Personality, concerned about the truth, for He Himself is Truth (Isaiah 65:16a; John 14:6,17).

Thus we may accept the scientific data God gives us in his personal self-revelation, the Bible. The information about our natural world found in scripture is rarely described explicitly as such, but usually is presented in an offhand, incidental manner. Ronald Simkins explains the sometimes puzzling nature of Old Testament storytelling.

> **This distinction between low and high context societies provides a helpful model for understanding the type of texts each society produces. On the one hand,**

low context societies tend to produce very detailed texts. Because little culture is shared among its members, texts written for low context audiences must describe in detail all the relevant cultural features that are necessary to understand the text. The texts produced by high context societies, on the other hand, frequently lack this detail. They are written by insiders for insiders, and so most aspects of culture can be assumed. All the members of the society have been socialized into shared ways of perceiving and acting... The Bible was produced by a high context society for high context readers. It assumes a rich culture that the biblical writers felt no need to describe. It is not surprising, then, that the Bible lacks any explicit articulation of the Israelites' worldview and value toward the natural world.[17]

Nor is the Bible self-consciously a textbook or even a volume of theology, but rather is largely a telling of the mighty acts of God, from which we may glean surprisingly accurate historical, theological, scientific and other data.

Man can study this information and upon the basis of his study can make true statements concerning Creation. The study of this revealed material is as truly the study of history as is the study of Caesar's accounts of ancient Gaul.[18]

Therefore, since science and religion (not the biblical revelation) are historically found commingled, their joint conclusions cannot always be trusted and, consequently, must be reexamined continually. But science and the Bible together allow much more accurate conclusions, and an increasingly viable model of Earth's origins continues to be extrapolated from sincere Bible study and historical and scientific research in conjunction with all—not selective—available data from the natural world. We cannot legitimately separate theology from geology: the Spiritual created the Physical.

---

17. *Op. cit.,* pp. 41-42.
18. E.J. Young, *op. cit.,* p. 24.

The burden of bankrupt eighteenth-century assumptions lies heavily upon modern science. A scientist—be he evolutionist or creationist—who rejects the miraculous out-of-hand has already prejudiced his conclusions, severely restricting the possibility of his arriving at correct results in his investigation of Earth's origins. God was, and continues to be, sovereign!

To restate the whole problem of the age of the Earth and its solution, we must examine critically all of our axioms. Since the Bible is truth and it obviously tells of a *young* Earth, and since significant scientific data have accumulated indicating an *old* Earth, we must check out every aprioristic statement. The resolution must never be a strained *ad hoc* compromise, but rather must be sought in the simplest, most evidential answers. Occam's razor still shaves painfully close. The truth may be disconcerting, even iconoclastic, and probably will injure a sacred cow or two, but, after all, truth is what we want.

Chapter 11

The Waters

I once heard a creationist lecturer make a statement to the effect that "the Bible does not specifically describe an antediluvian vapor canopy." I accosted him following the lecture, presenting the biblical evidence for the canopy that I was aware of, and he graciously challenged me to demonstrate my case in writing. This chapter is the result of that challenge.

Historically, a number of scholars have proposed a pre-Flood canopy. Jerome, translator of the fourth century Latin Vulgate, proposed a canopy that he called *compactae et densiores aquae*.[1] White interprets Jerome's words as an icy canopy.

The eighteenth-century philosopher Immanuel Kant suggested that the Flood might have been caused by the collapse of a vapor "ring" similar to Saturn's rings.[2] More recently, Isaac Newton Vail proposed in 1874 a ring-canopy similar to Kant's, although Vail was unaware of the priority of Kant's hypothesis.[3] Modern creationists usually accept some sort of antediluvian canopy.

But does the *Bible* speak about a vapor canopy? Or is the vapor canopy a pious *ad hoc* attempt by Bible believers to devise

---

1. Letters, LXIX, 6, in J.-P. Migne, Patrologia Latina, Vol. XXII, p. 659, quoted in White, *op. cit.*, Vol. I, p. 234.
2. Haber, *op. cit.*, p. 150.
3. Isaac N. Vail, *The Earth's Annular System*, 4th ed., Pasadena: Annular World Co., 1912, p. v.

a rational explanation for the antediluvian world and the enormity of a 40-day rainfall described in Genesis?

A vapor canopy is suggested or described by the following scriptures: Genesis 1:6-7; 2:5-6,10; 3:8; 6:17; 7:6-12,17; 8:2; 9:11,15,18; 10:1,32; 11:10. Additional allusions are found in Psalm 18:11; 29:10; and 2 Peter 3:5-6. The picture occasionally becomes even clearer when read in the original Hebrew or in a literal translation.

Genesis 1:2 speaks of "the deep," the typical translation of the Hebrew *t^{e}hom*. Driver says that *t^{e}hom* as used in this verse does not mean what the deep or the oceans would denote to the modern world, but rather "...the primitive *undivided* waters, the huge watery mass which the writer conceived as enveloping the earth" (italics added).[4]

Driver, of course, perceives these waters mythologically, so we must demythologize *his* language. In modern terms, Driver is telling us that prior to Genesis 1:6-7 these waters covered the earth, forming a hydrosphere upon this planet *and* a hot, steamy atmosphere above "the face of the waters"—an utterly uninhabitable chaos.

Following the creation of light, God dealt firmly with *t^{e}hom*, those chaotic waters. Two acts were necessary to make the earth habitable: the separation of the vaporous waters above the earth from the waters below and the raising of the land to force the remainder of *t^{e}hom* into its allotted areas. In verse 7, literally, "God made the sky [firmament]" and He used the sky to "separate [i.e., establish order between] the waters *under* the sky from the waters *above* the sky." The waters above were then called *mabbul*, a specific Hebrew designation to distinguish them from the remaining waters of *t^{e}hom* below, the oceans. Verse 7 thus describes the actual establishment of the antediluvian "vapor canopy."

Mabbul, the vapor canopy, has been difficult for moderns to identify because that Hebrew word does not appear until Genesis 6:17. Had it been used in chapter 1, its identification would have been simple. The Flood narratives refer to *mabbul's* existence, but because of our modern uniformitarian thinking, few scholars have grasped the full significance of *mabbul*. Among

---

4.   *Op. cit.*, p. 4.

them, von Rad has properly understood its prominence, and that only because he perceives *mabbul* mythologically, so it doesn't disturb his personal uniformitarian geogeny.

> An understanding...of the Flood depends materially on the correct translation of the word *mabbul*. *Mabbul* does not mean "flood," "inundation," or even "destruction," but it is a technical term for a part of the world structure, namely, the heavenly ocean. This heavenly sea, which is above the firmament (*raqia'*), empties downward... We must understand the Flood, therefore, as a catastrophe involving the entire cosmos. When the heavenly ocean breaks forth upon the earth below, and the primal sea beneath the earth, which is restrained by God, now freed from its bonds, gushes up through yawning chasms onto the earth, then there is a destruction of the entire cosmic system according to biblical cosmogony. The two halves of the chaotic primeval sea, separated—the one up, the other below—by God's creative government, are again united; creation begins to sink again into chaos. Here the catastrophe, therefore, concerns not only men and beasts..., but the earth—indeed, the entire cosmos.[5]

Sarna adds, "The Deluge is directly connected with Creation. It is, in fact, the exact reversal of it."[6]

Mabbul then is the technical Hebrew term for the vapor canopy, "the waters above," just as *tᵉhom*, following the separation of the waters, remains the technical name for the oceans, "the waters below."

Mabbul is found 13 times in the Old Testament. It is dealt with here in detail because of its common mistranslation, noted by von Rad. Twelve are in Genesis; here are the first eight (literal translations):

(1) For behold, I am bringing the *mabbul* of waters upon the earth... (6:17a).

(2) And Noah was 600 years old when the *mabbul* of waters was on the earth (7:6).

---

5. Von Rad, *op. cit.*, p. 247f.
6. Sarna, *op. cit.*, pp. 2-3.

(3) And Noah...went into the ark because of the waters of the *mabbul* (7:7).
(4) And after seven days the waters of the *mabbul* were upon the earth (7:10).
(5) And the *mabbul* was 40 days upon the earth (7:17a).
(6) And never again shall all flesh be cut off by the waters of the *mabbul* (9:11b).
(7) And there shall no longer be *mabbul* to destroy the earth (9:11c).
(8) And there shall no longer be the waters—namely, *mabbul*—to wipe out all flesh (9:15b).

Notice in these last two references that *mabbul* no longer exists following these frightful 40 days of precipitation. Further, the definite article is missing in both usages, strongly suggesting a titular quality for *mabbul*. Beginning in chapter 9, *mabbul* clearly takes on the character of a proper name, no longer a vapor canopy, but an event, a universal disaster. The disaster includes the sudden precipitation of the *mabbul* during the Flood.

For example, prior to April 15, 1912, "Titanic" meant an exciting new—"unsinkable"—transatlantic ship; but since that day this word has signified a horrible event in twentieth-century marine history. Prior to December 7, 1941, "Pearl Harbor" was an obscure naval base in Hawaii; since that day "Pearl Harbor" has been the epitome of a massive sneak attack by one nation against another. So it was with the *mabbul* after the "event" of its collapse. Witness the literal language as the subsequent verses of Genesis look back upon *mabbul*.

(9) And Noah lived after the *mabbul* 350 years (9:28).
(10) And sons were born to them after the *mabbul* (10:1b).
(11) And from these were the nations divided upon the earth after the *mabbul* (10:32b).
(12) And he became the father of Arpachshad two years after the *mabbul* (11:10c).

References 9 through 12 clearly look back upon *mabbul* as a catastrophic *event*, not merely a vapor canopy.

The final biblical appearance of *mabbul* is found in Psalm 29:10, where the psalmist is obviously fully aware that the *mabbul* had once been the antediluvian vapor canopy.

(13) The LORD sat [enthroned] above mabbul;
the LORD has been sitting [enthroned] as King forever.

The Hebrew verb in line one is in the perfect (punctiliar) tense, while in line two the verb is in the imperfect (continuing) tense.[7] That is, the Lord was once enthroned above the *mabbul*, but no longer, since the *mabbul* doesn't exist; however, He continues to be enthroned throughout eternity. This usage of *mabbul* in Psalm 29:10 demonstrates once and for all that *mabbul* cannot possibly be translated "flood" or "destruction" or any similar expression, but that the *mabbul* is part of the antediluvian structure of the heavens, a localized natural artifact. Again, the psalmist in 29:10 knows that the vapor canopy was once in the heavens but was precipitated out at the time of the Flood.

Subsequent scholars, including the third-century B.C. translators of the Septuagint, with their Greek worldview, had forgotten the very ancient meaning of *mabbul*. But the Bible exhibits the quality of inerrancy. Second Peter 3:5-13, which is such a helpful albeit brief New Testament commentary on Creation and the Flood, confirms the two "waters"—*t^ehom* and *mabbul*.

> ...*An earth formed out of water and by means of water,* **through which** [Greek *di hon,* plural] *the world that then existed was deluged with water and perished* (2 Peter 3:5-6).

The writer's choice of the genitive *plural* "which" again shows his astute perception of the actual conditions prior to the Flood: There were two waters, *t^ehom* and *mabbul*. He had not lost the national memory of the antediluvian vapor canopy, even if the Alexandrian Septuagint translators had.[8]

---

7.   Cf. Dahood, *Psalms I, op. cit.*, pp. 175, 180; Craigie, *op. cit.*, pp. 242-49; Young, *op. cit.*, p. 362. Brown, Driver and Briggs, op. cit, translate Psalm 29:10a, "The LORD at the Flood sat enthroned," considering that *mabbul* "seems in all other passages to be almost equal to a proper name of the Flood" (p. 55). Their statement, while not revealing the whole picture, as does von Rad's, is still quite helpful in understanding the nature of *mabbul*.

8.   Cf. James Moffatt, *The General Epistles,* The Moffatt New Testament Commentary, New York: Harper & Brothers, n.d., p. 204.

Mabbul then is the specific term or title for "the waters above," and our English translators should use the terms "the canopy" or an appropriate synonym each time *mabbul* appears.

As we have seen from Genesis 9:11c and 9:15b, *mabbul* is today only a meteorological memory; almost all of it was precipitated some millennia ago. The modern atmosphere scarcely contains even inches of water vapor. Still, using radio telescopes, scientists have found what might be assumed to be remanent traces of the canopy—water molecules "in the far reaches of outer space."[9]

Without a perception of the antediluvian canopy, modern Bible students remain mystified about the significance of the Creation's second day's work. What does it mean to "separate the waters from the waters"? In that ignorance we simply cannot understand what really took place on Day Two, nor are we able even to grasp why it is mentioned.

Scientific challenges to the canopy theory are beside the point: The Bible speaks of the canopy, names it, notes its proximity to the Earth (close enough for Earth's gravitational pull to cause most of it to drop and not dissipate into space), describes its demise, and recalls its former existence. Appeals to modern science in opposition to the canopy are meaningless; what commonly is called "science" today is in a state of constant change, while the Bible is immutable. In addition, the amount of water suspended in *mabbul* may not have been so very critical; massive volcanic upheavals in *t^{e}hom* obviously accomplished most of the damage during the Flood. The canopy would have needed only enough water to provide the 40 days of rain. And, as noted in Chapter 1, it was obviously *scalding rain.*[10]

Von Rad has proposed from his exegesis of Genesis that the Flood involved the entire cosmos; certainly it involved some or all of the visible planets and moons of the Solar System. Second Peter 3:5-6 likewise pictures the cosmos having been violently reordered during the Flood, and then verse 7 follows with the most specific New Testament portrayal of the future destruction by fire of *the entire cosmos.*

---

9.   *National Geographic,* May 1974, p. 625, noted in Baker, *op. cit.,* p. 4.

10.   Cf. Vardiman & Bousselot, *op. cit.,* pp. 607-618.

> *But by the same word the heavens and earth that now exist have been stored up for fire, being kept until the day of judgment and destruction of ungodly men (2 Peter 3:7).*

The Creation-Deluge sequence in Genesis 1–9 actually reveals a pattern of chaos to cosmos to chaos to cosmos. As the violent flood waters repeatedly rose and receded, God was re-creating the earth with quite different topographical and climatic characteristics. Anderson observes that the Flood narrative "flows in a sequence of units toward a turning-point and then follows the same sequence in reverse."[11] Quoting McEvenue,[12] he describes the narrative as chiastic, or palindromic.

Transitional Introduction (6:9-10)
1. Violence in God's creation (6:11-12)
2. First divine address: resolution to destroy (6:13-22)
3. Second divine address: command to enter the ark (7:1-10)
4. Beginning of the flood (7:11-16)
5. The rising flood waters (7:17-14)
GOD'S REMEMBRANCE OF NOAH
6. The receding flood waters (8:1-5)
7. The drying of the earth (8:6-14)
8. Third divine address: command to leave the ark (8:15-19)
9. God's resolution to preserve order (8:20-22)
10. Fourth divine address: covenant blessing and peace (9:1-17)
Transitional Conclusion (9:18-19)

The first part of the story represents a movement toward chaos... The second part represents a movement toward a new creation.[13]

Noah stepped out of the ark into a brand-new world, now more *tᵉhom* than *'erets* after 40 days of rain. The sons of Noah,

---

11.   Bernhard W. Anderson, "From Analysis to Synthesis: the Interpretation of Genesis 1–11," *Journal of Biblical Literature*, 97, 1978, p. 37.

12.   Sean E. McEvenue, "The Narrative Style of the Priestly Writer," *Analecta Biblica*, 50, 1971, pp. 27-32.

13.   Anderson, *op. cit.*, pp. 37-38; Gordon J. Wenham gives an alternative and more detailed chiastic structure: "The Coherence of the Flood Narrative," *Vetus Testamentum*, July 1978; XXVIII, Fasc. 3, pp. 336-48.

no longer threatened by hostile "giants," found a new threat—an increasingly severe climatic regime, probably leading to a housing situation producing a new people, the "cave men," exacerbated by what we now term "the Ice Age."

The Ice Age would have been the direct result of the scalding rain's having warmed the oceans from pole to pole, followed by the sudden chilling of the polar atmosphere and a resultant prolonged snowfall. Thus we see ancient Jewish literature and modern science confrming one another.

Mount St. Helens, which first erupted in May 1980, is an excellent demonstration in our own generation of the Flood and some of its aftermath. Called a "living laboratory," the volcano and the adjacent areas demonstrate conclusively that Earth's surface as we know it today was largely formed quickly and catastrophically. Types of natural formations that customarily are dated to millions of years of development are seen at Mount St. Helens to have occurred in hours, weeks or months.

We are reminded by the Flood sequence of von Rad's assessment of the chaos of Genesis 1:2: "Thus this second verse speaks not only of a reality that once existed in a preprimeval period, but also of a possibility that always exists."[14] Zimmerli warns, "You who feel so secure under your heaven, do you not know that God holds this whole world together? And that the space in which you breathe is totally in his hand and He does as He pleases?"[15] Although God has assured us in Genesis 9:11 that, literally, "there is no longer a *mabbul* to wipe out the earth," and some day *tehom* will be no more (Revelation 21:1), yet there remains the *tohu wabohu* of Genesis 1:2 and the prospect of future judgment, not by water, but by fire.[16] As God once exercised his privilege of restoring temporarily the watery chaos, so He will some day return the Earth to its preprimeval fiery condition, in preparation for one final New Creation.

---

14.   Von Rad, *op. cit.*, p. 48.
15.   Walter Zimmerli, *I Mose 1–11, Die Urgeschichte*, Zürich: Zwingli, 1943, p. 4 (trans. from the German).
16.   See next chapter for exposition.

Chapter 12

A Fiery Mass

Although the prior portions of this book are as factual as could be written, these final chapters include materials that are necessarily somewhat speculative.

During the research for this volume it was joyfully discovered once again that the Bible is capable of providing believers with as much revelation as they are able to receive. The Spirit of God continued to reveal through the study of dozens of commentaries. There are scriptural hints—reasonable indications—concerning the condition of "Earth" *prior* to Genesis 1. These clues appear, not in scriptures that look back to the Creation, but rather in passages that refer ahead to the fiery judgment.

Tohu wabohu, the Hebrew words of Genesis 1:2, are typically translated "formless and void" or "a formless void." The usual interpretation of verse 2 implies a chaotic, or even "empty," condition, but in Isaiah and Jeremiah those two Hebrew words describe—in context—a condition typified by destruction, heat, fire and/or smoke. Although *tohu* is occasionally found alone, *tohu wabohu* are used together only these two additional times.

> [Her] *streams...shall be turned into pitch,*
> *and her soil into brimstone;*
> *her land shall become burning pitch.*
> *Night and day it shall not be quenched;*
> *its smoke shall go up for ever.*

> *From generation to generation it shall lie waste;*
> *none shall pass through it for ever and ever.*
> *...He shall stretch the line of **tohu** over it,*
> *and the plummet of **bohu**...* (Isaiah 34:9-11).

"The picture is that of a ruined city surrounded by a land on fire, whose 'smoke shall go up forever.' "[1]

Then "Jeremiah compose[d] a little poem on the subject 'a vision of cosmic destruction....' His poetic eye sees...the invasion of chaos itself, as though the earth were returned to its primeval condition of 'waste and void'—the *tohu wabohu* that prevailed before the creation...."[2]

> *I looked on the earth, and lo, it was **tohu wabohu**,*
> *and to the heavens, and they had no light.*
> *I looked on the mountains, and lo, they were quaking,*
> *and all the hills moved to and fro.*
> *...I looked, and lo, the fruitful land was a desert,*
> *and all its cities were laid in ruins*
> *before the Lord, before his fierce anger.*
> *"...For this the earth shall mourn,*
> *and the heavens above be black"* (Jeremiah 4:23-28).

Both of these passages appear to be apocalyptic visions, future catastrophic reversals of the creation pattern.[3]

Tohu wabohu together form a figure of speech known as "hendiadys," in which two nouns connected by "and" actually use one noun to qualify the other. An example would be, "He approached with kindness and words," meaning, "He approached with kind words," a construction rarely found in English. Therefore *tohu wabohu* could hardly mean "unformed and void," because one would have to modify the other.[4] Genesis 1:2 and Jeremiah 4:23 are both examples of hendiadys, while the two words are separated within the same clause in Isaiah 34:11.

What does *tohu* mean? And what does *bohu* mean? And what do the two words mean in hendiadys? Some of the ancient Jewish sages suggested that *tohu* was the raw material from

---

1.   R.B.Y. Scott, "Isaiah," *The Interpreter's Bible*, Vol. 5, *op. cit.*, p. 357.

2.   Anderson, *Creation versus Chaos*, *op. cit.*, p. 12.

3.   Fishbane, *op. cit.*, pp. 151-67.

4.   Speiser, *op. cit.*, p. 5.

which light was formed, and *bohu* the source of darkness.[5] Scholars today are not at all certain of the precise meaning of *tohu wabohu*. Keil and Delitzsch note that its etymology is lost.[6] Skinner adds, "The exact meaning...is difficult to make out."[7] Ryle says the words are "untranslatable."[8] Franz Delitzsch, however, suggests that these two Hebrew words...

> **...go near to representing primitive matter as a fiery stream; the process of formation was indeed prepared for by the *tohu* being flooded over by the *t^{e}hom*... Darkness...settled over this flood of waters, in which the fervid heat of chaos was quenched.[9]**

Here we discover a most interesting clue to the meaning of these words. As was noted at the end of the previous chapter, perhaps *tohu wabohu* means just that: "a fiery mass." The ancient rabbis perceived *tohu wabohu* as being restricted deep within the earth during the present age.[10] *Tohu wabohu* seemed to the rabbis to possess almost a personality, and it strains impatiently at its bonds, anticipating the Day of its release in judgment, much like the "four angels who are bound at the great river Euphrates" in Revelation 9:14. The apocryphal book Ecclesiasticus (Sirach) 39:28-31 enlarges upon this theme.

> *There are winds that have been created for vengeance,*
>   *and in their anger they scourge heavily;*
> *in the time of consummation they will pour out their strength*
>   *and calm the anger of their Maker.*
> *Fire and hail and famine and pestilence,*
>   *all these have been created for vengeance;*
> *the teeth of wild beasts, and scorpions and vipers,*
>   *and the sword that punishes the ungodly with destruction;*

---

5. Jaki, *op. cit.*, p. 37.
6. C.F. Keil and F. Delitzsch, *Biblical Commentary on the Old Testament*, Vol. I, trans. James Martin, Grand Rapids: Eerdmans, 1951, p. 48.
7. Skinner, *op. cit.*, p. 16.
8. H.E. Ryle, *The Book of Genesis*, Cambridge: Cambridge Univ. Press, 1914, p. 4.
9. Delitzsch, *op. cit.*, pp. 80-81.
10. Ginzberg, *op. cit.*, Vol. I, pp. 10-11.

> *they will rejoice in his commands,*
>   *and be made ready on earth for their service,*
>   *and when their times come they will not transgress his word.*

Even *tohu* used apart from *bohu* seems to indicate more of heat or burning than our Hebrew lexicons suggest, particularly as found in Deuteronomy 32:10a; Job 6:18b; and Isaiah 24:10a.

Hugh Ross suggests that *tohu wabohu* was "the state of the earth just after it had condensed from a primordial ball of gases."[11] Although there is little evidence for such a "condensation," his proposed picture is otherwise rather reasonable.

Consider a creation model suggested by this exposition. A small, degenerate igneous mass is moving through the near-emptiness of space. This preprimeval Earth approaches a smaller, icy body, which reaches the Roche limit and disintegrates violently as the result of tidal stresses, much of the debris inundating the surface of fiery Earth with enormous mountains of ice.[12] Most of the ice would become steam prior to striking proto-Earth due to conversion of initial potential energy of separation into kinetic energy from its acceleration to Earth's flaming surface.[13]

The catastrophic nature of this encounter can be imagined, and the results would be intriguing: The igneous Earth retains its molten core (*tohu wabohu*); a thin layer of basement rock is congealed instantly by the shocking interaction of water/ice and magma; and a watery ocean of melted ice (*t^e hom*) covers the rock to a depth of thousands of feet. Much of the moisture remains suspended in a steamy atmosphere (*mabbul*) adjacent to the surface.

There we find a most plausible model of proto-Earth to which Genesis 1:2 may well be referring. It is at this point, according to Genesis 1, that God becomes aggressively involved—verse 3, the first "day" of Creation Week.

This model, incidentally, provides a most satisfying alternative explanation for Gentry's pleochroic halos in pre-Cambrian bedrock. Massive torrents of ice, water and vapor would have hardened the surface magma to create Earth's lithosphere quite

---

11. Quoted in Sailhamer, *op. cit.*, p. 63.
12. Patten, *op. cit.*, p. 161, hints at such a cosmogony.
13. Apparently this phenomenon of scalding rain occurred again later, during the Flood, as was noted in Chapter 1 (Ginzberg, *op. cit.*, Vol. I, p. 159).

suddenly. It may also explain the igneous rising plutons such as Stone Mountain, Georgia.[14]

This cosmic deluge of ice could be described as an event preceding the Creation of Genesis 1 or possibly implied in verse 1 as the initial creative act of Day One. Psalm 104:6 may be confirming just such an interpretation: "Thou didst cover [the earth] with [t*e*hom] as with a garment...." If this verse is referring to the Creation (as many feel it is), then the inundation of *tohu wabohu* by *t*e*hom* would indeed have been God's first creative act on behalf of the Earth; Day One would have included two distinct works, as did Days Third and Sixth. God used a catastrophic event in order to accomplish his will (a new creation), as He did in the later Flood, looking ahead again to another new creation.

Vail notes the Roman myth of the...

> **...titanic contest between the powers of Vulcan and Neptune. How the waters on high descended, while yet the earth was a hot and seething mass, and were again and again flung into space by the irritated fires; till, finally, worried by the eternal attacks of Neptune, the fires grew tame, and the oceans of vapor settled upon the earth.**[15]

Again we find a mythological distortion of the record available to Earth's earliest survivors of the Flood, where in this case fire and water were considered by the later Romans to be controlled by, and were themselves, gods. The sons of Noah knew the true story, but their increasingly paganized descendants gradually "re-mythologized" the memory. Seventeenth- and eighteenth-century scientists disputed among themselves concerning whether primeval Earth was molten or watery. *Tohu wabohu* and *t*e*hom* suggest that, in a sense, both were correct. In any case, the waters have already inundated the fiery chaos prior to Genesis 1:3, the proclamation of light.

---

14. Carl R. Froede, Jr., "Stone Mountain, Georgia: A Creation Geologist's Perspective," *Creation Research Society Quarterly*, Vol. 31, No. 4, March 1995, pp. 214-224; Andrew A. Snelling and John Woodmorappe, "The Cooling of Thick Igneous Bodies on a Young Earth," *Fourth International Conference on Creationism, op. cit.*, pp. 527-545.

15. *Op. cit.*, p. 14.

The proposed icy visitor's demise adjacent to the molten Earth, so fascinatingly portrayed in Roman mythology, would thus have provided the "raw material" for the waters that were separated on the second day. The near atmosphere of the Earth must have been like a vast steam bath until, in Genesis 1:7, God lifted the intense moisture—perhaps by some natural means—into the higher atmosphere to separate *mabbul,* the antediluvian vapor canopy. Our waterless planet may have received its entire water supply[16] in two stages—all of it originating from this proposed initial cosmic intruder—first, in the Creation, and second, in the later Flood as *mabbul* was condensed to fall as rain.

Patten has similarly proposed an icy model for the later Deluge and its attendant Ice Epoch.[17] If his model for the Flood is correct, Earth might have received its hydrosphere centuries apart as the result of two separate bodies of ice shattering near this planet. Patten estimates the rise in ocean levels during the Ice Age/Deluge to have totalled 12 million to 14 million cubic miles of water, with a significant amount of this water having been already in the atmosphere in the form of the vapor canopy (from the earlier ice dump at the Creation). Dillow[18] estimates the vapor canopy to have contained 6.219×10^{21} cubic centimeters of precipitable water, thus (if Dillow's estimate is correct) reducing the necessary size of Patten's proposed invading ice mass by nearly 1.5 million cubic miles of available water (ice).

Perhaps the suddenness of the "attack" upon fiery proto-Earth by the pre-creation icy body could also suggest an explanation for the presence of iron and other heavy metals in the Earth's crust rather than, as we would expect, in the core alone. Of further interest, most deposits of iron ore for commercial mining are found between 45 and 65 degrees north latitude. Could the proposed explosive violence to our originally molten planet explain those anomalies?

The igneous nature of proto-Earth would conform to what has been similarly learned in recent years about the composition

---

16.   According to Champ Clark (*Flood,* Alexandria, VA: Time-Life Books, 1982, p. 24), Earth's current total quantity of water is 326 million cubic miles.

17.   Patten, *op. cit.,* pp. 143f.

18.   Dillow, *op. cit.,* p. 268.

and "high" temperatures of Venus and the four Jovian planets. This primeval planet too would have been giving off excess heat, as most of our neighbors in the Solar System continue to emit to this day. The water-covered Earth would probably also have been experiencing gale-force winds and extremely high tides when God set about his creation. They were part of the chaos the Lord was about to "muzzle."

As God once appropriated his privilege of returning planet Earth to its earlier watery condition during the Flood, so He will some day seize that privilege again to restore his creation to its primal, *fiery* preexistence. At this point 1 Corinthians 3:13; 2 Peter 3:7,10; and Revelation chapters 8 and following, provide quite graphic reading. As *t^ehom* tries repeatedly to overflow the earth in its diurnal tides and is muzzled each time by Earth's Sustainer, so too *tohu wabohu* continually strains to break its bonds through volcanism, but God's restraining power will not release the fire before its time. Amos 7:4 predicts that day of "...judgment by fire, and it devoured the great deep [*t^ehom*]...." At the prophet's plea, the Lord God suspends the judgment temporarily. "But by the same word the heavens and earth that now exist have been stored up for fire..." (2 Peter 3:7a). Revelation also pictures that final release of *tohu wabohu*, which will indeed "devour," delivering the Earth at last from its partial domination by the waters: "...and the sea was no more" (Revelation 21:1). In mythological terms, as Neptune once tamed Vulcan, so Vulcan will have "the last laugh." *Tohu wabohu* will obtain its revenge against *t^ehom*, but only briefly, for God will have the final victory over both!

Thus the following is suggested as an alternative translation of Genesis 1:2: "The earth being [more plausibly, *having been*][19] *a fiery mass* and darkness being upon the face of the deep and the Spirit of God sweeping over the face of the waters." Certainly this proposal deserves further investigation.

The very reasonable model proposed as a direct result of the exegesis—conforming remarkably to the natural evidence provided by the Earth and its nearest neighbors—is another indication of the *revelatory* nature of the Bible. No man could have

---

19.   See W.R. Lane's similar translation in the Appendix.

seen what is described, yet the narrative exhibits a startling aura of accuracy. How utterly fascinating to study Earth's natural history and discover that God's word described it first!

Chapter 13

Further Contributions Toward a Creation Model

God is consistent. "For I the Lord do not change" (Malachi 3:6a). "Jesus Christ is the same yesterday and today and for ever" (Hebrews 13:8). God operates within his own established laws. The limitations of the First Law of Thermodynamics (conservation of energy) and the Second Law (entropy) are apparent throughout scripture as well as in this natural world. However, the interruptions of those natural laws that occurred during Creation Week are also found to be in accordance with God's laws; such interruptions have occurred repeatedly since—during the Exodus, in the ministries of the Old Testament prophets, of Jesus of Nazareth, and of the Church to this day. God's creative power continues to function—in his normal sustentative capacity and also in miraculous response to prayer and faith—in this modern world. Such miracles *reverse* the natural entropy.

Creation Week was apparently a fascinating and purposeful combination of the catastrophic and the creative. All but one of the five acts of Creation's first four days appear to have been catastrophic, "natural" events, having provoked major convulsions in the heavens and on the earth. The remaining two days were composed totally of three creative, life-giving acts.

The creative miracles are supernatural, but the catastrophes are natural, the precise *timing* and *placing* of the latter events characterizing God's miraculous interventions. A correct perception of these cataclysmic events is a necessity for understanding parts of the Bible. Two contrasting examples will suffice. The multiplication of food for Elijah and the widow in 1 Kings 17 was a creative miracle; the damming of the Jordan River in Joshua 3 was the result of a local catastrophe, miraculous specifically in its exact timing and location. Such an occasional slide of the Jordan River bank occurred as recently as the year 1927. The catastrophic "miracles" of Genesis 1 involved the inanimate world: the establishment of light, the vapor canopy, the dry land and the placement of the heavenly bodies. The creative miracles provided life: vegetation, the various orders of the animal kingdom and, finally, Man himself. "In him was life..." (John 1:4).

If such an invoking of the miraculous seems strained to the western mind, consider the widely accepted theory of evolution, which requires far greater miracles in both quality and magnitude. We are asked by the majority of the scientific community to accept a theory that clearly violates several natural laws. A *deus ex machina*, to be sure!

As the exegesis has already established, at least some of the later biblical catastrophes must have been cosmic, involving more than Earth alone. Terrestrial forces are far too insignificant to have caused all of these biblical events—a Deluge, a splitting apart of the continents, an apparent slowing of the Earth's rotation (Joshua 10), an apparent slight backward motion of the rotating earth (2 Kings 20:11),[1] as well as the future onslaught seen in Revelation. Earthbound forces—primeval or present— could hardly have caused "all the fountains of the great deep" to erupt almost simultaneously.[2] From the world of evolutionary science similar questions are raised by K. Krauskopf:

---

1.   The "long day" and the later backward movement of the shadow on the sundial were perhaps the experienced effects of spin axis precessions caused by near misses with passing celestial bodies. See Patten, Hatch, Steinhauer, *op. cit.*, pp. 113-29.

2.   But see John R. Baumgardner, "Runaway Subduction as the Driving Mechanism for the Genesis Flood," *Proceedings of the Third International Conference on Creationism, op. cit.*, pp. 63-75. However, Baumgardner's model might have vaporized Earth's water supply.

> "What are the irresistible forces which can twist and break the strongest rocks?" "Where do the forces originate which can raise and lower continental masses vertically?" With questions like these we have long since reached an impasse.[3]

Krauskopf asks compelling questions. We must find additional dynamics.

Since the Old Testament authors wrote from an earthbound perspective, cosmic events would have tended to be viewed quite provincially. Indeed, most biblical catastrophes were pictured only from the standpoints of their local terrestrial effects: celestial upheavals often passed unmentioned. However, the earlier chapter, "The Waters," demonstrated that the cosmos also was understood by the ancient author to have been implicated in the Deluge. Certainly the future dissolution by fire is cosmic: "...the heavens will be kindled and dissolved..." (2 Peter 3:12b).

Thus a reasonable geogeny must posit natural factors that are not specifically mentioned in the Bible. At least some of these factors must have been *extra-terrestrial*: they provided the dynamics needed to accomplish the catastrophes that God commanded in Genesis 1 and the subsequent massive changes that have occurred to that creation. Two or more icy bodies have already been proposed. For explicit descriptions (albeit couched in mythological language), we look also to the vast body of ancient literature. It is replete with countless sources of information concerning catastrophes in historical times, with remarkable confirmations of each other in widely separated cultures. Tragically, the modern scientific community, wearing its uniformitarian glasses, usually chooses to ignore these informative records.

Is the universe stable? Patten *et al.* propose a series of cosmic catastrophes, all of them noted in the Old Testament.

It is our contention that the concept of a serene solar system cannot be defended at all; it cannot be defended

---

3. Allan O. Kelly and Frank Dachille, *Target: Earth, The Role of Large Meteors in Earth Science*, Carlsbad, CA, 1953, p. 76, quoted in Alfred de Grazia, *The Lately Tortured Earth*, Princeton: Metron Publications, 1983, p. 282.

for the last 5,000 years (much less for the last 500,000,000 years).[4]

Isaac Newton, perhaps the greatest scientific intellect of any generation, stated his belief that the planets were not stable in their orbits—in spite of the natural laws he had formulated. He saw this instability as necessary if he were to reconcile his science with the chronology of Genesis.[5] Some catastrophists today would insist that Newton was quite correct. However, any assumptions of such recent cosmic catastrophes must undergo two critical tests:

(1) They must conform to the evidences of such enormous events as depicted in the literatures of various ancient cultures.

(2) They must be able to survive all scientific attempts to falsify them. Otherwise the proposed events are to be abandoned or, more optimistically, emended until they can finally endure such rigorous examination.

If the literary and/or scientific data were to succeed in disproving the idea of proposed specific, historical, cosmic catastrophes, such proposals would thus be demonstrated to be mere *ad hoc* explanations, no more authentic than the concordistic theories described earlier.

The reader is encouraged to refute all or part of the present proposals from appropriate disciplines—biblical, historical and mythological, and the pertinent scientific disciplines—without resort to post-Enlightenment categories of thought. Surely errors are to be found in this book, but those errors should cause no one to "throw the baby out with the bath water."

The planets of the Solar System possess a great deal of angular momentum—very much unequally distributed—a fact that seems to indicate cosmic catastrophes in the past. A violent

---

4.   Patten, *op. cit.*, p. 26. Thomas Burnet, in *The Sacred History of the Earth* (1690), proposed that the Flood might have been caused by the near passage of a comet (Brewster, *op. cit.*, p. 130); William Whiston, in his *New Theory of the Earth* (1696), suggested the same. The comet theory is once again finding respectability in scientific circles during the present generation.

5.   Jaki, *op. cit.*, p. 199.

history is clearly suggested by a number of additional conditions, such as the moon craters, the asteroids, Venus' retrograde rotation, the battered surface and huge, dry channels of Mars (a planet that apparently never had an ocean[6] or an extensive atmosphere), Saturn's (and others') rings and Pluto's anomalous orbit. Earth's mid-Atlantic rift, the Great Rift Valley in the eastern hemisphere, the incredible amount of violently buried fossils in sedimentary strata, and orogeny in general, provide ample evidences of probable cosmic catastrophes directly affecting our planet. Many additional silent witnesses could be noted. These enormous scars, some of them quite recent,[7] speak forcefully of natural disasters that the Bible says simply were ordained by God. Uniformitarians are extremely offended by the suggestion that such catastrophes might have occurred within the past few thousand years, but the literary and geological evidences are overwhelming.

Even evolutionary paleontologists are today increasingly looking to the skies for the causes of what they perceive to be sudden, mass extinctions of life in the past, in particular the abrupt, global termination of what they arbitrarily term the Cretaceous Period. Scientists are beginning to realize that the simultaneity of massive catastrophes worldwide requires extraterrestrial agents. How slowly, how painfully is modern science inching toward the truth concerning Earth's cataclysmic history!—as

---

6. Australia's Wallace Thornhill, in *The Electric Solar System* (slide presentation, 1997), demonstrates that the apparent water channels on Mars could not have been caused by water, since they flow up and over ridges. Rather, physicist Thornhill states, the channels were created by huge interplanetary electrical strikes. If Thornhill is proven correct, then one of the occasional areas of agreement between evolutionists and creationists will also disappear into history's graveyard.

7. Patten, Hatch and Steinhauer (*op. cit.*, pp. 259-60) suggest that a widening of the Great Rift Valley, from Israel to southern Africa, occurred during the Sodom and Gomorrah holocaust as depicted in Genesis 19. De Grazia, in *Chaos and Creation* (*op. cit.*, p. 166), describes the memory of adjacent peoples of the horrors surrounding this geologic event in not-so-ancient history. The "division" of the earth (Genesis 10:25) is also recent, North America apparently breaking off from Europe and South America from Africa. The Americas' joining at Panama is even more recent, attested by the fact that the fauna and flora are quite different north and south of the Isthmus.

long as the proposed events are not considered to have been recent.

Earlier there was proposed a model for the initial catastrophe involving the Earth, a cosmic "accident" in which this proposed molten proto-planet was "attacked" by shattered ice and other debris, congealing the Earth's basement rock and adding its hydrosphere. Thus was provided the raw material for God's Creation.

Day One brought the creation of light. The Earth was apparently already rotating in order to provide the daily alternation of light and darkness. Again, all events in Genesis 1 are viewed as from the earth.

> **The most advanced astronomer of our day will speak of the sunrise and the sunset and of sending *up* a rocket. Such language is geocentric, but it is not in error. Genesis one...does not claim that the earth is the physical center of the universe.**[8]

The source of that light on Day One? Second and first millennium B.C. Israelites, not having been schooled in uniformitarianism and rationalistic philosophies, would have been untroubled by the light appearing three days before the sun found its permanent place.[9] Scripture does not answer this question. However, having said that, the source of the light was in all probability our very own sun. How could that be? An ancient Israelite might have responded scornfully: "Of course the light was from the sun! It just wasn't yet in its proper place, which was accomplished on Day Fourth." Everything was oriented from the Earth—the stars included. There was a reorientation of Earth on that day in relation to the rest of the heavenly bodies, quite similar to an interior decorator putting the final touch on her new "creation" by adding that last key piece of furniture.

Although God is light (1 John 1:5), Genesis 1:3 suggests that the light of Day One could not have emanated from Him (yet it will in the New Jerusalem). Here is the most obvious difference between Genesis and pagan cosmogonies, where in the latter a

---

8.   E.J. Young, *op .cit.*, p. 93; cf. *ibid.*, p. 32; Leupold, *op. cit.*, p. 45.

9.   Ginzberg, Vol. I, *op. cit.*, pp. 8-9; Jaki, *op. cit.*, p. 29.

god (or, gods) not only controls but is also identified with the substance out of which matter is created. The true Creator of this universe is not part of it; He *commands* the various components, all of which are totally material and subservient to the unique God who is spirit.

Occasionally exegetes will perceive a difference between the Hebrew words *or* ("light") in 1:3-5 and *maor* ("luminary") in 1:14-16, suggesting that perhaps the "light" of Day One was a different kind of illumination (at least until Day Fourth). However, *or* is also used to mean the same luminaries elsewhere, such as the stars (Ezekiel 32:8), the sun (Job 31:26) and sunlight and moonlight (Isaiah 30:26). So the biblical *maor* is not reserved solely for light sources as opposed to the light they produce.

Sailhamer, who draws some unwarranted conclusions, gives his opinion of the first day's light.

> **The text does not imply that this was the first "sunrise." Since the sun had already been created in Genesis 1:1, the narrative assumes there may have been countless sunrises before this particular one. When the text says "and there was light," it means simply that the first day of that [particular] week had begun... The narrative has clearly stated that God already created the sun "in the beginning."[10]**

Sailhamer is close to the truth, but proper exegesis does not allow all of these statements.

We are led by the "light question" to skip ahead to Day Fourth, when "God made the two great lights...he made the stars also." Verses 14-18 describe a putting into their proper places of "the greater light," "the lesser light" and the stars. *Neither the sun nor the moon is specifically named.*

Strangely, the world's most ancient pagan cosmogonies insist that "the lesser light to rule the night" was none other than what we today call the planet *Saturn*! And in times recent enough to be remembered and recorded by our forefathers! Such a suggestion would seem preposterous if the tradition were not so widespread. Many ancient sources around the world universally recall an

---

10.   *Op. cit.*, p. 113.

antediluvian "Golden Age" when Saturn (the gas giant that may be the dark remains of a star) prominently ruled the night skies. Saturn's ancient Greek name, Chronos, still connotes the measurement of time: "...and let them be for signs and for seasons and for days and years" (Genesis 1:14b). If this is true, an incredibly violent cosmic upheaval must have occurred centuries later, provoking (on the Earth) the Flood and the Ice Age and restructuring at that time a significant part of the Solar System. I add this possibility not because I necessarily believe it—indeed, the dynamics of such a proposed planetary grouping and reordering seem incredible, but mythological records in a number of ancient cultures confirm one another in this statement. Thornhill (*op. cit.*) provides the proposed physical evidences for such an alignment. If this scenario were to be proven correct, Saturn's nighttime brilliance would have contributed significantly to the extremely lush growth of the antediluvian biosphere and the resultant vast supply of carbon in the Earth's sedimentary strata. The Semitic god El was often noted as the "father of gods"—the creator, consistently identified with the planet Saturn—who later "retired" from the scene. Our moon would have been rather insignificant or, perhaps, an astronomical "newcomer." Just what did occur has been the subject of continuing investigations by a number of modern scholars.[11]

Another bit of speculation: perhaps our gracious God rearranged the Solar System at the Flood, placing Saturn and Jupiter's orbits well outside the Earth, in order to "sweep" the

---

11.   See, e.g., Cardona, "Let There Be Light," *Kronos*, Vol. III, pp. 34-55; Immanuel Velikovsky, "On Saturn and the Flood," *ibid.*, Vol. V, No. 1, pp. 3f. David N. Talbott, *The Saturn Myth*, Garden City, New York: Doubleday, 1980; de Grazia, *Chaos and Creation, op. cit.*, pp. 179f; Georgio de Santillana and Hertha von Dechend, *Hamlet's Mill: An Essay on Myth and the Frame of Time*, Boston: Gambit, 1969; Patten, *op. cit.*, pp. 309f. David N. Talbott, "The Saturn Thesis," *Aeon*, Vol. IV, No. 3, 1996, pp. 10-37; for a visual animation, see the video by David N. Talbott, "Remembering the End of the World": Beaverton, OR: Kronia Communications, 1996.

The ancient rabbis apparently agreed: Cf. Velikovsky, "Khima and Kesil," *Kronos*, Vol. III, No. 4, 1978, p. 23, where he translates the Jewish Talmud (Tractate Brakhot, Fol. 59), "Two stars erupted from the planet Saturn and caused the Deluge." Incidentally, Saturn and some of its satellites are all or partially composed of water.

inner space surrounding our own planet. Thus the Jovian planet's screening effect protected Earth from its possible destruction by the Comet Shoemaker-Levy 9 in 1994's massive collision with Jupiter. The Almighty Sustainer was active.

Why do secular scientists typically resent the evidence for recent catastrophism on the Earth and in the cosmos? As noted earlier, the reason is not scientific, but rather, religious: Catastrophes in historical times speak of *judgment*, and secularists will always deny divine judgment.

But why should *Christians* have difficulty with such a proposed upheaval in the recent history of the Solar System? Repeatedly the scriptures promise a not-too-distant future demise of the sun (e.g., Isaiah 13:10; 24:23; 34:4; Ezekiel 32:7; Joel 2:10,31; 3:15; Amos 5:20; 8:9; Zephaniah 1:15; Matthew 24:29; Mark 13:24; 2 Peter 3:10; Revelation 6:12; 8:12; 16:8; 21:23; 22:5). If we believe in such a *future* astronomical catastrophe within the millennia pictured in the New Testament, our worldview should allow for similar disasters as recorded in the Old Testament era. Is it not true that even Christians who study origins are also deeply affected by uniformitarian thinking?

So, although the Bible does not describe specifically Saturn's possible nighttime prominence as do many other ancient records, still the unnamed "lesser light" of Genesis 1:16 clearly allows for this possibility. Whatever took place at the word of God on the fourth day necessarily entails some speculation. However, the exegesis maintains that Day Fourth was the *ordering* of the Earth in relation to the other components of the Solar System and beyond. It was not a creation *ex nihilo*.

The preexistent Earth thus was established in an orbit revolving around the preexistent sun. Or perhaps, was the pre-Flood Earth a satellite of Saturn, which itself was orbiting the sun? Kepler's Third Law would seem to preclude such a system, *unless* Earth, Mars and Venus were all satellites of Saturn, as the worldwide ancient cosmologies seem to insist. Kepler's Third Law would not apply in that case.

The source(s) of Earth's light on Day One remains a matter for speculation with so little data available, although there will one day be "...no need of sun or moon to shine upon it, for the glory of God is its light, and its lamp is the Lamb" (Revelation 21:23). Day One, Day Fourth.

The Earth after that first day was a steaming chaos. So God separated *mabbul*, the waters above the earth, from *t^ehom*, the ocean waters below, to institute the vapor canopy, perhaps a temperature inversion high above the earth.[12] Whatever natural mechanism God utilized to institute this remarkable "separation" would make an interesting study. Perhaps at God's word Earth's primeval heat alone would have been sufficient to establish the canopy. Today there are two bands of heat surrounding the earth high in the stratosphere. Are they the remains of *mabbul*? A rather uniformly warm, moist climate enveloped the earth; the percentage of oxygen in the atmosphere was significantly higher than today; air pressure was perhaps twice the modern figure[13] (otherwise the winged pterosaurs would have been unable to fly); but the surface was still all *t^ehom*, the rebellious ocean waters. Day Second.

Another planned catastrophe occurred on Day Third. "And God said, 'Let the waters under the heavens be gathered together into one place, and let the dry land appear.' And it was so" (Genesis 1:9). Again it is suggested that God had scheduled a *larger* cosmic body to pass near the geoidal Earth, the resulting tidal forces, electrical and gravitational—this time on the Earth—causing a massive upheaval in the crust to expose the land mass. Would two interplanetary bodies engaging the Earth within what may have been a brief time seem far-fetched? Not if the first (the icy one) were a mere satellite of the much larger mass that later passed near the Earth on the third day. In fact, Patten proposes just such a two-body invasion as the cause of the Deluge centuries later.[14] Violent tidal convulsions of both hydrosphere and lithosphere were the order of the day, Day Third. Thus is pictured a catastrophic sequence for the first four days of the Creation. Including the third day's creation of the plant kingdom, the remainder of God's acts were all creative miracles.

---

12.   See Dillow, *op. cit.*, for an examination of the varieties of possible vapor or ice canopies.

13.   *Ibid.*, p. 233.

14.   Patten, *op. cit.*, p. 137f.

Surely some inspired speculation could suggest additional possibilities. Perhaps the largely molten proto-Earth, only recently relieved of its fiery surface, might account in part for the universal "warmth" of the antediluvian period.[15] Earth's molten core surely would have included more of what is today the thick (1,800 miles), plastic mantle beneath the very thin lithosphere. We need not place the full burden of the Paleozoic calefaction on the "greenhouse" effect alone. A slowly cooling Earth could perhaps contribute to the long-range instability of Dillow's model of a temperature inversion; sooner or later his proposed vapor canopy had to collapse.[16]

Certainly all the discrepancies between biblical and uniformitarian chronologies have not been resolved, but only the age of *inorganic* Earth. The dating of the creative results of Days Fifth and Sixth—*hayah nephesh*, "life itself"—will still remain embroiled in controversy. This book has spoken primarily to the former, and little to the origins of life upon the Earth. Although the point is not central to this study, I also remain convinced that, in agreement with scripture, life is quite young in geological terms. And I continue to maintain that there need be no conflict between theology and geology; Genesis 1 makes good sense and good science!

The drama of Creation—*inorganic*—then may be described as God's *ordering*, much as a designer "creates" the interior of a home by selecting and arranging the various pieces of furniture and accessories. "And God set them in the firmament of the heavens..." (Genesis 1:17).

Apparently He chose selectively from his universe, bringing together disparate components to "furnish his house." Previous theories of planetary origins seem to be ruled out by their great variety: the planets' diverse composition, varied orbits, angular momentum, temperatures and size, retrograde rotation, strongly tilted axes and other incongruous characteristics. God gathered

---

15. The eighteenth-century Comte de Buffon attempted to date the Earth's age by how rapidly its interior was cooling from a presumed once-molten state; cf. Hallam, *op. cit.*, p. 82. This technique figured largely in subsequent prognostications until the continental drift, or plate tectonics theory, began gaining acceptance in very recent years.

16. *Op. cit.*, pp. 263f.

together (in what we today would term catastrophes) wandering, dissonant participants, impressing them into his own symphony, and allowed the descendants of Adam to title it the Solar System.

"Thus the heavens and the earth were finished, and all the host of them" (Genesis 2:1).

Conclusion

(1) Scriptural exegesis reveals that the Bible does not speak of creation *ex nihilo*, but tells of a creation out of existing material—material that stubbornly resisted God's creativity.

(2) This exegesis provides the only interpretation of Genesis 1:1-3 that is not self-contradicting. It confirms itself throughout the Bible.

(3) We have traced historically the heretical origin of the doctrine of *creatio ex nihilo* and its subsequent, almost-but-never-complete adoption by the Christian Church.

(4) Creation out of nothing should now be removed from scientific creationism's biblical expositions.

(5) The creation narrative of Genesis 1 need not be demythologized; it had already been demythologized when first written. The chapter is almost all historical prose, presented in deliberate chronological order.

(6) What has hitherto appeared to be a most awkward, even mythological, order of the events of creation in Genesis 1 now seems more plausible scientifically.

(7) Some commentators permit a chronology that Genesis 1 does not demand, while others demand a chronology that Genesis 1 does not permit.

(8) The chronology detailed in Genesis 1 allows for certain old-Earth indicators and certain young-Earth indicators,

contributing toward a resolution of creationists' disagreement over our planet's age.

(9) Concordistic theories are not only invalid, but also unnecessary. Scientific creationists should not compromise with the pagan culture about us by accepting *scientistic* dogma that varies with each generation.

(10) Contrary to much creationist literature, the natural and supernatural laws in effect during Creation Week are indeed the same laws that are quite operative to this day.

(11) A more valid Creation-and-Flood model can be inferred from a detailed study of relevant scriptures in conjunction with other appropriate disciplines.

(12) By the inclusion of this treatise's insights, scientific creationism will be both more scriptural and more logical.

(13) The Bible and modern science can now speak more nearly in agreement.

(14) Creation science should be making a more significant contribution to our perception of the overall unity of the Bible and God's working in history.

(15) Our Creator is highly exalted, yet remains ever-so-much involved in our daily lives.

Creationists should courageously reexamine Earth's age indicators in the light of scripture. My hope is that this treatise will strengthen a Christian's trust in the inerrancy of the Bible and of the great God who in it revealed his very personal story of the Creation: "...I the LORD your God am a jealous [read, passionate] God..." (Exodus 20:5). I have attempted to accomplish this goal simply by allowing the Hebrew text to speak on its own (non-modern) terms. A literal acceptance of the relevant historical and revelatory portions of scripture, in their ancient contexts, is the only valid way to understand them.

I have been greatly encouraged in this study by the discovery that, for the first time in the modern world, some evangelical scholars today are finding for themselves the improbability of *ex nihilo* creation in Genesis 1. Realizing too that some readers may be partially or totally unconvinced, I present this thesis to the Christian world for its heuristic value, trusting that it will stimulate further discussion, research and, surely, prayer.

Ridicule and personal scorn are the final resorts of the defeated intellectual; let them not be heard in the creationist camp. I trust that open-minded creationists will expose this presentation to the process of falsification, not using the yard-sticks of tradition or rationalism. It is hoped that interested scientists who are creationists will pursue the various scientific questions and suggestions raised.

There are yet many unanswered questions, but the reader may take comfort in knowing that those Christian commentators who claim competing concepts of creation confront a more clamorous covey of cacophonous contradictions.

Appendix

Following are 16 modern translations of Genesis 1:1-3 that vary from the Septuagint tradition. The first five are modeled after Rashi's interpretation; the remainder copy Ibn Ezra.

(1) In the beginning when God created the heavens and the earth, and while the earth was still unformed and chaotic, with darkness on the surface of the deep, and the Spirit of God brooding over the waters, God said, "Let there be light," and there was light" (Charles F. Kent, *The Old Testament*, 1921).

(2) When God began to create heaven and earth—and the earth was chaotic and empty, and darkness was over the primordial ocean, and the spirit of God was hovering over the water—, (then) God said, Let light come into existence, and light came into existence (William F. Albright, "Contributions to Biblical Archaeology and Philology," *Journal of Biblical Literature*, Vol. 43, 1924).

(3) When God began to create the heaven and the earth—the earth being unformed and void, with darkness over the surface of the deep and a wind from God sweeping over the water—God said, "Let there be light"; and there was light (Jewish Publication Society of America, *The Torah*, 1962).

(4) When God began to create the heavens and the earth, the earth having been without form and void, darkness being upon the face of the deep and the spirit of God soaring over the face of the waters, God said, "Let there be light"; and there was light (W.R. Lane, "The Initiation of Creation," *Vetus Testamentum*, Vol. XIII, 1963, p. 72).

(5) When God set about to create heaven and earth—the world being then a formless waste, with darkness over the seas and only an awesome wind sweeping over the water—God said, "Let there be light." And there was light (E.A. Speiser, *The Anchor Bible*, 1964).

(6) In the beginning of God's preparing the heavens and the earth—the earth hath existed waste and void, and darkness is on the face of the deep, and the Spirit of God fluttering on the face of the waters, and God saith, "Let light be"; and light is (Robert Young, *Young's Literal Translation*, 1887).

(7) When God began to form the universe, the world was void and vacant, darkness lay over the abyss; but the Spirit of God was hovering over the waters, God said, "Let there be light," and there was light (James Moffatt, *A New Translation of the Bible*, 1922).

(8) When God began to create the heavens and the earth, the earth was a desolate waste, with darkness covering the abyss and a tempestuous wind raging over the surface of the waters. Then God said, "Let there be light!" And there was light (J.M.P. Smith & Edgar Goodspeed, *An American Translation*, 1931).

(9) When God began to create the heavens and the earth, the earth was without form and void, and darkness was upon the face of the deep; and the Spirit of God was moving over the face of the waters. And God said, "Let there be light!"; and there was light (*Revised Standard Version* [footnote], 1952).

(10) In the beginning of creation, when God made heaven and earth, the earth was without form and void, with darkness over the face of the abyss, and a mighty wind

that swept over the surface of the waters. God said, "Let there be light," and there was light (*New English Bible*, 1961).

(11) When God began to order heaven and earth, the earth was chaotic with darkness on the face of the Deep and with the Spirit of God flying over the surface of the waters; and [then] God said: "Let there be light!" and so there was light (Cyrus H. Gordon, *Biblical Motifs: Origins and Transformations*, 1966).

(12) In the beginning, when God created the heavens and the earth, the earth was a formless wasteland, and darkness covered the abyss, while a mighty wind swept over the waters. Then God said, "Let there be light," and there was light (*New American Bible*, 1970).

(13) When God began creating the heavens and the earth, the earth was at first a shapeless, chaotic mass, with the Spirit of God brooding over the dark vapors. Then God said, "Let there be light." And light appeared (*The Living Bible*, 1971).

(14) In the beginning, when God created the universe, the earth was formless and desolate. The raging ocean that covered everything was engulfed in total darkness, and the power of God was moving over the water. Then God commanded, "Let there be light"—and light appeared (*The Bible in Today's English Version*, 1976).

(15) In the beginning when Elohim had created the heavens and the earth, the earth was formless and waste; and darkness lay upon the face of the deep, and the spirit of Elohim brooded over the waters (Harold G. Stigers, *A Commentary on Genesis*, 1976).

(16) In the beginning when God created the heavens and the earth, the earth was a formless void and darkness covered the face of the deep, while a wind from God swept over the face of the waters. Then God said, "Let there be light"; and there was light (*New Revised Standard Version*, 1989).

Bibliography

Aalders, G. Ch., *Genesis*, Bible Student's Commentary, Vol. I, trans. William Heynen, Grand Rapids: Zondervan, 1981.

Allis, Oswald T., *God Spake by Moses*, Nutley, NJ: Presbyterian & Reformed Publishing Co., 1976.

Anderson, Bernhard W., *Creation versus Chaos*, New York: Association Press, 1967.

Archer, Gleason, *Encyclopedia of Bible Difficulties*, Grand Rapids: Zondervan, 1982.

Baker, Mace, *Dinosaurs*, Redding, CA: New Century Books, 1991.

Barnhouse, Donald Grey, *The Invisible War*, Grand Rapids: Zondervan, 1965.

Barth, Karl, *Church Dogmatics*, Vol. III, part I, Edinburgh: T. & T. Clark, 1958.

Bergman, Ringgren, Bernhardt, Botterweck, *Theological Dictionary of the Old Testament*, ed. G. Johannes Botterweck & Helmer Ringgren, trans. John T. Willis, Grand Rapids: Eerdmans, 1975.

Beveridge, W.I.B., *The Art of Scientific Investigation*, London: Heinemann, 1950.

Blocher, Henri, *In the Beginning*, trans. David G. Preston, Downers Grove, IL: Inter-Varsity Press, 1984.

Boman, Thorlief, *Hebrew Thought Compared with Greek*, Philadelphia: Westminster Press, 1960.

The Book of Jasher, faithfully translated from the Original Hebrew into English, Salt Lake City: J.H. Parry & Co., 1887.

Brewster, Edwin Tenney, *Creation: A History of Non-Evolutionary Theories*, Indianapolis: Bobbs-Merrill, 1927.

Brongers, H.A., *De Scheppingstradities bij de Profeten*, Amsterdam: H.J. Paris, 1945.

Brown, Francis, S.R. Driver and Charles A. Briggs, *A Hebrew and English Lexicon of the Old Testament*, Oxford: The Clarendon Press, 1907 (reprinted 1959).

Brueggemann, Walter, *Genesis*, Atlanta: John Knox Press, 1982.

Burnet, Thomas, *The Sacred Theory of the Earth*, 1690.

Calvin, John, *Commentaries on the Book of Genesis*, Vol. I, trans. John King, Grand Rapids: Eerdmans, 1948.

_____, *Commentary on the Epistles of Paul the Apostle to the Corinthians*, trans. John Pringle, Grand Rapids: Baker, reprinted 1979.

Cassuto, Umberto, *A Commentary on the Book of Genesis*, trans. Israel Abrahams, Jerusalem: Magnes Press, 1944.

Charles, R.H., ed. *Pseudepigrapha*, Oxford: Clarendon Press, 1913.

Charlesworth, James A., *The Old Testament Pseudepigrapha*, 2 vols., Garden City, NY: Doubleday, 1983.

Childs, Brevard S., *Myth and Reality in the Old Testament*, Naperville, IL: Alec R. Allenson, 1960.

Clark, Champ, *Planet Earth: Flood*, Alexandria, VA: Time-Life Books, 1982.

Cohen, A., *The Soncino Chumash*, Hindhead, Surrey: Soncino Press, 1947.

Corvin, R.O., *Home Bible Study Course*, Vols. I, V, Charlotte: PTL Club, 1976.

Craigie, Peter C., *Psalms 1–50*, Word Biblical Commentary, Waco: Word Books, 1983.

Dahood, Mitchell, *Psalms I, Psalms II, Psalms III*, Anchor Bible: Garden City, NY: Doubleday, 1966.

Davidson, Robert, *Genesis 1–11*, London: Cambridge University Press, 1973.

Day, J., *God's Conflict with the Dragon and the Sea*, Cambridge: 1985.

de Grazia, Alfred, *Chaos and Creation*, Princeton: Metron Publications, 1981.

_____, *Homo Schizo I*, Princeton: Metron Publications, 1983.

_____, *The Lately Tortured Earth*, Princeton: Metron Publications, 1983.

Delitzsch, Franz, *A New Commentary on Genesis*, Edinburgh: T. & T. Clark, 1888.

de Santillana, Giorgio, *The Crime of Galileo*, Chicago: University of Chicago Press, 1955.

_____ and Hertha von Dechend, *Hamlet's Mill: An Essay on Myth and the Frame of Time*, Boston: Gambit, 1969.

Dillmann, August, *Genesis Critically and Exegetically Expounded*, trans. William B. Stevenson, Edinburgh: T. & T. Clark, 1897.

Dillow, Joseph C., *The Waters Above*, Chicago: Moody Press, 1981.

Diodati, John, *Pious Annotations upon the Holy Bible*, London: Nicholas Fussell, 1543.

Dods, Marcus, *The Book of Genesis*, Edinburgh: T. & T. Clark, 1911.

Driver, S.R., *The Book of Genesis*, London: Methuen, 1904.

Eichrodt, Walter, *Theology of the Old Testament*, trans. J.A. Baker, Philadelphia: Westminster, 1967.

Field, Fridericus, *Origenis Hexaplorum supersunt*, Vol. I, Oxford: 1875.

Fields, Weston W., *Unformed and Unfilled*, Phillipsburg, NJ: Presbyterian & Reformed Publishing Co., 1978.

Finegan, Jack, *In the Beginning*, New York: Harper & Bros., 1962.

Francis, Wilfrid, *Coal: Its Formation and Composition*, 2nd ed., London: Edward Arnold, 1961.

Geiger, Abraham, *Urschrift and Uebersetzungen der Bibel in ihrer Abhängigkeit von der innern Entwickelung des Judenthums*, 1857.

Gentry, Robert V., *Creation's Tiny Mystery*, Knoxville: Earth Science Associates, 1986.

Gerstner, John, *Wrongly Dividing the Word of Truth: A Critique of Dispensationalism*, Brentwood: TN: Wolgemuth and Hyatt, 1991.

Gilkey, Langdon, *Maker of Heaven and Earth*, Garden City, NY: Doubleday, 1959.

Ginzberg, Louis, *The Legends of the Jews*, Vols. I & V, Philadelphia: The Jewish Publication Society of America, 1947.

Gordon, Cyrus H., *Ugaritic Textbook*, Rome: Pontifical Biblical Institute, 1965.

Graves, Robert & Raphael Patai, *Hebrew Myths, The Book of Genesis*, Garden City, NY: Doubleday, 1964.

Gray, Gordon, *The Age of the Universe: What Are the Biblical Limits?* Washougal, WA: Morning Star Publications, 1996.

Gunkel, Hermann, *Genesis*, 6th ed., Göttingen: Vanderhoeck & Ruprecht, 1964.

_____, *Schöpfung und Chaos in Urzeit and Endzeit*, Göttingen: Vanderhoeck & Ruprecht, 1895.

Guthrie, W.K.C., *In the Beginning*, Ithaca, NY: Cornell University Press, 1957.

Haardt, Robert, *Gnosis: Character and Testimony*, trans. J.F. Hendry, Leiden: E.J. Brill, 1971.

Haber, Francis C., *The Age of the World: Moses to Darwin*, Baltimore: The Johns Hopkins Press, 1959.

Hallam, Anthony, *Great Geological Controversies*, Oxford & New York: Oxford University Press, 1983.

Hanna, William, *Posthumous Works of Thomas Chalmers*, Vol. I, New York: Harper, 1849.

Hastings, James, *The Great Texts of the Bible*, Vol. I, New York: Charles Scribner's Sons, 1911.

Heidel, Alexander, *The Babylonian Genesis*, 2nd ed., Chicago: University of Chicago Press, 1951.

Heim, Karl, *Christian Faith and Natural Science*, New York: Harper & Brothers, 1953.

Hogben, Lancelot, *Mathematics for the Millions*, New York: W.W. Norton, 1937.

Howley, G.C.D., F.F. Bruce, H.L. Ellison, eds., *The New Layman's Bible Commentary*, Grand Rapids: Zondervan, 1979.

Hyers, Conrad, *The Meaning of Creation*, Atlanta: John Knox Press, 1984.

Jacob, Edmond, *Theology of the Old Testament*, trans. Arthur W. Heathcote and Philip J. Allcock, London: Hodder & Stoughton, 1958.

Jaki, Stanley L., *Genesis 1 Through the Ages*, London: Thomas More Press, 1992.

Keil, C.F. and F. Delitzsch, *Biblical Commentary on the Old Testament*, Vol. I, trans. James Martin, Grand Rapids: Eerdmans, 1951.

Kelly, Allan O. and Frank Dachille, *Target: Earth, The Role of Large Meteors in Earth Science*, Carlsbad, CA, 1953.

Kidner, Derek, *Genesis, An Introduction and Commentary*, Downers Grove, IL: Inter-Varsity Press, 1967.

Kinney, LeBaron W., *Acres of Rubies*, New York: Loizeaux Brothers, 1942.

Kittel, Rudolph, *Biblia Hebraica*, Stuttgart: Württembergische Bibelanstalt, 1937.

Klaaren, Eugene M., *Religious Origins of Modern Science*, Grand Rapids: Eerdmans, 1977.

Kravitz, Nathaniel, *Genesis: A New Interpretation of the First Three Chapters*, New York: Philosophical Library, 1967.

Leeming, David A. & Margaret A. Leeming, *A Dictionary of Creation Myths*, New York: Oxford University Press, 1994.

Leupold, H.C., *Exposition of Genesis*, Grand Rapids: Baker, 1950.

Loretz, O., *Schöpfung und Mythos*, Stuttgart: 1968.

Luther's Commentary on Genesis, Vol. I, trans. J.T. Mueller, Grand Rapids: Zondervan, 1958.

Maher, Michael, *Genesis*, Wilmington, DE: Michael Glazier, 1982.

Malina, Bruce J., *Christian Origins and Cultural Anthropology: Practical Models for Biblical Interpretation*, Atlanta: John Knox.

Moffatt, James, *The General Epistles*, The Moffatt New Testament Commentary, New York: Harper & Brothers, n.d.

Morris, Henry M., *Scientific Creationism*, San Diego: Creation-Life Publishers, 1974.

————, *The Long War Against God*, Grand Rapids: Baker Book House, 1989.

Murphy, James G., *A Critical and Exegetical Commentary on the Book of Genesis*, Boston: Estes & Lauriat, 1873.

The Natural History of Pliny, Vol. I., trans. John Bostock and H.T. Riley, London: George Bell & Sons, 1893.

Neville, Robert C., *God the Creator*, Chicago: University of Chicago Press, 1968.

Patten, Donald W., *The Biblical Flood and the Ice Epoch*, Seattle: Pacific Meridian, 1966.

_____, Ronald R. Hatch, Loren C. Steinhauer, *The Long Day of Joshua and Six Other Catastrophes*, Seattle: Pacific Meridian, 1973.

Paul, William, *Analysis and Critical Interpretation of the Hebrew Text of the Book of Genesis*, Edinburgh & London: William Blackwood & Sons, 1852.

Peake, Arthur S., *A Commentary on the Bible*, London: T.C. & E.C. Jack, 1931.

Pearson, John, *An Exposition of the Creed*, (first pub. 1659), rev. W.S. Dobson, New York: D. Appleton, 1844.

Pedersen, Johannes, *Israel: Its Life and Culture*, 2 vols., London: Oxford University Press, 1926.

Pember, G.H., *Earth's Earliest Ages*, New York: Fleming H. Revell, 1876.

Phillips, J.B., *Your God Is Too Small*, New York: Macmillan, 1953.

Pope, Marvin H., *Job*, Anchor Bible, Garden City, NY: Doubleday, 1965.

Price, Ira M., Ovid R. Sellers, E. Leslie Carson, *The Monuments and the Old Testament*, Philadelphia: The Judson Press, 1958.

Quispel, Gilles, *Gnostic Studies*, I, Istanbul: Nederlands Instituut voor het Nabije Oosten, 1974.

Ramm, Bernard, *The Christian View of Science and Scripture*, Grand Rapids: Eerdmans, 1955.

Ramsey, F.P., *An Interpretation of Genesis*, New York: Neale, 1911.

Rashi, *The Pentateuch and Rashi's Commentary, Genesis*, ed. Abraham ben Isaiah & Benjamin Sharfman, Brooklyn, NY: S.S. & R. Publishing Co., 1949.

Ridderbos, N.H., *Is There a Conflict Between Genesis 1 and Natural Science?* Grand Rapids: Eerdmans, 1957.

Rifkin, Jeremy, with Ted Howard, *Entropy: A New World View*, New York: Viking Press, 1980.

Rohl, David, *A Test of Time: The Bible—from Myth to History*, Vol. One, London: Century Ltd., Random House, 1995.

Ross, Hugh, *The Creator and the Cosmos*, Colorado Springs: NavPress, 1993.

_____, *Creation and Time*, Colorado Springs, NavPress, 1994

Ryle, H.E., *The Book of Genesis*, Cambridge Bible for Schools & Colleges, Cambridge: Cambridge University Press, 1914.

Sailhamer, John H., *Genesis Unbound*, Sisters, OR: Multnomah Books, 1996.

Sarna, Nahum M., *Understanding Genesis*, New York: McGraw-Hill, 1966.

Schaff, Philip, *The Creeds of Christendom*, Vol. II, Grand Rapids: Baker, 1983.

Schonfield, Hugh, *The Passover Plot*, New York: B. Geis Associates, 1966.

Simkins, Ronald A., *Creator and Creation*, Peabody, MA: Hendrickson Publishers, 1994.

Skinner, John, *A Critical and Exegetical Commentary on Genesis*, International Critical Commentary, Edinburgh: T. & T. Clark, 1910.

Smith, William and Henry Wace, eds., *A Dictionary of Christian Biography, Literature, Sects and Doctrines*, Vol. III, reprint of the 1877 edition, New York: AMS Press, 1974.

Speiser, E.A., *Genesis*, The Anchor Bible, Garden City, NY: Doubleday, 1964.

Spurrell, G.J., *Notes on the Hebrew Text of the Book of Genesis*, London: Methuen, 1904.

Stigers, Harold G., *A Commentary on Genesis*, Grand Rapids: Zondervan, 1976.

Strahler, Arthur N., *Physical Geology*, New York: Harper & Row, 1981.

Talbott, David N., *The Saturn Myth*, Garden City, NY: Doubleday, 1980.

Thackeray, Henry St. John, *The Letter of Aristeas*, London: Society for the Promotion of Christian Knowledge, 1917.

Thompson, Bert, *Creation Compromises*, Montgomery, AL: Apologetics Press, Inc., 1995.

Thornhill, Wallace, *The Electric Solar System* (Slide presentation, 1997).

Tucker, Gene M., *Form Criticism of the Old Testament*, Philadelphia: Fortress Press, 1971.

Unger, Merrill F., *Archaeology and the Old Testament*, Grand Rapids: Zondervan, 1954.

Vail, Isaac N., *The Earth's Annular System*, or, *The Waters Above the Firmament*, 4th ed., Pasadena: Annular World Co., 1912.

Van Groningen, G., *First Century Gnosticism*, Leiden: E.J. Brill, 1967.

Vardiman, Larry, *Ice Cores and the Age of the Earth*, El Cajon, CA: Institute for Creation Research, 1993.

Vawter, Bruce, *A Path Through Genesis*, London: Sheed & Ward, 1957.

Velikovsky, Immanuel, *Worlds in Collision*, New York: Doubleday, 1950.

_____, *Earth in Upheaval*, New York: Doubleday, 1955.

von Rad, Gerhard, *Genesis*, Philadelphia: Westminster, 1961.

_____, *Wisdom in Israel*, Nashville: Abingdon, 1972.

Wakeman, Mary K., *God's Battle with the Monster*, Leiden: E.J. Brill, 1973.

Weigle, Luther A., *The Genesis Octapla*, New York: Thomas Nelson, 1952.

Wellhausen, Julius, *Die composition des Hexateuchs*, 3rd ed., Berlin, 1899.

Wernecke, Herbert H., *The Book of Revelation Speaks to Us*, Philadelphia: Westminster Press, 1954.

Westermann, Claus, *The Genesis Accounts of Creation*, trans. Norman E. Wagner, Philadelphia: Fortress Press, 1964.

Whiston, William, *A New Theory of the Earth*, 1696; New York: Arno Press, 1978.

Whitcomb, John C., Jr. and Henry M. Morris, *The Genesis Flood*, Grand Rapids: Baker, reprint 1978.

White, Andrew Dickson, *A History of the Warfare of Science with Theology in Christendom*, Vol. I, New York: D. Appleton & Co., 1898.

Wilkin, Robert L., *The Christians as the Romans Saw Them*, New Haven: Yale University Press, 1984.

Young, Davis A., *Creation and the Flood*, Grand Rapids: Baker Book House, 1977.

_____, *Christianity and the Age of the Earth*, Grand Rapids: Zondervan, 1982.

Young, Edward J., *Studies in Genesis One*, Phillipsburg, NJ: Presbyterian & Reformed Publishing Co., 1979.

Young, Robert, *Concise Commentary on the Holy Bible*, Edinburgh: George Adam Young, 1904.

Zimmerli, Walter, *I Mose 1–11, Die Urgeschichte*, Zürich: Zwingli, 1943.

Journal and Encyclopedia Articles

Albright, W.F., "Book Review of Alexander Heidel, *The Babylonian Genesis*," *Journal of Biblical Literature*, Vol. 62, 1943, pp. 366-70.

_____, "Contributions to Biblical Archaeology and Philology," *Journal of Biblical Literature*, Vol. 43, 1924, pp. 363-93.

_____, "The Old Testament and Archaeology," *Old Testament Commentary*, ed. Herbert C. Alleman & Elmer E. Flack, Philadelphia: Muhlenberg Press, 1948.

Alvarez, Luis W., *et al.*, "Extraterrestrial cause for the Cretaceous-Tertiary extinction," *Science*, 208, 1980, pp. 1095-1108.

Anderson, Bernhard W., "Creation," *Interpreter's Dictionary of the Bible*, Vol. I, Nashville: Abingdon Press, 1962.

_____, "From Analysis to Synthesis: the Interpretation of Genesis 1–11," *Journal of Biblical Literature*, 97, 1978, pp. 23-29.

_____, "The Earth is the Lord's," *Interpretation*, Vol. IX, 1955, pp. 3-20.

Austin, Stephen A., "Excess Argon within mineral concentrates from the new dacite lava dome at Mount St. Helens Volcano," *Creation Ex Nihilo Technical Journal*, Vol. 10 (3), 1996, pp. 335-343.

Baumgardner, John R., "Runaway Subduction as the Driving Mechanism for the Genesis Flood," *Proceedings of the Third International Conference on Creationism*, ed. Robert E. Walsh, Pittsburgh: Creation Science Fellowship, Inc., 1994.

Bergman, Jerry, "The Establishment of a Heliocentric View of the Universe," *Journal of the American Scientific Affiliation*, Vol. 33, No. 4, Dec. 1981, pp. 225-30.

Berner, Robert and Gary Landis, *Science*, Nov. 13, 1987, p. 890.

Berthault, Guy, "Experiments on Stratification," *Proceedings of the Third International Conference on Creationism*, ed. Robert E. Walsh, Pittsburgh: Creation Science Fellowship, Inc., 1994.

Bible Science Newsletter, Book review, Feb. 1998, p. 18.

Bloch, Joshua, "The Influence of the Greek Bible on the Peshitta," *American Journal of Semitic Languages and Literatures*, XXXVI, Jan. 1920, pp. 161-66.

Brown, Robert H., "Moses' Creation Account," *Ministry*, Sept. 1978.

Cardona, Dwardu, "Let There Be Light," *Kronos*, Vol. III, No. 3, pp. 34-55; Vol. IV, No. 3, Forum: "Creation and Destruction," pp. 71-74.

Chemical and Engineering News, Oct. 11, 1976.

Childs, Brevard S., "The Enemy from the North and the Chaos Tradition," *Journal of Biblical Literature*, Vol. 78, 1959.

Christianity Today, Vol. XXVI, No. 16, October 8, 1982, editorials.

"Constitutions of the Holy Apostles," *Ante-Nicene Fathers*, Vol. VII, ed. Alexander Roberts and James Donaldson, Buffalo: Christian Literature Publishing Co., 1985.

Creation Research Society Quarterly, Book review, Vol. 24, No. 4, pp. 197-200.

Dahood, Mitchell, "Mišmār 'Muzzle' in Job 7:12," *Journal of Biblical Literature and Exegesis*, 80, 1961.

DeVries, S.J., "Chronology of the Old Testament," *Interpreter's Dictionary of the Bible*, Vol. I, Nashville: Abingdon Press, 1962.

DeYoung, Don B., "Origins: Spontaneous or Supernatural," *Creation Perspectives*, May 1997.

Dods, Marcus, "The Book of Genesis," *The Expositor's Bible*, New York: A.C. Armstrong and Son, 1903.

Encyclopaedia Britannica, 15th ed., Vol. 1, art., "Arithmetic"; Vol. 11, art., "History of Mathematics."

Ferté, Thomas, "A Record of Success," *Pensée*, Special Issue, Vol. II, No. 2, May 1972, pp.11-15,23.

Fischer, Michael J., "A Giant Meteorite Impact & Rapid Continental Drift," *Proceedings of the Third International Conference on Creationism,* ed. Robert Walsh, Pittsburgh: Creation Science Fellowship, Inc., 1994, pp. 185-197.

Fishbane, Michael, "Jeremiah IV 23-26 and Job III 3-13: A Recovered Use of the Creation Pattern," *Vetus Testamentum,* Vol. XXI, 1971, pp. 151-167.

Froede, Carl R., Jr., "Stone Mountain, Georgia: A Creation Geologist's Perspective," *Creation Research Society Quarterly,* Vol. 31, No. 4, March 1995, pp. 214-224.

_____ and Don B. DeYoung, "Impact Events within the Young-Earth Flood Model," *Creation Research Society Quarterly,* Vol. 33, No. 1, June 1996, pp. 23-24.

Gaster, T.H., "Cosmogony," *Interpreter's Dictionary of the Bible,* Vol. I, Nashville: Abingdon Press, 1962.

Gordon, Cyrus H., "Leviathan: Symbol of Evil," *Biblical Motifs: Origins and Transformations,* ed. Alexander Altmann, Cambridge: Harvard University Press, 1966.

Guth, Alan H. and Paul J. Steinhardt, "The Inflationary Universe," *Scientific American,* Vol. 250, No. 5, May 1984.

Ham, Ken, "Do the Days Really Matter?" *Back to Genesis,* Institute for Creation Research, Sept. 1990.

Hasel, Gerhard F., "Recent Translations of Genesis 1:1: A Critical Look," *The Bible Translator,* Vol. 22, No. 4, Oct. 1971.

_____, "The 'Days' of Creation in Genesis 1: Literal 'Days' or Figurative 'Periods/Epochs' of Time?", *Origins,* Loma Linda, CA: Geoscience Research Institute, Vol. 21, No. 1.

Helwig, Otto J., "How Long an Evening and Morning?" in Hugh Ross, *Facts and Faith,* Vol. 9, No. 3, 1995.

Hippolytus, "The Refutation of All Heresies," *Ante-Nicene Fathers,* ed. Alexander Roberts and James Donaldson, Buffalo: Christian Literature Publishing Co., 1985.

Humphreys, D. Russell, "The Creation of the Earth's Magnetic Field," *Creation Research Society Quarterly,* Vol. 20, No. 2, Sept. 1983.

Irenaeus, "Against Heresies," *Early Christian Fathers,* Vol. I, The Library of Christian Classics, Philadelphia: Westminster Press, 1953.

James, Peter, *Society for Interdisciplinary Studies Review*, Vol. IV, 3,4.

Jerome, "Letters, LXIX, 6," in J.-P. Migne, *Patrologia Latina*, Vol. XXII, Paris: 1864.

Kiessling, Nicholas K., "Antecedents of the Medieval Dragon in Sacred History," *Journal of Biblical Literature*, LXXXIX, pp. 167-77.

Krause, David J., "Astronomical Distances, the Speed of Light and the Age of the Universe," *Journal of the American Scientific Affiliation*, Vol. 33, No. 4, Dec. 1981.

Lane, W.R., "The Initiation of Creation," *Vetus Testamentum*, Vol. XIII, 1963, pp. 63-73.

Lee, Robert E., "Radiocarbon: Ages in Error," *Anthropological Journal of Canada*, Vol. 19, No. 3, 1981; reprinted in *Creation Research Society Quarterly*, Vol. 19, No. 2, Sept. 1982.

L'Heureux, Conrad, "Understanding Old Testament Prophecies," *The Bible Today*, Vol. 23, No. 1, Jan. 1985, pp. 56-57.

Linde, Andrei, "The Self-Reproducing Inflationary Universe," *Scientific American*, Nov. 1994, pp. 48-55.

Lucretius, "On the Nature of Things, Book I, 146," trans. H.A.J. Munro, *Great Books of the Western World*, Vol. 12, Chicago: Encyclopaedia Britannica, 1952.

McEvenue, Sean E., "The Narrative Style of the Priestly Writer," *Analecta Biblica*, 50, Rome: 1971.

"Monitor," Workshop, Vol. 6, No. 3, *Society for Interdisciplinary Studies*, Feb. 1986.

Morgenstern, Julian, "The Sources of the Creation Story," *American Journal of Semitic Languages and Literatures*, XXXVI, 1920, pp. 169-212.

Morris, Henry, "The Literal Week of Creation," *Back to Genesis*, May 1998, Institute for Creation Research, El Cajon, CA.

National Geographic, May 1974, p. 625, noted in Baker, *op. cit.*, p. 4.

Origen, "Hexapla," in J.-P. Migne, *Patrologiae Graecae*, Vol. XV, Paris: 1857.

Overn, William, "The Creator's Signature," *Bible Science Newsletter*, Vol. 20, No. 1, Jan. 1982.

Peiser, Benny Joseph, "Catastrophism and Anthropology," *Chronology and Catastrophism Review*, Special Issue, The Society for Interdisciplinary Studies, July 1994, pp. 130-34.

Pun, Pattle P.T., "A Theory of Progressive Creationism," *Journal of the American Scientific Affiliation*, March 1987.

Scott, R.B.Y., "Isaiah," *The Interpreter's Bible*, Vol. 5, Nashville: Abingdon, 1952.

Setterfield, Barry, "The Velocity of Light and the Age of the Universe," *Ex Nihilo*, Vol. 4, No. 1, March 1981, and Vol. 5, No. 3, Jan. 1983.

Sewell, Curtis, Jr., "The Faith of Radiometric Dating," *Bible-Science Newsletter*, Vol. 32, No. 8, pp. 1-6.

"The Shepherd of Hermas," *The Apostolic Fathers*, trans. Graydon F. Snyder, Camden: Thomas Nelson, 1968.

Simpson, Cuthbert A., "The Book of Genesis," *The Interpreter's Bible*, Vol. I, Nashville: Abingdon, 1952.

Smith, J.M. Powis, "The Syntax and Meaning of Genesis 1:1-3," *American Journal of Semitic Languages and Literatures*, 44, 1928, pp. 108-115.

Steidl, Paul M., "The Velocity of Light and the Age of the Universe," *Creation Research Society Quarterly*, Vol. 19, No. 2, Sept. 1982.

Stuhlmueller, Carroll, "The Theology of Creation in Second Isaias," *Catholic Biblical Quarterly*, Vol. 21, 1959, pp. 429-67.

Talbott, David N., "The Saturn Thesis," *Aeon*, Vol. IV, No. 3, 1996, pp. 10-37.

Tertullian, "Against Hermogenes," *Ante-Nicene Fathers*, Vol. III, ed. Alexander Roberts and James Donaldson, Buffalo: Christian Literature Publishing Co., 1985.

Unger, Merrill F., "Creation," *Unger's Bible Dictionary*, Chicago: Moody Press, 1957.

_____, "Rethinking the Genesis Account of Creation," *Bibliotheca Sacra*, Vol. 115, 1958, pp. 27-35.

Vadja, Georges, "Notice sommaire sur l'interprétation de Genèse 1:1-3 dans le judaisme post-biblique," In Principio: Interprétation des Premier Versets de la Genèse, Paris: Etudes Augustiennes, 1973.

Vardiman, Larry and Karen Bousselot, "Sensitivity Studies on Vapor Canopy Temperature Profiles," *Proceedings of the*

Fourth International Conference on Creationism, ed.
Robert E. Walsh, Pittsburgh: Creation Science Fellowship,
Inc., pp. 607-618.

Velikovsky, Immanuel, "Khima and Kesil," *Kronos,* Vol. III,
No. 4, 1978, pp. 19-23.

_____, "On Saturn and the Flood," *Kronos,* Vol. V, No. 1,
pp. 3f.

Wallace, Howard, "Leviathan and the Beast in Revelation," *The
Biblical Archaeologist,* Vol. XI, No. 3, pp. 61-68.

Waltke, Bruce K., "The Creation Account in Genesis 1:1-3," *Bibliotheca Sacra,* Parts 1-5, Jan. 1975–Jan. 1976.

Watson, David C.C., "Dare We Reinterpret Genesis?" *Bible-
Science Newsletter,* Vol. 22, No. 5, May 1984.

Wenham, Gordon J., "The Coherence of the Flood Narrative,"
Vetus Testamentum, July 1978, XXVIII, Fasc. 3, pp. 336-348.

Whitelaw, Robert L., "The Fountains of the Great Deep, and the
Windows of Heaven," *Science at the Crossroads: Observation
or Speculation?* Richfield, MN: Onesimus Publishing, 1985,
pp. 95-104.

Wilson. R.J., "Wilhelm Vischer on 'God Created,' " *Expository
Times,* LXV, 1953, pp. 94-95.

Wolbach, Wendy S., Roy S. Lewis, Edward Anders, "Cretaceous
Extinctions: Evidence for Wildfires and Search for Meteoritic Material," *Science,* Vol. 230, No. 4722, Oct. 11, 1985,
pp. 167-70.

_____, I. Gilmore, E. Anders, "Major Wildfires at the Creta-
ceous/Tertiary Boundary," in V.L. Sharpton and P.D. Ward
(editors), *Global Catastrophes in Earth History,* Boulder,
CO: Geological Society of America Special Paper 247,
pp. 391-400.

Wonderly, Daniel, "Non-Radiometric Data Relevant to the Question of Age," *Journal of the American Scientific Affiliation,*
Vol. 27, No. 4, Dec. 1975.

Young, Edward J., "The Relation of the First Verse of Genesis
One to Verses Two and Three," *Westminster Theological
Journal,* Vol. XXI, No. 2, May 1959.

Zimmern, Heinrich and T.K. Cheyne, art., "Creation," *Encyclopaedia Biblica,* Vol. I, ed. T.K. Cheyne and J. Sutherland
Black, New York: Macmillan, 1899.

General Index

Scripture Index

Old Testament

Apocrypha

New Testament

Other
Destiny Image *titles*
you will enjoy reading

FAITH WORKS
by R. Russell Bixler.
The story of Russ and Norma Bixler's pioneering work in Christian television for Pittsburgh is a testimony to the power of faith in God! From a tiny trailer on a hilltop to a massive earth station and satellite uplink, Cornerstone TeleVision has touched multitudes of lives with the good news and healing power of Jesus Christ. This book will encourage you to pursue God's call on your life no matter what obstacle you face!
ISBN 1-56043-338-8

THIS GOSPEL OF THE KINGDOM
by Bertram Gaines.
What is your definition of the Kingdom of God? Some think that it's Heaven. Some think that it won't come until Jesus does. But Jesus said the Kingdom of God would come with power before all His disciples passed away! Here Bertram Gaines, teacher of the Kingdom Life Bible Seminars and a pastor, explains that the Kingdom of God is a spiritual system of righteous government. It's available to believers today, and God wants you to have a part in it!
ISBN 1-56043-323-X

FIRE IN THE WAX MUSEUM
by Hugh "Bud" Williams.
Is your church cold and frozen in tradition and religion or on fire and flowing with the power of the Holy Spirit? Today, like fire in a wax museum, the Holy Spirit is melting old forms and remolding the Church into a vessel fit for the challenges that lie before her. This awe-inspiring story tells how the Holy Spirit caught a denominational church and its pastor by surprise—and launched an international ministry out of it! Rev. Hugh "Bud" Williams, an Episcopal priest and now international minister, tells of both the joy and the pain of being in the fires of revival. *Fire in the Wax Museum* will cause you to examine the role of tradition and religion—and make you hungry for a closer and more intimate walk with the Lord.
ISBN 1-56043-344-2

THE COSTLY ANOINTING
by Lori Wilke.
In this book, teacher and prophetic songwriter Lori Wilke boldly reveals God's requirements for being entrusted with an awesome power and authority. She speaks directly from God's heart to your heart concerning the most costly anointing. This is a word that will change your life!
ISBN 1-56043-051-6

Available at your local Christian bookstore.
Internet: http://www.reapernet.com

Exciting titles by Tommy Tenney

GOD'S FAVORITE HOUSE

The burning desire of your heart can be fulfilled. God is looking for people just like you. He is a Lover in search of a people who will love Him in return. He is far more interested in you than He is interested in a building. He would hush all of Heaven's hosts to listen to your voice raised in heartfelt love songs to Him. This book will show you how to build a house of worship within, fulfilling your heart's desire and His!
ISBN 0-7684-2043-1

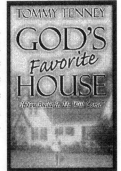

THE GOD CHASERS (Best-selling **Destiny Image** book)

There are those so hungry, so desperate for His presence, that they become consumed with finding Him. Their longing for Him moves them to do what they would otherwise never do: Chase God. But what does it really mean to chase God? Can He be "caught"? Is there an end to the thirsting of man's soul for Him? Meet Tommy Tenney—God chaser. Join him in his search for God. Follow him as he ignores the maze of religious tradition and finds himself, not chasing God, but to his utter amazement, caught by the One he had chased.
ISBN 0-7684-2016-4

GOD CHASERS DAILY MEDITATION & PERSONAL JOURNAL

Does your heart yearn to have an intimate relationship with your Lord? Perhaps you long to draw closer to your heavenly Father, but you don't know how or where to start. This *Daily Meditation & Personal Journal* will help you begin a journey that will change your life. As you read and journal, you'll find your spirit running to meet Him with a desire and fervor you've never before experienced. Let your heart hunger propel you into the chase of your life...after God!
ISBN 0-7684-2040-7

Available at your local Christian bookstore.

Internet: http://www.reapernet.com

Other *Destiny Image titles* you will enjoy reading

FATHER, FORGIVE US!
by Jim W. Goll.
What is holding back a worldwide "great awakening"? What hinders the Church all over the world from rising up and bringing in the greatest harvest ever known? The answer is simple: sin! God is calling Christians today to take up the mantle of identificational intercession and repent for the sins of the present and past; for the sins of our fathers; for the sins of the nations. Will you heed the call? This book shows you how!
ISBN 0-7684-2025-3

AN INVITATION TO FRIENDSHIP: From the Father's Heart, Volume 2
by Charles Slagle.
Our God is a Father whose heart longs for His children to sit and talk with Him in fellowship and oneness. This second volume of intimate letters from the Father to you, His child, reveals His passion, dreams, and love for you. As you read them, you will find yourself drawn ever closer within the circle of His embrace. The touch of His presence will change your life forever!
ISBN 0-7684-2013-X

THE THRESHOLD OF GLORY
Compiled by Dotty Schmitt.
What does it mean to experience the "glory of God"? How does it come? These women of God have crossed that threshold, and it changed not only their ministries but also their very lives! Here Dotty Schmitt and Sue Ahn, Bonnie Chavda, Pat Chen, Dr. Flo Ellers, Brenda Kilpatrick, and Varle Rollins teach about God's glorious presence and share how it transformed their lives.
ISBN 0-7684-2044-X

THE HIDDEN POWER OF PRAYER AND FASTING
by Mahesh Chavda.
The praying believer is the confident believer. But the fasting believer is the overcoming believer. This is the believer who changes the circumstances and the world around him. He is the one who experiences the supernatural power of the risen Lord in his everyday life. An international evangelist and the senior pastor of All Nations Church in Charlotte, North Carolina, Mahesh Chavda has seen firsthand the power of God released through a lifestyle of prayer and fasting. Here he shares from decades of personal experience and scriptural study principles and practical tips about fasting and praying. This book will inspire you to tap into God's power and change your life, your city, and your nation!
ISBN 0-7684-2017-2

Available at your local Christian bookstore.

Internet: http://www.reapernet.com

B6:141

Other
Destiny Image titles
you will enjoy reading

THE LOST PASSIONS OF JESUS
by Donald L. Milam, Jr.

What motivated Jesus to pursue the cross? What inner strength kept His feet on the path laid before Him? Time and tradition have muted the Church's knowledge of the passions that burned in Jesus' heart, but if we want to—if we dare to—we can still seek those same passions. Learn from a close look at Jesus' own life and words and from the writings of other dedicated followers the passions that enflamed the Son of God and changed the world forever!

ISBN 0-9677402-0-7

THE ASCENDED LIFE
by Bernita J. Conway.

A believer does not need to wait until Heaven to experience an intimate relationship with the Lord. When you are born again, your life becomes His, and He pours His life into yours. Here Bernita Conway explains from personal study and experience the truth of "abiding in the Vine," the Lord Jesus Christ. When you grasp this understanding and begin to walk in it, it will change your whole life and relationship with your heavenly Father!

ISBN 1-56043-337-X

THE MARTYRS' TORCH
by Bruce Porter.

In every age of history, darkness has threatened to extinguish the light. But also in every age of history, heroes and heroines of the faith rose up to hold high the torch of their testimony—witnesses to the truth of the gospel of Jesus Christ. On a fateful spring day at Columbine High, others lifted up their torches and joined the crimson path of the martyrs' way. We cannot forget their sacrifice. A call is sounding forth from Heaven: "Who will take up the martyrs' torch which fell from these faithful hands?" Will you?

ISBN 0-7684-2046-6

Available at your local Christian bookstore.

Internet: http://www.reapernet.com

Other
*Destiny Image **titles***
you will enjoy reading

USER FRIENDLY PROPHECY
by Larry J. Randolph.
Hey! Now you can learn the basics of prophecy and how to prophesy in a book that's written for you! Whether you're a novice or a seasoned believer, this book will stir up the prophetic gift God placed inside you and encourage you to step out in it.
ISBN 1-56043-695-6

ENCOUNTERS WITH A SUPERNATURAL GOD
by Jim and Michal Ann Goll.
The Golls know that angels are real. They have firsthand experience with super-natural angelic encounters. Go on an adventure with Jim and Michal Ann and find out if God has a supernatural encounter for you!
ISBN 1-56043-199-7

ANOINTED OR ANNOYING?
by Ken Gott.
Don't miss out on the powerful move of God that is in the earth today! When you encounter God's Presence in revival, you have a choice—accept it or reject it; become anointed or annoying! Ken Gott, former pastor of Sunderland Christian Centre and now head of Revival Now! International Ministries, calls you to examine your own heart and motives for pursuing God's anointing, and challenges you to walk a life of obedience!
ISBN 0-7684-1003-7

WOMAN, THOU ART LOOSED!
by T.D. Jakes.
This book offers healing to hurting single mothers, insecure women, and bat-tered wives; and hope to abused girls and women in crisis! Hurting women around the nation—and those who minister to them—are devouring the com-passionate truths in Bishop T.D. Jakes' *Woman, Thou Art Loosed!*
ISBN 1-56043-100-8

Available at your local Christian bookstore.
Internet: http://www.reapernet.com

B6:80